CIVIL WAR
BY
OTHER
MEANS

CIVIL WAR
BY
OTHER
MEANS

AMERICA'S LONG AND UNFINISHED
★ FIGHT FOR DEMOCRACY ★

JEREMI SURI

PUBLICAFFAIRS

New York

PublicAffairs
Hachette Book Group
1290 Avenue of the Americas, New York, NY 10104

www.publicaffairsbooks.com

@Public_Affairs

Printed in the United States of America

First Edition: October 2022

Published by PublicAffairs, an imprint of Perseus Books, LLC, a subsidiary of Hachette Book Group, Inc. The PublicAffairs name and logo is a trademark of the Hachette Book Group.

The Hachette Speakers Bureau provides a wide range of authors for speaking events. To find out more, go to www.hachettespeakersbureau.com or call (866) 376-6591.

The publisher is not responsible for websites (or their content) that are not owned by the publisher.

Unless otherwise attributed, illustrations are in the public domain.

Library of Congress Cataloging-in-Publication Data has been applied for.

ISBNs: 9781541758544 (hardcover) 9781541758551 (e-book)

LSC-C

Printing 1, 2022

To Alison, Natalie, and Zachary—
advocates and defenders of democracy

Contents

CIVIL WAR
BY
OTHER
MEANS

Introduction

Confederates in the Capitol

Now this is not the end. It is not even the beginning of the end.
—Winston Churchill[1]

Worries about a new civil war in America are misplaced because the Civil War never fully ended. Its lingering embers have burst into flames at various times, including during our own.

On January 6, 2021, thousands of American citizens, self-proclaimed patriots, marched up the Mall in Washington, DC, crossed a line of barricades, and broke into the U.S. Capitol. They interrupted the House of Representatives and the Senate in session, sending the vice president and others scuttling to secure locations. Capitol Police were wholly unprepared for the crowd's desire to break the windows, ransack the offices, and assault the occupants of the building.

The bright Capitol dome symbolizes the peaceful transfer of power in a united country, but this mob would have nothing of it. They were an insurrection against the Union and the electoral process. The timing of the march was meant to prevent the inauguration of a new president with whom they disagreed. Some rioters posed proudly for selfies, displaying self-righteous anger and intolerance. They sent videos around social media, documenting their break-in.

"Look at me," so many shouted on Facebook, "I am here, taking back our government!"

Not all in the crowd were violent, but if you were a Black law enforcement officer on duty that day, you felt the brutality personally.

James Blassingame, a police officer with seventeen years of experience, recounted the fury:

> My squad, we head over to the Capitol, to the Crypt. Then I hear somebody yell, "They're coming through a window." I look north. I wish I could come up with a better analogy, but it's just a horde of zombies running at us full speed. I mean, the whole length of the hall. There's maybe like eight, ten of us. People are yelling. They're throwing stuff. We're holding the line. Somebody broke a wood stanchion in half and threw it at a guy next to me; he just dropped.... People were pissing on walls. People were dumping water coolers on the ground.... It was mob mentality.[2]

The fanatical rage had roots in the Civil War, which explains why the mob flagrantly displayed the Confederate Battle Flag. The loudest insurrectionists proclaimed a connection to the Confederacy and its defense of white families and privileges. They targeted those who placed democracy—particularly the will of the majority of voters—above their needs and desires.

The mob wanted to stop the certification of the 2020 election, one of the freest and securest in American history. They echoed old Southern claims of "fraud," first articulated when nonwhite votes had turned Confederate partisans out of office. A renunciation of white power at the ballot box was unacceptable—a cause for vigilante justice, authoritarianism, and worse. The mob came prepared for battle, with guns, knives, handcuffs, and pepper spray.

Kevin Seefried was a foot soldier in this forever war. A stout, short-haired, bearded, fifty-one-year-old white man from southern Delaware, he carried a life-size Confederate flag into the seat of American democracy, threatening to murder the vice president. Those around him shouted, "Kill Mike Pence!" as he waved the symbol of slaveholders under the majestic white rotunda. Some members of the mob had already used their flagpoles to impale police officers. Others prepared to do much worse.

On the grass field in front of the Capitol, Seefried's confederates had assembled a wooden gallows with a noose, a uniquely American symbol of racist vengeance. They were ready to lynch the vice president and other elected leaders who undermined their control of the government.

It did not matter that the vice president had been a loyal servant to his party. "Kill Mike Pence!" "Hang [Speaker] Nancy Pelosi!" The mob knew what they were saying. They would not permit people to gain power who were different from them—Black, Brown, Asian, female—even if elected by millions of votes. Power mattered more than justice. Status, especially for those fearful of losing it, mattered more than freedom. The Confederate flag symbolized it all.

Like many others in the mob, Seefried brought his son, Hunter, to the insurrection. It was a proud moment for a father who had spent many of his years in and out of work, living in an economically depressed area two hours from the Capitol. He and his son were taking back their country, showing that they could make a difference, standing up for fellow working-class families who felt forgotten. They would not accept a president elected by nonwhite voters. The Confederate flag was *their* battle flag.

On January 6, 2021, insurrectionists built a public gallows in front of the Capitol, evoking the long history of mob lynchings in the United States. They shouted, "Kill Mike Pence!" and "Hang Nancy Pelosi!" *Credit: Tyler Merbler, Creative Commons Attribution 2.0 Generic license*

The Confederate Battle Flag, originally designed in 1863, remains a widespread symbol of racial and political defiance in the United States.

Some might find it odd that the symbol of a defeated regime should fly so high for insurrectionists, but that is part of this American history. The flag that Seefried carried into the Capitol emblazoned the jackets, shirts, trucks, and homes of millions of citizens. The Confederate emblem, in fact, became more popular after the collapse of the Confederacy. As this book shows, the image of the flag was resilient because defeat was not followed by a sustained uprooting of the cause behind it. Although the battles were lost—at Gettysburg, at Vicksburg, at Atlanta, and beyond—the racial hatred was not given up. Ironically, the legend of the "Lost Cause" was added to a creed that wasn't lost at all, and to a conflict that ended only militarily at Appomattox but sinuously continued through other means.

Originally designed as a battle flag for Robert E. Lee's army, the blue diagonal cross with stars on a red background was adopted by Confederate army veterans and placed around their communities as a statement of defiance. It was a marker of protest against helping Black men at the cost of whites. The flag became a trigger for resistance to civil rights, and it spread widely among families who felt attacked by reformers, activists, and federal law enforcement.

Politicians used the Confederate flag to advocate for white supremacy without saying those words. Their followers knew what they meant, but they could not be quoted by their critics, especially in a court of law. The flag allowed for violent provocation without responsibility. Southern Democrats who sponsored Jim Crow violence against African Americans, especially the Dixiecrats after the Second World War, found the flag a very effective tool. It aroused attacks on "uppity" African Americans who pushed for improved treatment, and it promised to preserve a "traditional" America. Dixiecrats contended that they were defending a "historical symbol," not the repression. They blamed "race agitators" for undermining "law and order."

This was a terrible fiction. In reality, the flag was an advertisement for inhumane cruelty. It was not very different from the Nazi swastika or the straight-armed fascist salute. And it continues to send the same message—threatening to its targets, empowering to those who display it. The Confederate flag is the bullhorn of the racist bully.

When lynch mobs hung a man from a tree, as happened frequently and without punishment during the first half of the twentieth century, the people in the crowd displayed the Confederate flag. When white groups, including local police officers, beat peaceful marchers in the 1960s, they carried the flag. When white supremacists besieged the University of Virginia campus in 2017, they showed off the flag. Seefried and other insurrectionists in 2021 were loyal to this ugly tradition, and they knew it.

The Seefrieds had felt themselves falling further behind educated, economically mobile, and often nonwhite Americans for more than a decade, following the worst financial crisis since the Great Depression. The economic downturn that began in late 2007 hit working families hard. Jobs dried up and bank loans were denied. Struggling main streets became ghost towns.

Sussex County, Delaware, where the Seefrieds resided in a rundown house, fit the pattern. This rural region of chicken farms entered a tailspin that triggered higher crime and drug dependence, lower incomes, and diminished expectations for the future. Everything seemed to be going the wrong way, and the election of the first African American president in 2008 only made things feel worse. Barack Obama symbolized an emerging country that the Seefrieds believed they could never enter. They lacked the education and pedigree to compete in a multiracial meritocracy that promised so much for some, leaving many others out. Obama's diverse supporters were winning, while the traditional white families in Sussex and other rural counties were not. The Seefrieds felt like losers.

The losers wanted to fight back. They were desperate. They searched for a cause and found it, as others had before, in the Confederacy—a rebellion of white people to protect themselves.

In 2004, a group of white residents in Sussex County created the Delaware Grays, a chapter of the nationwide Sons of Confederate Veterans. They quickly became a major presence in county parades, on the internet, and in the community as a whole. They even visited schools, sharing the stories of the "good" Confederates who had fought to protect their homes and their slaves.

In May 2007, the Delaware Grays built their own monument. They dedicated a nine-foot-tall gray granite obelisk with the inscribed names of the 140 Delaware residents who had fought for secession. Two flagpoles surrounded the monument—one flying the state emblem, the other the Confederate flag. The purpose was clear: "to recognize the valor and sacrifices of Delaware's citizens and soldiers who fought for the Confederacy" in what the monument's supporters called "the War between the States."[3]

The monument drew immediate controversy, including condemnation from the state legislature and a withdrawal of public funding from the local historical society, which owned the land. Efforts to remove the Confederate flag, however, only encouraged resistance. The Delaware Grays raised money to replace state grants, and they doubled down on their commitment to honor those who had fought for secession and slavery.

Jeff Plummer, the Delaware Grays' camp commander, told reporters: "I am proud to carry the torch.... When you don the uniform of the Confederate soldier, there is a feeling of pride that cannot be equaled. It is 'in your heart,' as we say. You are preserving for future generations history of the sacrifices and valor for the cause, the memory and the pride of the gallant Southern dead."

The hunger for personal dignity through Confederate emulation filled his words. One implication is unmistakable: only white men could "don the uniform of the Confederate soldier."

"I stand up at the playing of Dixie," Plummer continued in a defiant tone. "I well-up at the scene of Pickett's Charge in the movie *Gettysburg*. I am committed to honoring my ancestors, and will defend ferociously their good name and deeds."

In addition to venerating the Confederate flag and its anthems, the Delaware Grays adopted the infamous pledge of Confederate veteran and Mississippi politician Stephen Dill Lee: "We submit the vindication of the Cause for which we fought; to your strength will be given the defense of the Confederate soldier's good name, the guardianship of his history, the *emulation of his virtues*, the *perpetuation of those principles he loved* and which made him glorious and which you also cherish. Remember, it is your duty to see that the true history of the South is presented to future generations."[4]

The Delaware Grays repeat those words at every meeting. Through their monument building and flag waving, they have encouraged the suffering white families in Sussex County to claim dignity in resistance to nonwhite rule. They have surfaced the awful old tradition. In 2016, Donald Trump won nearly 60 percent of the votes in the county.

Four years later, when a Delaware Democrat was elected president, the Confederate flag still flew in Sussex County, and the Delaware Grays continued to encourage white men to stand up for themselves. Kevin Seefried was part of this movement. When asked by FBI agents where he acquired the Confederate flag that he carried into the Capitol, he explained that he brought it from home, where it was "usually displayed outside." He depicted his actions as the legitimate behavior of a white American patriot. That is how he saw it.[5]

Even after the insurrection, the Delaware Grays' website still promoted a defiant "salute to the Confederate flag." The group asked its followers to pledge "affection, reverence and undying devotion to the Cause." The Delaware Grays do not call for insurrection, but they offer the Confederacy as a model for citizens unhappy with the changes in a more diverse country. This message resonated with Seefried and millions of others. By most accounts, it still does.[6]

The Confederacy was a brief, chaotic, illegal, and beaten regime composed of a handful of Southern states. It failed as absolutely as any government could—it did not protect its people, it accomplished nothing but devastation and economic misery. But its memory and promise (and threat) are still alive. If anything, its twisted legacy has expanded its reach into depressed communities in Wisconsin, Michigan, Pennsylvania, and, of course, Delaware. The presence of Confederate flags in small towns as far north as the Canadian border attests to its appeal for citizens distant from the traditional land of Dixie.

The Seefrieds and thousands of others who invaded the Capitol believed they were showing the "undying devotion to the Cause" that would save their country. Their boldness was surprising; their reliance on ideas and symbols from the past was predictable. They were fighting the Civil War by other means—a campaign that began immediately after the Army of Northern Virginia, under General Robert E. Lee, surrendered at Appomattox.

More than 150 years after Appomattox, I watched the events of January 6 on television with horror. Although I am a historian and a scholar of politics, I had never before paid attention to the certification of the electoral votes for president. Most Americans did not even know such a thing occurred every four years, two months after citizens voted. Although the United States has had numerous close and contested elections, the acceptance of the results by Congress has rarely been anything more than an empty ritual. Not this time.

The National Guard did not come to restore order until hours after the attack on the Capitol began, but the Confederate flag was there, carried by Kevin Seefried and the trespassers who rummaged through the Senate chamber, sat in Nancy Pelosi's office, and killed a police officer. Four more police officers died from the lingering trauma in later days.

It happened so suddenly. Just like that, a stable democracy with the most peaceful tradition of transferring power was under siege. This was not the America that I had studied and taught for years. This was surely not the America I grew up in, where elections were hard-fought but then respected by winners and losers alike.

As I looked back at the history that I had studied, I realized that I had underappreciated the long-standing domestic forces of destruction and exclusion. Alongside the growth and development of American democracy, the country had remained mired in unresolved debates about who should have power and who should not.

These issues were most urgent after the military battles of the Civil War, when four million former slaves became citizens. Where would they live? Where would they work? Would they vote?

The fights over these questions in the nineteenth century were still sharp on January 6, 2021. The beginnings of the insurrection at the Capitol started much earlier, in the years after the Confederacy was defeated but remained alive in the imaginations of the dispossessed. The two decades after Robert E. Lee's surrender were years when the seeds of voter suppression, segregation, and vigilantism were planted.

This book is about those beginnings—the history of the two decades after Appomattox, when some Americans tried to build a multiracial nation and others refused. It tells the story of difficult transition years for the United States, and it shows how they created a pattern for exclusion, violence, and coup plotting that repeated into the twenty-first century.

This is a history that reaches far back but remains terrifyingly present. The civil rights struggles in the years after Abraham Lincoln's death are harrowingly similar to our own. The past and present efforts to deny voting rights are almost identical.

The threads of the Confederate flag weave it all together, connecting nineteenth-century slaveholding secession to twenty-first-century white supremacist rioting. Kevin Seefried and the other insurrectionists at the Capitol were reenacting the two decades after Appomattox described here. We can only understand what happened on January 6, and remove its causes, if we start with this history—with the long shadow of a civil war that still has not ended.

CHAPTER I

Dying for Country

Tell my mother I die for my country.

John Wilkes Booth was surrounded. He had shot the president, fled across the Potomac River, and was hiding in a barn in Virginia. He had found sympathizers along the way, as he had expected. But his actions had not triggered the intended avalanche of renewed Confederate violence. At least not yet.[1]

Vainglorious to the end, Booth blamed the cowering citizens who failed to take up arms with their self-appointed savior. He saw himself as the hero of his age, cutting down the tall, dark oppressor to free the hardworking people. As he fled through the Virginia countryside, Booth compared his predicament, in his diary, with the roles he had performed, created by famous playwrights William Shakespeare and Friedrich Schiller:

> After being hunted like a dog through swamps, woods, and last night being chased by gunboats till I was forced to return wet, cold, and starving, with every man's hand against me, I am here in despair. And why? For doing what Brutus was honored for. What made [Wilhelm] Tell a hero? And yet I, for striking down a greater tyrant than they ever knew, am looked upon as a common cutthroat. My action was purer than either of theirs.

"I cannot see my wrong," Booth scribbled, "except in serving a degenerate people." He bemoaned his suffering as a servant who bravely sacrificed against grave odds for a higher cause. "I hoped for no gain.

I knew no private wrong. I struck for my country and that alone. A country that groaned beneath this tyranny, and prayed for this end, and yet now behold the cold hands they extend to me."

Referring to President Lincoln, Booth lashed out in his diary: "Our country owed all her troubles to him, and God simply made me the instrument of his punishment. The country is not what it was." Paraphrasing Shakespeare's Brutus—who exclaims, "I love the name of honor more than I fear death"—Booth wrote: "I care not what becomes of me. I have no desire to outlive my country."[2]

He kept repeating that word, *country*. Booth did not mean a place or even its people. He meant a way of life, with free white men controlling land and government, masters of their houses and overseers of slaves. The privileges of white men were essential for freedom, in Booth's eyes. Slavery gave white men wealth, and it gave them status. They were "white" because they ruled darker-skinned people; they were "men" because they used violence for personal gain.

The democracy of prosperous white men, including Booth, demanded slavery. From the Virginia planters who wrote the Constitution to the Jacksonian settlers who moved west and killed Indians, white men had built American prosperity on the backs of slaves who had cleared the land, tilled the soil, managed the homesteads, and even nursed the children. Slavery made white men, even those who did not own slaves but engaged in merchant activities, free and rich. Slaves were an essential capital resource for the economy of American democracy.

Booth took that as an article of faith. A man of the stage, he relied on the patronage of wealthy white Americans, many of whom owned slaves. That was his audience. He saw himself as a protector of the dominant racial culture that defined his beloved country.

Born in the border state of Maryland, Booth had performed frequently in the South, where he was revered among white theatergoers. In the society of rich gentlemen and pretty ladies, he was their muse, their mirror, their conscience, their entertainment. He depended on the affluent leisured class, the transplanted English squires, and would-be fine folk. And they depended on slaves. Booth was obsessed with Lincoln because the president did much more than conduct a

John Wilkes Booth—handsome, well dressed, and ready for the stage. *Credit: Wikimedia Commons*

war to defend the Union. By limiting and then abolishing slavery, Lincoln challenged the status of the polite, well-mannered society of white people whose inherited wealth and power Booth depended upon.

Although he did not believe in full racial equality, by war's end, Lincoln had slowly come to advocate for freed slaves participating in what had been exclusive white society—in businesses, in schools, and even at the ballot box. This was a personal affront to Booth, who imagined the hideous specter of a rising of four million dark-skinned enemies. The nightmare of angry ex-slaves attacking their former masters animated popular fears, even among those who did not necessarily defend slavery.

Booth was jolted by those fears; they contributed to a condition of perpetual agitation that his friends observed in him during the last months of the Civil War. He seemed often on edge, prone to violent rants and apocalyptic harangues. He became increasingly maudlin, sometimes morose. Booth envisioned a massive riot of former slaves, turning the tables of power in American society, triggered by a blood-thirsty president—a deranged, uneducated, backwoods Caesar who did not understand the true white male roots of democracy.

Booth was one of millions of Americans—from the South and North—who commonly spoke of Lincoln in violent terms. The language of war had seeped into all parts of society, and it divided families and neighbors far away from the battlefields. Hatred of secession defined the Republican Party; fear of Lincoln and a rising of freed slaves characterized Democrats, especially after the muskets around Richmond, the Confederate capital, went silent.

How would the "great emancipator" punish the suffering Southern people now that he had won the war? Booth expected the worst.

In the days between the surrender of Confederate general Robert E. Lee on April 9, 1865, and Booth's firing of his derringer pistol at Ford's Theatre six days later, Lincoln provoked the actor's worst nightmares. Freedom for former slaves, as promised by Union leaders, meant loss and indignity for Booth and others. Speaking to a rain-drenched crowd on April 11 from a second-floor window of the Executive Mansion, the president suggested giving the "colored man" the "elective franchise." "I would myself prefer," Lincoln announced, that voting rights "were now conferred on the very intelligent, and on those who serve our cause as soldiers."[3]

The president was careful and still limited in his suggestion. He did not advocate voting rights for all former slaves, only those who had proven themselves through education or military service. Lincoln's vision was pragmatic, connected to political reform and readmission to the Union for former Confederate states. He emphasized reconciliation.

Lincoln had crossed the color line that protected privileged white men from competition by anyone else. Lincoln's audience was grateful for the end of war but anxious—and frightened—about what would

Abraham Lincoln in 1865. His worn and tired face shows how the Civil War had taxed his body. He was only fifty-six but looked much older. *Credit: Alexander Gardner*

come next. Some, like Booth, were enraged. "That means nigger citizenship!" he exclaimed to his coconspirator David Herold. The next day, Booth went further: "We are all slaves now." He condemned Lincoln's words and what he had witnessed in the nation's capital: African American enlistees in the U.S. Army, guarding white prisoners.

The former slaves had risen, and the traditional white Americans with whom Booth identified had fallen fast. "If a man were to go out and insult a nigger now," he lamented, "he would be knocked down by the nigger, and nothing would be done to the nigger." Even partial racial justice meant an end to what Booth recalled as the old days of white male privilege. "Great God!" he exclaimed: "I have no longer a country! This is the end of constitutional liberty in America."[4]

Booth was not sure he, or anyone else, could reverse the course of events, but he believed he had to try. In his mind, he was a Shakespearean hero trapped in a violent tragedy; redemption only came from killing the man responsible for a train of misdeeds. He mixed revenge with self-righteousness. "Somebody ought to kill the old scoundrel," Booth postured as he also contended that he and his coconspirators were "men who love their country better than gold or life."[5]

He left a testimonial, designed to outlive him and influence those who followed. "I have ever held the South were right," he explained. "The very nomination of Abraham Lincoln, four years ago, spoke plainly, war— war upon Southern rights and institutions. His election proved it."

Lincoln used the power of the Union to crush the inherited institution of slavery and impose foreign rules on the South, according to Booth's analysis. The president violated the Constitution. He substituted his military might for the rights of the people. His actions led to what Booth called a "total annihilation" of slavery and democracy alike. Slavery made the Southern white population free, and Lincoln abolished both in the assassin's retelling.

With theatrical flourish, Booth declared: "I love justice more than I do a country that disowns it; more than fame and wealth; more (Heaven pardon me if wrong,) more than a happy home." And then he turned, ominously, to religious fatalism: "For four years have I waited, hoped and prayed for the dark clouds to break, and for a restoration of our former sunshine. To wait longer would be a crime. All hope for peace is dead. My prayers have proved as idle as my hopes. God's will be done. I go to see and share the bitter end."[6]

On Good Friday, April 14, 1865, Booth brought on the bitter end—for him and for Lincoln. Months earlier, Booth had plotted to kidnap the president and other members of his administration. When he shifted to an assassination plot at the time of Lee's surrender, it happened fast, and it seemed so easy in retrospect. No one had ever assassinated an American president before, and few had even tried. Presidents, including Lincoln, had very little protection during the nineteenth century. They were elected by the people. Why would they need protection from their voters?

Booth did not come to his idea of assassinating Lincoln from common conversation, even among Confederate sympathizers. And he was not mentally ill. Booth was reenacting the historical role of the assassin as slayer of tyrants, often glorified on the stage. The assassins remembered by playwrights were prophetic defenders of democracy against monstrous usurpers.

Few nineteenth-century Americans perceived presidents in these terms before the Civil War, in part because earlier presidents had limited influence over daily lives. Presidents were distant from most citizens, unseen and unheard. Why would anyone bother to assassinate a politician with such pitiful powers? Presidential opponents more often ignored the man and the office.

Lincoln changed that. He expanded the capabilities of the president enormously by leading the Union in the Civil War, emancipating slaves, and pushing federal influence across the growing country. Freeing slaves meant removing the claimed property of slaveholders, taking away their forced labor, and creating new citizens in their communities with new rights. Lincoln also promoted homesteading, railroad construction, and higher education as no president had before. He empowered thousands of immigrants and poor whites, as well as former slaves. Lincoln turned George Washington's distant and dispassionate presidency into a commanding office that transformed cities, towns, and rural areas. The president mattered more than ever for ordinary citizens.[7]

A more powerful presidency inspired more violent forms of resistance. Booth was ahead of his time in understanding how assassinations—of presidents and other figures—would become part of the political struggles over democracy. Assassins were mostly absent from antebellum society; they became a major presence in post–Civil War America. Previous republics, including ancient Rome and the Italian city-states of the Renaissance, experienced frequent assassinations of popular leaders who appeared to violate long-accepted limits on their power. From Machiavelli to John Locke, Western political theory probed the legitimate uses of political violence to defend the freedoms of citizens against demagogues and tyrants. Rulers had to show restraint, or they would lose their lives. Political violence was part of the historical process surrounding democracy—deployed by leaders and those who resisted them. The framers of the U.S. Constitution knew this history well, and it is one of many reasons they wanted a small and nonthreatening presidency.

Despite all his self-taught wisdom, Lincoln did not appreciate this history or how the growth of the presidency would transform political violence in the United States. Lincoln had confronted personal threats to his safety, as early as his train ride while president-elect from his home in Springfield, Illinois, to Washington, DC, in February 1861. Following repeated warnings four years later, he still did not take the threats very seriously. He was not heavily guarded when he traveled, nor when he entertained visitors in the Executive Mansion.

Lincoln understood that people often tried to kill tyrants, but he did not believe the same violence would be directed toward democratically elected leaders. Since Lincoln was the latter, he did not expect political opposition would bring the violence of the battlefields to the nation's capital. He was a leader who had experienced death all around him, and he had many dark forebodings, but he failed to appreciate how the defense of democracy, as perceived by Booth and millions of others, could motivate men to kill the elected leader of what was the world's largest democracy. The Civil War empowered the democratic claims of both the president and those who demanded his death.

Booth and Lincoln shared something else: They loved the theater. Worn out from four years of war, and countless nights following events in the Telegraph Office of the War Department, the president was eager to attend a performance of the lighthearted comedy *Our American Cousin*. After premiering in New York before the war, it was restaged at Ford's Theatre, a short carriage ride from the Executive Mansion. Booth, who knew the theater well, planned for Lincoln's visit.

The main character in *Our American Cousin* is Asa Trenchard, a naive American farmer from Vermont who inherits a grand English estate. The comedy revolves around his ill-prepared visit to his sophisticated yet empty-headed relatives across the Atlantic. American audiences loved Trenchard and his younger cousin Florence because they were honest and free of pretensions (and also very patriotic), while their English counterparts were corrupt and outdated. The characters humorously talk past one another throughout the play, and although the English sophisticates seek to manipulate their bumbling American cousin, Trenchard outsmarts them in the end, of course. He also finds love and reverses a long-standing crime.[8]

Harry Hawk, the twenty-seven-year-old actor playing Trenchard, remembered that on the evening of April 14, "the play was going off so well." The audience, including the Lincolns, was in a very festive mood, with continuous laughter "from the time the curtain went up until it fell." Hawk remembered that Mrs. Lincoln, despite her dour reputation, showed many signs of happiness. "She was laughing at my speech when the shot was fired."[9]

Booth had quietly entered the president's box at Ford's Theatre during act 3. He stood behind Lincoln, awaiting what he knew would be a high point for laughter after one of Trenchard's funniest lines. As the audience laughed, Booth fired into the president's skull, behind his left ear. When he shot, Booth shouted, "Freedom!" echoing the Shakespearean assassins of Caesar.

He then stabbed Major Henry Rathbone, who had accompanied the Lincolns to the play. Booth jumped from the box to the stage, a twelve-foot fall that he had practiced. During his jump, he shouted, "Sic semper tyrannis!"—"Thus always to tyrants."

Booth caught his spur in the flag draping the presidential box, causing him to land awkwardly, breaking his leg. For some in the audience, this all seemed like a surprising addition to the evening's entertainment. Most attendees remained still in their seats, shocked and bewildered by the unexpected theatrics.

Before escaping, Booth had a message to convey from center stage, with his customary self-importance. Holding the dagger dripping Rathbone's blood above his head, Booth looked into the eyes of the 1,700 shocked men and women before him. He delivered his line: "The South is avenged."

And then he staggered out the side stage door, stabbing the orchestra leader along the way. He jumped on his horse and rode off into the night.[10]

Depiction of Lincoln's assassination, published soon after the horrible event. Booth is shown firing point-blank into the head of the president, who is unprepared and unprotected. Lincoln clutches the American flag. To his right are his wife, Mary Todd Lincoln, socialite Clara Harris, and Major Henry Rathbone. Rathbone did not try to stop Booth from shooting, as shown here. He did not see the assassin approach and reacted only after the fatal shot was fired. *Credit: Currier and Ives*

The shock of Booth's actions gave way to a frenzy of activity in Ford's Theatre. At least three doctors pushed their way to the president's comatose body. A group of soldiers carefully carried the body across the street to the row house built by William Petersen, a local tailor from Germany. The soldiers laid Lincoln's long, limp body diagonally across a bed in the first-floor bedroom. More physicians arrived, filling the cramped building with what became a crowd of medical personnel and other government officials, many of whom had treated countless savage gunshot wounds during the war.

Despite their best efforts, the doctors quickly concluded that Lincoln would not survive. The president's brain continued to hemorrhage. His breathing was calm, but he was nonresponsive. Lincoln held on until early Saturday morning, April 15. He died at 7:22 a.m. Three hours later, Salmon Chase, chief justice of the Supreme Court, administered the oath of office to the new president, Andrew Johnson, in his residence just a block away. He was the first vice president to replace a slain commander in chief. The Civil War had claimed its greatest victim.

More death would follow. Booth's coconspirators failed to assassinate Vice President Johnson and Secretary of State William Seward, as planned. Booth fled to Maryland, where he connected with his friend and coconspirator David Herold, who had participated in the failed effort to kill Seward. The fugitives traveled twenty miles on horseback to the home of rural doctor and acquaintance Samuel Mudd. They spent the night in his home, where Mudd set Booth's broken leg and provided him with crutches. Booth and Herold then traveled farther south, eventually making their way into Virginia, the heart of the defeated Confederacy.

The manhunt for the assassins, led by the Sixteenth New York Volunteer Cavalry, lasted twelve long days. In the early dark hours of April 26, after 2:00 a.m., Union soldiers cornered Booth and Herold in a barn on a farmstead near the small town of Port Royal, Virginia. "We are guilty of no crime!" Booth shouted to the soldiers surrounding him. "If I have done anything, I did it for the good of my country. At least I fancied so."

"You have spoiled my plans," Booth continued. "I was going to Mexico to make my fortune." Booth would not be the last stubborn defender of the Confederacy to seek escape south of the border.[11]

Herold surrendered. Booth refused. The twenty-nine soldiers surrounding the barn lit it on fire to flush out the assassin. Booth still refused to surrender, and he raised his weapons to shoot his captors as his own body was engulfed by flames. Sergeant Boston Corbett, a thirty-three-year-old soldier who had survived five months as a prisoner of war in the Confederacy's infamous Andersonville prison, shot a defiant Booth in the neck. The soldiers wanted to take the fugitive alive, but they feared for their own lives.

After Corbett fired, Booth fell to the ground. The neck wound left him paralyzed throughout most of his body. He could breathe only with great effort. He managed one final statement, a last testament: "I die for my country. I did what I thought was best."[12]

The remorseless assassin stopped breathing before 7:00 a.m. Union soldiers returned his body to the nation's capital, where he was identified and given an undignified burial in the old prison attached to the Washington Arsenal. The other conspirators, including Herold, were later tried and hanged in the same location. These were military tribunals and executions, for a country still at war.

Lincoln's assassination was the opening to the second phase of the Civil War—the longer, more difficult, and less predictable struggle over conflicting conceptions of democracy. Before his death, Lincoln promoted a more inclusive, but still unequal vision of political participation, with some African American voters. The Republican Party called this expansive concept of democracy "free labor"—freedom to work for pay, to own land, and to participate in political decision-making for most American males. Women remained largely excluded.

Booth stood firmly against free labor. His view exemplified the resistance of millions of Americans who still raised their weapons to keep American democracy white. The Democratic Party, the party of Booth, defined its vision of democracy around "local control," later "home rule" and "states' rights." These phrases emphasized freedom for communities to define their own rules of conduct, to protect inherited property, and to preserve power for those who had long held it. The end of slavery was the end of one peculiar institution, as Southerners later called it, but Democrats clung to the folkways and habits that had surrounded its existence for more than two centuries. That was what democracy meant to Booth and much of his audience in April 1865.

The question was not whether democracy, but what kind? The debate remained violent as it bled back into farm towns and cities—including theaters—far from the battlefields with famous names.

CHAPTER 2

Martyrs

Funerals are battlefields of a different kind. Remembering the dead presents an opportunity to promote the cause for which they died.

Abraham Lincoln's Gettysburg Address mastered the funeral battlefield. It quickly became the most famous and enduring eulogy in modern history. The president had spoken on November 19, 1863, to a crowd assembled on the grounds of one of the bloodiest battles of the Civil War. The fields were filled with bones and other human remains; the stench of death was still in the air. Lincoln memorialized more than 3,500 fallen Union soldiers on that late autumn day.

"We have come," Lincoln explained, "to dedicate a portion of that field as a final resting-place for those who here gave their lives that that nation might live." The soldiers had turned back a Confederate force invading Union territory, a force aiming to sack the nation's capital and capture the president. In his address, Lincoln invoked the Union soldiers' valor to inspire greater dedication from those still living "to the great task remaining before us":

> that from these honored dead we take increased devotion to that cause for which they gave the last full measure of devotion—that we here highly resolve that these dead shall not have died in vain, that this nation under God shall have a new birth of freedom, and that government of the people, by the people, for the people shall not perish from the earth.

The remembrance of the soldiers' sacrifices boosted the cause for which they had fought. Their deaths were justified by the continued pursuit of something greater than their lives. And their memory, thanks to Lincoln's soaring words, was now bound to the creation of an expanded, more inclusive democracy.

The funeral at Gettysburg transformed mass death into collective resurrection. Lincoln called it a "new birth"—a renewal of flagging Republican ideals, bloodied but pure, free from compromise and half measures that characterized standard political rhetoric. Lincoln's Gettysburg Address memorialized recent death to motivate expanded action.

For generations, Lincoln's 271 words were widely read and spoken because they turned soldiers into martyrs. The president's advocacy of a stronger, more inclusive democracy for more people passed from one generation to the next, a family heirloom and an article of faith that defined Republican Party politics for the next half century. Republicans, including millions of freed slaves, waved the bloody shirt of the sacrifices in the war to demand payment on the promise of democratic participation in the Union, for which their fathers had fought and died. Lincoln used death to demand freedom for generations of different citizens.

The president's assassination deepened the memory of Gettysburg, attaching an indelible image to the inspiring words of his address. Undertakers worked feverishly to prepare Lincoln's damaged body for public display. On April 18, 1865, three days after the president's death, thousands of citizens lined up early in the morning to pay their respects, visiting the embalmed body in the East Room of the Executive Mansion.

The crowd was large and diverse—the largest to visit the president's home since Andrew Jackson's time in office thirty years earlier. Unlike in Jackson's era, the visitors after Lincoln's assassination included thousands of freed slaves and other African Americans, who, according to some estimates were more than half the crowd. Union veterans, widows, and children also visited in large number.

People came from near and far over the course of the long day. As the number of visitors continued to swell, officials hurried emotional people past the body. The air in the East Room was dense from the heavy breathing and tears of many onlookers. Some visitors cried out in pain. Numerous men and women wept as they passed the body.

Ushers struggled to silently control the distraught crowd. Many on-lookers wanted to linger and pray. Lincoln's body, limp and discolored, was venerated like that of a saint. By some.

The reverence for the slain president grew in coming days. On April 19, a horse-drawn hearse carried Lincoln's body to the Capitol, where it lay in state in the Rotunda, under the nearly finished dome. The fu-neral procession imitated George Washington's, sixty-five years earlier. A riderless horse, symbolizing the missing leader, followed the hearse. Thousands lined the streets, and the presence of African American sol-diers was overwhelming. This might have been the largest multiracial crowd ever assembled, to that time, in the nation's capital or any other American city. Booth's nightmare of mass race mixing had ironically come to fruition because of his violent act.

The mourning on April 19 extended far beyond Washington, DC. Cities and towns throughout the North and the West held public, multiracial processions to remember Lincoln. Even occupied Southern areas witnessed gatherings of white and Black Union soldiers to honor their late commander in chief. Shared grief united citizens, shocked by the assassination and shaken by the loss of their leader. Even those Union supporters who did not revere Lincoln before had trouble resist-ing the urge to glorify him in death.

"O Captain! my Captain!" wrote the poet Walt Whitman, describ-ing how the martyred president's demise cast a long shadow across the nation.

Confederate general Robert E. Lee's surrender and Lincoln's assas-sination, within days of each other, opened new uncertainties about the future of the country. As in any other period of prolonged and repeated suffering, citizens felt a disorienting mix of dread and anxiety, as well as relief and hope. What was happening, and what would it mean? Millions of Americans held tight to Lincoln's paternal, religious image ("Father Abraham") as an anchor of stability.

Whitman closed his poem with Lincoln's body symbolizing both the hope and dread of the moment:

Exult O shores, and ring O bells!
But I with mournful tread,
Walk the deck my Captain lies,
Fallen cold and dead.[1]

Confederate critics were moved by Lincoln's death, but in a different way. They did not share the same grief as Whitman in Lincoln's departure. He was their enemy, not their captain. He was not their president; that was Jefferson Davis. If Lincoln symbolized lost innocence and renewed promise for his followers, he embodied abolitionist degeneracy and Yankee tyranny for his adversaries. His assassination did not temper bitter and vindictive feelings. "Lincoln was a man of low, vulgar instincts," the *Texas Republican* reminded its large reading audience shortly after his funeral.[2]

The Union's displays of fealty to Lincoln only reinforced the revulsion toward his image in the South. If anything, the public outpouring for the president in the North made him and his followers more threatening to Confederate critics. The *Texas Republican* condemned Lincoln's supporters for "exulting over the supposed prostrate condition of the South." The crowds mourning the president appeared dangerously poised to punish the region his assassin defended.[3]

Lincoln's inclusive democratic vision seemed more popular, and threatening, to opponents than ever. Expressions of sympathy for Lincoln, therefore, became highly dangerous political acts in the former Confederacy. One newspaper in the capital of South Carolina, burned during Union occupation, warned that Lincoln's death could create a "pretext," "eagerly seized upon by thousands at the North, to whom the sudden suspension of hostilities is a serious loss."

Speculators will be glad to renew their games, practicing with their own wits upon the fluctuating moods of the country; soldiers will be glad of the pretext for rifling defenceless towns and villages; and

thousands of jackals, in the wake of the tiger, will rush along our high-
ways, gleaning whatever shall remain in the stores of the miserable
population.[4]

One week after Lincoln's fateful visit to Ford's Theatre, his embalmed and much-viewed body boarded a special nine-car train waiting at the New Jersey Avenue Station in the northwest corner of the
nation's capital. Four years earlier, Lincoln had first arrived there,
lightly guarded, for his inauguration. Now he began his final journey
home from the same spot, with a much larger crowd of spectators and
a full train of three hundred dignitaries.

Lincoln's departure was particularly sad. He was murdered in his
moment of long-suffering triumph. He died without an opportunity to
leave a final testament or say his goodbyes. And he died heartbroken.
The body of his eleven-year-old son, Willie, who died in early 1862
from typhoid fever, accompanied his father's corpse on the funeral
train. At the time of his assassination, the president and his wife had
still not recovered from the blow of losing Willie.

The presence of the two bodies together, father and son, conveyed the
suffering of the family—like thousands of other families—during the
Civil War. The president had given so much personally for something
much larger than himself. The Lincoln family pain on display to the nation was a pain many others felt.

Elizabeth Keckley, who remembered her suffering as a slave in Virginia before becoming a free woman in the Lincoln household, captured
the sentiments of many former slaves: "No common mortal had died.
The Moses of my people had fallen."[5]

The shared sacrifice and pain made Lincoln's remembered words
personal, even religious, for those now mourning his death. His beautiful turns of phrase became literal as the weeping citizens observed the
bodies: "Let us strive on to finish the work we are in, to bind up the
nation's wounds, to care for him who shall have borne the battle and
for his widow and his orphan."

The message of Lincoln's death to Union supporters was clear. There
could be no "just and lasting peace," as the president had promised,

without continued commitment to the cause: what Lincoln had called "firmness in the right as God gives us to see the right." [6]

Sadness, pain, and faith followed the funeral train across nearly seventeen hundred miles of track, zigzagging from the nation's capital to the Lincoln family's final burial place in Springfield, Illinois. The cars moved slowly along the rails, often only five miles per hour. Crowds of men, women, and children from all races and backgrounds lined the route—some waiting in the rain and cold for hours to catch a last glimpse of the president. They removed their hats, they knelt, and they most often wept, even as the train traveled past them.

When the train stopped in cities and towns, an escort of military veterans would remove the president's body from its carriage and take it to a location where local residents could view it up close. The crowds were so large that they frequently became disorderly, with men and women pushing and shoving to see the corpse. Citizens felt more connected to their leader than ever before, and they wanted to feel that connection as near as possible. To be "there" was to enact the larger mission of Union and emancipation that defined Lincoln.

Mourning was a mobilization of men and women, a continuation of the conscription for war. More than twenty million people attended events honoring Lincoln, millions more witnessed his last train ride. The commemoration of his life constituted the largest funeral in American history to that time. In a world without radio, television, or social media, the simultaneity of the experience for so many was unprecedented.

People remembered and told their children where they were when they learned of Lincoln's assassination and witnessed his funeral. And like the Pearl Harbor bombing three generations later, Lincoln's death stiffened public resolve to punish the wrongdoers and promote the very policies that they attacked. Charles Niles, a soldier escorting Lincoln's funeral procession, spoke for countless others when he wrote to his father that he felt his hatred for the Confederates "added to tenfold." [7]

Surveying the sentiment among mourners from the far west, one California newspaper reported: "The universal feeling seems to be to mete out the sternest justice to all sympathizers with the rebellion."

The crowded procession of New Yorkers who came out to pay
their respects to Abraham Lincoln after his assassination. The
open second-floor window in the last building on the left shows
six-year-old Theodore Roosevelt and his brother, Elliott, watch-
ing the procession. Theodore never forgot this moment of sadness and inspiration.

Another newspaper went further: "No words at our command can express our abhorrence of the damning act of his assassination."

> The contempt of the civilized world, as well as the righteous judgments
> of both human and divine governments, will follow the instruments—
> direct and remote—of the foul deed, and well may they cry unto the
> rocks and mountains to fall upon them and hide them from the swift
> coming wrath which is their just due. To Abraham Lincoln no harm
> was done—a martyr's crown but added glory to his other rewards. The
> tears of the millions who have wept over the grave of this Father of his
> country are the best eulogy of his excellence and worth.[8]

The meaning of the cause differed among the diverse population of mourners. African Americans and the more radical members of the Republican Party pursued Lincoln's promises to promote freed slaves' right to vote and other forms of full participation. Suffragists demanded that white women now get the same rights as freed slaves. Skeptics, who had long criticized Lincoln but now mourned him, hoped for a rapid return to stability with minimal disruptions.

The vast majority of Lincoln's mourners did not support the most radical calls for equality but sought some uncertain mix of expanded democracy and stability. The president had famously balanced these two goals in his cautious, gradual pursuit of emancipation, emphasizing Union above all. His tragic death deepened the urgency of debates about his true legacy, motivating millions of citizens to carry on what they saw as his work. The mourners were a new and larger army of soldiers, following the trails Lincoln left behind.

The collective memory of Lincoln became the foundation for constructing a more inclusive post-slavery democracy across the continent. The three constitutional amendments ratified after his death—ending slavery (1865), affirming equal protection under the law (1868), and prohibiting racial restrictions on voting (1870)—were relics of Lincoln's life imprinted by his followers on the American founding document. Confederate states and new states had to pledge loyalty to these manifestations of Lincoln's memory before they joined (or rejoined) the Union.

Those looking for an antithesis of Lincoln did not alight on Jefferson Davis or Robert E. Lee, commanders of Confederate forces in the Civil War, but on John Wilkes Booth. There were no statues built for Davis or Lee in 1865. Confederate resistance embraced the image of Lincoln's assassin.

A villain in the North, he was treated sympathetically by Southern writers. "There is no reason to believe," the *Texas Republican* explained, "that Booth in killing Lincoln was actuated by malice or vulgar ambition." Newspaper coverage of the assassination described the famous actor as a humble, God-fearing man, devoted to those who suffered from Northern aggression. He acted in selfless ways to free people, and he modeled honor, faith, and tradition, in this widely repeated account.[9]

Booth was, of course, famous before his final night at Ford's Theatre, but the reports of his deed generally failed to mention that. In his death, Confederates remade Booth into someone new. They defined him by his last act and the purposes they wanted to see in it. Booth became a Confederate martyr unrecognizable to those who knew Booth the stage actor.

In memory, Booth was treated as a faceless everyman, a representative for the suffering white citizens of the Confederacy. Booth mirrored the sacrifice of those who lost so much in the war. He symbolized for thousands of demoralized men and women how they could still fight back with hope and God on their side. His martyrdom was made prophetic, a foil to Lincoln's.

Booth allegedly acted for higher forces. "God Almighty ordered this event or it could never have taken place," the *Houston Telegraph* proclaimed. The newspaper warned against wanton violence, but it refused to criticize Booth. It valorized his act because, in the newspaper's view, it brought justice: In Lincoln's death "the finger of God's providence is manifest." The assassin "freed us from the threatened yoke of a tyrant. We look upon him as God's instrument, and as such have him with his maker, praying for infinite mercy to succor him in his hour of need."[10]

This became a common account of the assassination. Booth was a Christian soldier performing his highest duty. His murder of the president replayed the biblical parable of the young, innocent David slaying the mighty Goliath: "He slew him as a tyrant, and the enemy of his country." The *Texas Republican* wrote: "We honor the deed. Would that we could impress the sentiment upon the heart of every man North and South, that resistance to tyrants is obedience to God; that we could place in Southern man's hand a dagger, with the resolute, virtuous purpose to use it against tyrants, whenever the opportunity offered." In this telling, Booth had righteousness and democracy on his side. He would be a traitor to his cause and his people if he did *not* act.[11]

The popular Southern depiction of Booth would rationalize bringing violence into civilian areas—including theaters, schools, and voting places—where Booth's followers could continue their fight. Booth had fired a shot that replayed the long-told rising of the righteous against more powerful tyrants. This self-serving narrative, whether accurate or not, offered former Confederates proof that resistance was possible.

Booth also enacted the Confederate urge for revenge. More than a quarter of a million Southern white men had died on battlefields and from war-related disease. Hundreds of thousands of Southerners fled their homes, starved, and lost their property, including their slaves. They were deeply disoriented and profoundly humiliated. Countless families struggled to survive, let alone restore their prior prosperity or anything close. Men and women throughout the region felt beaten down, and they had severely wounded pride. Southern swagger and independence had given way; the region was on its knees, occupied, and indignant.

Booth's murder of Lincoln was a vengeful strike back, a solid blow of revenge. It brought the powerful man down, and it gave the suffering victims power of their own. Booth's act was personal violence as collective, regional therapy.

Southern newspapers carried this vengeful theme forward as they described why Lincoln and his supporters deserved death, why they had it coming to them. "Mr. Lincoln and Mr. Seward had by their malignity," one newspaper explained, "created only feelings of detestation and horror for them in the minds of our people." They had provoked this violence by invading the Confederacy and disrupting lives. Union leaders were responsible for the violence, including the assassination, according to this argument. Booth was the victim, not the villain.[12]

Lincoln became a monster in this telling, an Antichrist who had corrupted the nation. The *Texas Republican* reported: "For upwards of four years this man, remarkable for his iron will and malice, had carried on a war against these States, without a parallel in modern history for its atrocity and barbarism, with the declared purpose of subjugation or extermination."

To hammer home Lincoln's alleged degeneracy and enrage Southern readers, the *Texas Republican* claimed (without evidence) that the president was celebrating their suffering when he visited Ford's Theatre. He relished the destruction and danced on their graves, according to this account. And Lincoln's alleged braggadocio brought on his assassination. It was his comeuppance. "At the very time when in his heart he was exulting over the supposed prostrate condition of the South," the *Texas Republican* recounted, "he fell by the hand of one of his own people."

Making the case for divine retribution in Lincoln's assassination, the newspaper turned the biblical references of his Second Inaugural Address against the slain president: "How prophetically the lines, which he applied to the South, refer to himself: 'it must needs be that offences come, but woe to that man by whom the offence cometh.' "[13]

For the millions of Confederates who had spent the last four years hearing horrifying (and untrue) tales about Lincoln's hate for white civilization and his bloodthirsty intentions, the newspaper accounts of his death must have felt good—they were certainly popular, reprinted across the region, and eagerly read.

Booth was less prophet than avenger. His steadfast determination to punish Lincoln was evidence of his integrity and loyalty. Newspapers extolled these qualities and took them as touchstones for wider reactions to the Union occupation. Instead of giving in, white Southerners had to continue to resist, stand tall, and defend what was theirs. This was not a call for open rebellion but continued vigilance and determination against Northern intrusions. Booth's martyrdom gave readers a reason to believe that they could resist and even make the Northerners pay a high price for their crimes.

Inspired by Booth, the *Columbia Daily Phoenix* encouraged readers to "subside quietly from view—to avoid the highway and the thoroughfare; avoid all discussion, whether of past or future; submit to the inexorable fate which seems to have the sanction of the Most High God." This meant refraining from open conflict with Union forces but also foot-dragging and, when possible, strong reaction. Southern readers were told to lie in wait and then act forcefully when opportunities presented themselves.[14]

Southerners had learned that they could not defeat Union forces, any more than Booth could reverse the armistice at Appomattox. But they could use their resistance to raise the costs of Union efforts and bolster the defense of their local power. Pushing back as individual citizens would disrupt federal organization and leadership, especially in hostile Confederate territories.

Like other martyrs, Booth had shown that the defeated still had power. He gave Confederate supporters a reason to continue the fight by other means. His actions rejected submission, proposing renewed pride and control through continued violence. The suffering of the South at the end of the Civil War would provide motivation and means for resistance in new ways. The *Chattanooga Daily Rebel* told readers: "Our poverty is now our protection."[15]

Those words echoed Booth's militant defiance. Battlefield losses would inspire stronger self-protection closer to home. The former slave states were still stubbornly separate from the rest of the country, and many residents wanted them to stay that way. Booth was the martyr to that separation—the lodestar for demoralized Southern whites who refused to give up. Revering him, Southern whites affirmed their control over their destinies—their democracy, as they defined it.

Secretary of War Edwin Stanton understood the power of martyrdom. He was by the side of the president's body at death, and he managed the manhunt for his assassin. Stanton famously announced Lincoln's martyrdom—"Now he belongs to the ages"—while at the same time attempting to deny Booth's.[16]

He refused requests for the body from the assassin's family. "It would be a source of irritation to the loyal people of the country," Stanton predicted, "if his body was permitted to be made the instrument of rejoicing at the sacrifice of Mr. Lincoln."[17]

Instead of returning to his family, Booth's body was buried unceremoniously and secretly in the Washington Arsenal. Stanton kept the key to the locked room above Booth's grave. The secretary of war recognized how dangerously attractive Booth's body could become as a shrine for Confederate sympathizers.

Southern defenses of the assassin foiled Stanton's efforts to silence his legacy. In the years after Booth's death, his body drew increased attention. During the fall of 1867, the War Department, still under Stanton's leadership, exhumed the remains of Booth and the other conspirators to clear space for renovations of the Washington Arsenal. A trench in a nearby warehouse secretly became the new burial place for Booth. His family, particularly his elder brother Edwin, continued to demand the body. Stanton still refused.

Stanton was the Lincoln cabinet official most determined to erase Booth's influence over Southern minds. His efforts reached an abrupt end in May 1868 when, following the impeachment and failed conviction of President Andrew Johnson in the Senate, Stanton was forced to leave office. Early the next year, Johnson consented to return Booth's body to his family.

In February 1869, representatives of the Booth family retrieved the body from the trench near the Washington Arsenal and transported it by train to Baltimore. Already, the decaying corpse attracted attention from crowds as it was moved. The *Baltimore Sun* reported: "Many persons saw the remains. Some with a fondness for souvenirs tore off pieces of the blanket [draping the body] and secured locks of hair."[18]

Relics from Booth's cadaver became touchstones for Confederate loyalty and yet another condemnation of Lincoln and his followers. As Stanton predicted, connecting to Booth as a holy ghost was a way of rejoicing in his act and pledging loyalty to his cause. Confederates could now see (and sometimes touch) their martyr.

On June 26, 1869, Booth was buried in Baltimore's fancy and frequently visited Green Mount Cemetery. The rarefied grounds were modeled on Boston's Mount Auburn Cemetery, home to some of the nation's founders. Booth was laid to rest with a formal ceremony, and a distinguished memorial site, shared with his family. Tombstones for local dignitaries and Confederate soldiers surrounded his now public grave.

Immediately, the grave became a pilgrimage site. In the first year after Booth's burial, the *Baltimore American and Commercial Advertiser* reported that his grave received more decorations than any other—"a pyramid of flowers." The bright bouquets and other tokens of appreciation came from strangers. They were placed "to do honor to the Southern soldiers, and if the richness and profusion of the emblems is to be taken as the measure of affection in which the deceased soldier is held, John Wilkes Booth is the greatest hero of them all."

The majestic grave site for John Wilkes Booth and other family members in Baltimore became a place of pilgrimage for his continuing supporters. Booth's grave was regularly decorated with flowers, and a local newspaper called him "the greatest hero of them all." *Credit: James G. Howes, 2008*

Of course, Booth was never a soldier, but he became a heroic warrior in his public burial. Thousands of citizens would visit his memorial, pay tribute, and pledge devotion to his fight against Yankee law. In nostalgic prose, the *Baltimore American and Commercial Advertiser* described the "inspiration" gained from the "sacred graves" of Booth and other dead Confederates buried by his side:

It is a blessed privilege each returning year to be permitted to make them beautiful with flowers. It will keep alive the recollection of the heroism and truth and honor; and although the cause for which these men died is lost, yet that cannot detract from their noble devotion to what they believed to be right.... They died heroes and martyrs.[19]

The Civil War produced conflicting martyrs for a country that re-mained deeply divided. Their images would shadow the continuing de-bates about democracy in the United States. And their examples would inspire many imitators, including a group of men who left the country to continue their fight for the Confederate cause.

CHAPTER 3

Exiles

The soil of the American South plays a special role in the world economy. Since the seventeenth century, the region has tilled and excavated its land for profit. Tobacco, cotton, sugar, rice, oil, and gas have fueled industry far and wide, enriching the fortunate families that control these treasured commodities. Southern identity endures around a conspicuous affection for the land that has seeded a distinct culture.

The vivid Southern imagining of the land is immortalized in the song "Dixie," which became the most popular anthem in the region during the Civil War and remained ubiquitous through the next century. The song began as a blackface minstrel performance in the 1850s, describing the alleged harmony between slaves, masters, and Southern society. The song mixed nostalgia with pride in a place like none other:

> *I wish I was in the land of cotton,*
> *Old times dar am not forgotten,*
> *Look away! Look away! Look away! Dixie Land.*
> *In Dixie Land whar' I was born in,*
> *Early on one frosty mornin',*
> *Look away! Look away! Look away! Dixie Land.*

The refrain "Look away" became a call to glance back after the Civil War and force out those who challenged the past. The language of the song showcased regional dialect and pride, invoking traditional habits. And the chorus rose explicitly to a cry for resistance—to "take my stand," and to "live and die" on hallowed land. The song repeated the command "away" to all those who threatened inherited glory.

> *Den I wish I was in Dixie, Hoo-ray! Hoo-ray!*
> *In Dixie land, I'll take my stand to live and die in Dixie;*
> *Away, away, away down south in Dixie,*
> *Away, away, away, down south in Dixie.*

Joseph Shelby, one of the most revered Confederate cavalry officers of the Civil War, echoed these sentiments when he addressed more than one thousand soldiers on April 26, 1865—coincidentally, the same day as John Wilkes Booth's capture and death. Shelby called upon his tired and demoralized men to stand by one another and their slaveholding community:

> All that life holds nearest and dearest is there. Your bleeding mother land—pure and stainless as an angel guarded child is there. The proud imperial South—the nurse of your boyhood and the priestess of your faith is there, and calls upon you—her children, her best and bravest—in the pride and purity of your manhood, and your blood to rally around her altar's shrine—the blue skies and green fields of your nativity.

Born in Kentucky, like Lincoln, Shelby had followed a very different path. He moved to Missouri as a young man, where he became one of the largest and wealthiest slaveholders in the state. He was militant in his defense of what he believed was the "mother land" for his prosperity, security, and rightful ownership of other human beings. Union forces were foreign invaders who threatened to destroy "the pride and purity" of the South, especially by freeing the slaves.

Shelby's troops rejoiced at Lincoln's assassination. Although Shelby worried about what would come next, he shared their disdain for the Yankee emancipator.

"We will never surrender," Shelby announced to his men, even though his commander had laid down his arms at Appomattox more than two weeks earlier. Adopting the language of a zealot, Shelby

explained that surrender "is more terrible than death." He gave his soldiers very clear instructions: "We will do this: We will hang together,
we will keep our organization, our arms, our discipline, our hatred of
oppression, until one universal shout goes up from an admiring age,
that this Missouri Cavalry Division preferred exile to submission—
death to dishonor."[1]

Shelby's stubborn resistance to Union forces, even after defeat,
was in character. His call for exile was not. Southerners defined their
identity by their land—it was the container for their wealth (including slaves), the repository for their family lineages, and the foundation
for their faith. They prayed on, and to, their land. There could be no
Southern gentry without Southern land.

Yet the Southern leaders who revered their sacred land did not stick
to that land after their losses on the battlefield. When given the opportunity to return to their farms, without their slaves, many Confederate
soldiers chose otherwise. Some continued to fight as long as they could;
some, like Shelby, chose to leave. Soldiers, commanding officers, and
even governors fled their beloved South rather than face the difficult
consequences of their actions. They did not continue to resist; they chose
to leave. Exile was a widespread expression of freedom for these Confederates and a rejection of loyalty to their land, their country, and the more
inclusive democracy promoted by Union leaders.

At least fifty thousand white Southerners, probably many thousands
more, left in the days and weeks after Appomattox. Their families followed soon after. More than ten thousand men and women went west,
swelling the crowds of Southern settlers in these drier, sun-drenched territories. Others followed the paths of previous exiles from the American
Revolution and the War of 1812, migrating to Canada, England, and
other parts of the British Empire, where many had family and commercial
relations. Some Southerners even moved to the Northern states, especially
New York, where they found business opportunities and sympathetic
communities of Democrats, critical of emancipation and other "radical"
Republican efforts to expand political participation for freed slaves.

These exiles remained loyal to the Confederacy, but they recognized
that it was in retreat. Like Booth, they hoped to resurrect it through

violence. They continued to defend a narrow vision of democracy with white male dominance and inherited concentrations of wealth. The exiles tried to blend into their new homes by bringing much of the Confederacy with them, including, in the case of Brazil, their slaves.

The transition was hardest for leading military figures who were unwilling to accept defeat. This was particularly true for officers, like Shelby, who perceived themselves as victors in countless battles. Shelby spoke of their "spotless banner" that would be "tarnished by dishonor" in surrender, especially to an occupying force filled with African American soldiers.[2]

Major General John Bankhead Magruder, feted for his heroism in the Mexican-American War two decades earlier, and then his recapture of Galveston for the Confederacy in the Civil War, expressed the sentiment of those who still believed the South had a winnable cause. "Come what may," Magruder told his men, "I shall stand by my country, and I will never be a slave to Yankee power. I had rather be a Camanche Indian chief than bow the knee to Yankeedom."[3]

After Lee's surrender and Lincoln's assassination, the most defiant Confederate military leaders continued the Civil War by taking their armies farther south. They kept their forces organized, and they led them through Texas and across the Rio Grande, into Mexico. At least five thousand Southerners followed this path in the summer of 1865. More than twenty thousand traveled farther south, to Venezuela, Brazil, and other countries.

Exile was a strategic maneuver by Southern military men to continue the fight for their vision of a white male democracy. They had no remorse. And they did not believe their cause was lost.

Brigadier General Joseph Shelby led the Confederate flight south of the border. He kept his Iron Brigade together in North Texas until June 1, 1865, when he announced that "he was not going to surrender, but was going to Mexico." He offered his soldiers a choice: They could surrender individually, they could fall out and return to their homes, or they could stay in ranks and march to Mexico City. About one hundred and fifty of Shelby's soldiers, including most of his senior officers, pledged to continue their service with him and headed for a

General Joseph O. Shelby. *Credit: George Caleb Bingham*

foreign country. Other soldiers fled back to their families, mostly in Missouri. More than a thousand of Shelby's men surrendered to Union forces in Shreveport, Louisiana, where federal officials provided them rations and allowed them to return to their homes on "parole," with the condition that they would never again serve in any armed force of the Confederacy.[4]

As was true for Lee's soldiers in Virginia, the surrender terms for Shelby's troops were generous and humane. Exile in Mexico promised much more uncertainty and suffering, and yet many of the highest-ranking officers chose that route. The motivation to leave revealed a fear of multiracial democracy much more than a dread of punishment or deprivation. Exile allowed elite white men who would lose their status as slave masters to try to hold on. In Mexico, they hoped, they could keep their military status as accomplished warriors and white overlords, even without their slaves. They could avoid the adjustments of emancipation and defeat, which seemed more painful than the adjustments of exile.

Shelby and the soldiers who followed him to Mexico committed mutiny against the United States and their secessionist regime at the same time, disobeying both the commander in chief in Washington and the surrendering Confederate commander in Virginia. In their own eyes, overriding their military obligations to their commanders was a mystical attachment to the land for which they had fought; they were being true to that, even as they abandoned their homesteads.

The brigade of approximately one hundred and fifty soldiers grew quickly, as families joined the husbands and fathers in rank. Soldiers from other scattered units linked up as well. The Confederate stalwarts marched south through Waco and Austin before stopping in San Antonio. Over more than two hundred miles, Shelby's war-weary men hauled a large cache of Confederate weapons, many of which had been part of the federal arsenal before the war. This was now stolen matériel. The weapons included ten Napoleon howitzers, two thousand Enfield rifles, forty thousand rounds of small ammunition, five hundred dragon sabers, and numerous carbines, pistols, and cartridges. Their clothes were tattered and their bodies broken from years of war, but Shelby and his men were armed to continue the fight.[5]

Almost without exception, Texans welcomed them on their march south, greeting them as courageous heroes, not runaways or thieves. The soldiers treated the civilians they encountered with respect, sometimes offering protection against roaming bandits and other elements of disorder following the collapse of the Confederacy. In Austin, Shelby's troops helped to protect the state treasury and other assets. Governor Pendleton Murrah hailed them as protectors, and he then joined the exiles.

Shelby's zealousness for an exclusive white democracy, and his violent opposition to multiracial reforms, was widely popular from town to town and city to city. Austin was just one example. Most Confederates in the city could not leave their local livelihoods and move farther south on short notice, but they sympathized and approved. They hoped that Shelby's brigade would rebuild the power of the Confederacy in Mexico and then bring it back to the American South. Austin was one of many war-damaged cities in Texas, but its residents still had not given up on the conflict—they supported its continuation across the Rio Grande.

The southward marching exiles encountered so much goodwill that they decided to rest and entertain themselves in San Antonio, the vibrant missionary and trading city just 150 miles north of the border. Shelby lodged at the Menger Hotel, the fanciest establishment in town, with an ornate Victorian lobby, spacious rooms overlooking the famous Alamo square, a well-stocked bar, and the city's finest cuisine. Menger was more than a hotel; it was a hub for Confederate businessmen and military leaders to meet and plan for their future. As Shelby's men drank and danced around town, the general conspired with allies in the comforts of the fine hotel.

Although he was a fugitive, he stayed in plain sight, mostly at the Menger bar, for more than a week. Shelby shared drinks and Mexico schemes with a growing cabal of elite Confederate fugitives, including General Magruder, General Edmund Kirby Smith, Texas governor Murrah, Missouri governor Thomas Reynolds, and Louisiana governor Henry Watkins Allen. These were the leading men of the Confederacy west of the Mississippi. They were joined by Colonel William Broadwell, the cunning figure who oversaw the Confederate Cotton Bureau, smuggling cotton from Louisiana into Texas and across the Rio Grande in return for payment by foreign purchasers. These arrangements, begun in 1863 to circumvent the Union blockade on Southern trade, provided the cash to finance Confederate arms during the last two years of the war. Now Broadwell would help the fugitive Confederate leaders plan their resettlement in Mexico.

They did not worry about security during their march through the parched land sandwiched between the hill country of San Antonio and the river border with Mexico. Despite the presence of bandits and approaching Union forces, Shelby and his colleagues knew they could count on supportive local communities. And the former Confederates were very well armed.

The main question was what to do after crossing the border. At that moment, Mexico was divided by a civil war, often called the Reform War. During the early part of the 1850s, a growing group of young, educated reformers had taken up arms against the dictatorial presidency of Antonio López de Santa Anna and the landed elites who supported him. Exiled in Louisiana, the reformers appealed to citizens in their country for a new constitution that would guarantee individual freedoms, empower poor citizens, and limit the influence of the wealthy families around Santa Anna.

By 1855, the reformers had attracted enough support to force Santa Anna from office, and in 1857, Mexico adopted a new constitution. It included a number of rights protections that echoed, and in some ways advanced beyond, the U.S. Constitution. For example, the 1857 Mexican document prohibited slavery, abolished all forms of torture and the death penalty, and protected freedom of speech and conscience. Sympathizers in the Union, including Abraham Lincoln, hailed the new Mexican Constitution as an enlightened, liberal document, promising a brighter future for the country that had only achieved independence from Spain thirty-six years earlier. In the weeks before his inauguration, Lincoln wrote enthusiastically about the reforms in Mexico as steps toward "happiness, prosperity, and liberty."[6]

On December 21, 1860—the day after South Carolina voted to become the first state to secede from the Union—Benito Juárez was elected president of Mexico. In many ways, Juárez was the Lincoln of his country. Juárez and Lincoln were self-taught politicians who came from very modest roots. They both sought to break down inherited concentrations of power and create new economic opportunities for hardworking, disadvantaged citizens—which meant opposition to slavery and other forms of coerced labor. Lincoln was the controversial emancipator of slaves; Juárez advocated strongly for the rights of indigenous communities, often mistreated by the Mexican government.

Juárez's Liberal Reform Party echoed Lincoln's Republican Party. It was a new political organization connecting diverse men and women who sought to modernize Mexico by expanding access to land, education, wages, and political participation. The parties on both sides of the border drew on radical ideas about free markets and universal male franchise. Both had strong followings among young, upwardly mobile citizens, often in urban areas. Their opponents were landed traditional families, religious institutions, and long-standing political elites— including Jefferson Davis and Santa Anna. Lincoln's Republicans and Juárez's Liberal Reformers promoted a wider, more diverse vision of democracy.

That was precisely what General Shelby and his growing band of exiles wanted to escape and then destroy. The Confederacy had made some overtures to Juárez during the Civil War, hoping that he might help the Southern states break the Union blockade on selling cotton and other products abroad. Juárez had rejected any connection with the Confederacy, reaching out to the Union as his preferred partner. Lincoln pledged official "neutrality" as Juárez's government struggled with a violent opposition, but the American president helped where he could, including limited arms transfers. He recognized that Juárez's efforts to reform Mexico would help the cause of open, multiracial democracy in North America.[7]

Lincoln's encouragement was not nearly enough. The Mexican reformers confronted dangerous enemies abroad, as well as at home. Burdened with the costs of fighting adversaries and financing promised aid to citizens, Juárez's government suspended debt payments to European creditors in the summer of 1861. Within six months, a small coalition of British, Spanish, and French forces landed at the large trading port of Veracruz, in southeastern Mexico, demanding repayment. This military intervention bolstered Juárez's domestic adversaries, and Confederate leaders, like Jefferson Davis, welcomed European opponents of liberal reforms.

Despite their aggression, the foreign powers were not able to force payment on Mexican debts; Juárez's government simply did not have the money. The British and the Spanish also had other demands on their forces in the Caribbean and Southeast Asia. Within months, they withdrew, cutting their losses.

The French, however, decided to stay and exploit the debt crisis as an excuse to occupy Mexico. Napoleon III, the insecure but self-important nephew of the first Napoleon, had a vision of re-creating

Benito Juárez, elected president of Mexico in December 1860, pursued a series of reforms designed to expand the rights and opportunities of all Mexican citizens. He sought assistance from President Abraham Lincoln, who pledged neutrality but offered support (including arms) where he could. *Credit: Pelegrí Clavé*

the French empire in North America. He perceived the convulsions in Mexico and the Civil War in the United States as opportunities for expansion. After British and Spanish forces departed, he increased his contingent of soldiers in Mexico, reaching a total of almost forty thousand men under arms. On April 20, 1862, Napoleon III declared war on Juárez's government. By June of the next year—just weeks before the Battle of Gettysburg—French troops took control of Mexico City, forcing Juárez and his supporters to flee. Confederate soldiers under General Lee's command had failed to reach Washington, DC, but French imperial combatants had now conquered the capital of Mexico.

The French emperor appointed Maximilian, the younger brother of the Austrian Habsburg emperor, to build a conservative, pro-French government in Mexico that would crush the reformers, who soon launched an insurgency. Maximilian had no personal or familial connection to Mexico. Nonetheless, Napoleon III and his allies in North America believed they were restoring the power of traditional elites and preventing a descent into multiracial democracy. They promised a new political order, led by a powerful group of heavily armed men, across a war-torn continent.

Confederates, especially the exiles, expressed a strong and obvious preference for Maximilian's imported Mexican emperorship, just as Republicans in the Union nurtured an affinity with Juárez's Liberal Reform Party. Maximilian did not defend slavery, but he represented the continued power of white landholders, the enforcement of strict social hierarchy, and the prohibition of mass political participation. He opposed the emancipatory promises of the 1857 Mexican Constitution, and he made common cause with the conservatives who had previously backed Santa Anna and traded with Southern plantation owners. Maximilian had a powerful French army that remained in Mexico, and he looked for new allies in the north.

Shelby and his exiles were happy to oblige. Reflecting the near-unanimous preferences of his soldiers, the general announced: "We will fight under Maximilian." So no one would be mistaken, he elaborated: "You have chosen the Empire."[8]

When Shelby's group crossed the Rio Grande, they initially made contact with Juárez's forces. The soldiers treated one another with courtesy, avoiding unnecessary violence. Although they wanted to ally with Maximilian, the exiles were not at war with his enemies yet, and besides, Juárez's forces outnumbered the exiles, who were in unfamiliar territory.

The Liberal Reformers needed more equipment, which the exiles possessed. In the border town of Piedras Negras, Shelby sold Juárez's forces the Confederate howitzers and munitions he had stolen, in return for $16,000 in silver and $40,000 in the Liberal Reform government's currency. The exiles used this money to pay for food, shelter, and entertainment as they continued marching south to Mexico City.

Following their transaction, the Liberal Reformers and the Confederate exiles peaceably departed from Piedras Negras.

Moving deep into Mexican territory, the Americans were determined to reach Maximilian's court as quickly as possible. They wanted to offer their services to his regime and, by extension, Napoleon III's government in France. Shelby, Magruder, and other exile leaders expected that Maximilian would treat them as the heroic defenders of white civilization they believed they were. They also hoped the two emperors—Maximilian and Napoleon III—would help them rebuild the Confederacy, first in Mexico and then back across the American border.

The exiles were trying to recapture the lands they had abandoned by enlisting foreign invaders. They dreamed of a renewed Confederate empire, partnered with the French empire. They believed their treason was perversely patriotic.

Painting of General John Bankhead Magruder from early in his career. *Source: Egbert Watson Magruder, Year Book of the American Clan Gregor Society, 1914 (Richmond, VA: Ware and Duke, 1915), frontispiece*

General Magruder, who commanded a smaller group of soldiers than Shelby, reached Mexico City first, and he eagerly met with the emperor. Magruder recounted this meeting in detail soon after. He had visited the Mexican leader's palace (then occupied by Santa Anna) eighteen years before, when the American army captured the capital. This time, Magruder arrived as a fugitive from the United States, seeking employment and assistance. Although the tables had turned, the American visitor showed at least as much ambition as before.

Magruder described Maximilian in heroic terms: "Though tall and commanding in stature, his person was a model of manly beauty, and his face denoted greater firmness and strength than I had expected from the photographs I had seen of him."

Magruder, Shelby, and other Confederate leaders thought of themselves as landed aristocrats, and they clearly identified more closely with European royalty than with the poor citizens, especially the former slaves, in their home states. The same applied to their views of Mexican citizens. In their extensive writings about their travels south of the border, the exiles say almost nothing about the residents they encountered in the various communities they visited. Like European imperialists, the Confederates in Mexico were only attentive to the light-skinned warriors and politicians who fit their own self-image. The bond Magruder felt to Maximilian was based on a shared commitment to white man's rule over the rest of the people. Only strong, hierarchical leadership, he wrote, could ensure order and progress for the American South and Mexico.

Maximilian suspected the motives of Magruder, Shelby, and all the Confederate exiles. Would they strengthen his embattled government or seek to plunder it for their purposes? Were they reliable military and political supporters? Would collaboration with the exiles trigger more forceful opposition to Maximilian from the United States government? Union general Philip Sheridan had a large army poised north of the Mexican border, he was providing Juárez's soldiers with weapons, and there was growing evidence that he and his commander, General Ulysses Grant, considered invading Mexico to capture the fleeing Confederates. Maximilian did not want to provoke the massive military forces at the command of Sheridan and Grant by enlisting the much smaller exile army.

For that reason, Maximilian showed caution in his late August 1865 meeting with Magruder, followed by a meeting with Shelby soon after. The emperor rejected both of their offers for military assistance; he did not want to create a Mexican army of Confederate exiles, as they had proposed. Instead, he pushed the exiles toward a program of colonization.

Relations between the United States and Mexico had centered on colonization since the early nineteenth century. After 1821, the newly independent Mexican republic honored a Spanish grant that Stephen F. Austin, a prominent empresario, or land developer, had inherited from his father. To populate territory in Texas and other areas, the government in Mexico City hoped to attract able-bodied settlers from the United States. Austin recruited three hundred of the earliest white

Maximilian I, emperor of Mexico. *Credit: Ludwig Angerer*

American settler families to live in Texas. They became landowners in what was a northern province of Mexico. And they recruited many more.

In just fifteen years, the white settlers who colonized Texas demanded independence from Mexico, which they attained after a short war in 1836. They joined the United States as the twenty-eighth state at the end of 1845, nine months ahead of California. The Mexican colony had become an independent country and then a state in the Union. When Texas voted to secede from the Union in 1861, it had come full circle—a settler community attached to bigger states (Mexico and the United States) but also devoted to its independence. This ambivalence has carried forward into the twenty-first century.

Without sufficient understanding, Maximilian spread the complex colonial dynamics of Texas to other parts of Mexico. The exiles had a better sense of this history, and they recognized that Confederate colonization south of the border could construct a stepping-stone to the independent empire of white landed elites that they had fought to protect during the Civil War. They wanted to create another Texas in Mexico that would eventually expand, separate, and rejoin other Confederate territories—including the original Texas.

Maximilian viewed Confederate colonization as a tool for recruiting more supporters to his regime. He appointed Matthew Fontaine Maury, one of the Confederacy's most famous scientists and longtime advocates of Southern expansion, to the ostentatious position of Imperial Commissioner of Colonization. Maury and the emperor had corresponded before Maximilian's arrival in Mexico. The two figures saw themselves as modernizers of backward lands and protectors of white rule. They shared a deep interest in using science and colonization to project power.

Maury promised Maximilian that together they could transform Mexico into a "New Virginia." Maury believed that the damage to the South, caused by Union armies, would motivate some of the region's best men to support this project. Instead of reconstruction in the American South for multiracial democracy, he called for reconstruction in

Mexico to protect white planters. "In contemplating the shipwreck of country, kinsmen, and friends," Maury wrote of the defeated Confederacy, "I recognized among the debris of the wreck the very materials that are required to build upon good and solid foundations, the Mexican Empire." He continued, "From such a wreck, Mexico may gather and transfer to her own borders the very intelligence, skill, and labor which made the South what she was in her palmy days."[9]

The only exception that Maury allowed to this idyllic Southern vision was the exclusion of slavery in Mexico. He recognized that Maximilian and his European patrons had prohibited slavery in their empires by this time. The Mexican Republic had also abolished slavery after its independence from Spain. But Maury expected that Southern planters moving to Mexico would bring their former slaves in a permanent subordinate position: "apprentices bound by indentures," he explained.[10]

Maury promoted the old patriarchal assumption that freed slaves still needed their masters: "Though many of the negroes have been set free, and owing to the abrupt manner of closing it, have run riot, and are afflicted with pestilence and famine, there are many of them still true to their masters." The eagerness for freedom expressed by former slaves belied this argument. Former slaves almost universally sought to escape their previous masters.[11]

Extending his defense of racial patriarchy to the poor residents of Mexico, Maury believed that settlers from the South should conscript local labor. He envisioned Brown and Black apprentices working under the direction of newly arrived white overseers, a common practice in the European colonies.

Maury presented a detailed plan for Southern colonization to Maximilian in June 1865, two months before Shelby and Magruder arrived in Mexico City: the "Project of a Design to Encourage the Immigration into Mexico of Planters from Virginia and the South with their Freed Slaves." According to the plan, the emperor would provide land to white settlers from the South, who would re-create plantation life with intensive cash-crop agriculture and strict labor control. Each master who emigrated from the American South to Mexico would have "the proper and requisite police on his plantation" with the power "to compel these apprentices who may be

Commander Matthew Fontaine Maury. *Credit:*
Mathew Brady

disposed to idleness and vice to conform to the laws and to render service."
Substitute *slaves* for *apprentices* and this sounded like Virginia indeed.[12]

Southerners would immigrate to Mexico, Maury promised, because
colonization allowed them to preserve what they had lost at the hands
of Union soldiers: "It would be difficult to say which have suffered, or
are suffering, most—the whites from the ravages of war, or the blacks
from the so-called kindness of friends." Maury argued that colonization
was "the quickest, most certain and best means of affording relief to
their sufferings, of giving quiet to this country, stability to the throne,
and peace to America." Southern planters would reconstruct plantation
life, Maximilian would acquire loyal subjects, and the values of white
society would be preserved, temporarily relocated to a new country.[13]

Maury promised profits for Maximilian and the Southern exiles
too. He described Mexican planters as toiling "in a rude state." "A few

of our clever farmers, bringing with them their agricultural apprentices, would give new life and energy to the country," Maury explained. "By sprinkling the Empire with settlers of this sort, they and their improved implements of husbandry and methods of culture would serve as so many new centers of agricultural life, energy, and improvement."[14]

Maury calculated that colonization by white Southerners and their former slaves would grow annual Mexican agricultural exports from $4 million to as much as $300 million. The increased trade would enrich the exiles and Maximilian, as well as his European patrons. One can understand why the new Mexican emperor, in need of cash to build his state, found this proposition enticing, perhaps intoxicating.

Empire glittered with gold, or so it seemed.

The Confederate soldiers in Mexico conceived of colonization as both an opportunity and a respite from battle. The emperor granted 160 acres of land to each single man and 320 acres to each male-headed family. The new landholders were exempted from all Mexican taxes for a year and from military service for five years. The emperor made special provisions for former slaves, who were tied to their former masters as apprentices and required to work under their command for five to ten years. The apprentices were paid a wage, but only one-quarter of what white laborers earned, and they did not receive the money until their term of service finished. They were also prohibited from changing employers or resigning. Although slavery had been abolished, Confederate settlers in Mexico kept something very close. The freed slaves brought to the colony were hardly free.

The colonizers largely settled on five hundred thousand acres of abandoned land in the Córdoba Valley, about three days' journey southeast from Mexico City. The land was fertile for coffee growing, which required intensive daily labor. Similar to the plantation systems around cotton and tobacco in the American South, settlers designed vast agricultural fields, requiring large numbers of inexpensive laborers. The apprentices did the backbreaking work in the hot sun, with little equipment, overseen by white masters.

Adding to the aristocratic veneer that many American Southerners craved, Maximilian named the Confederate utopia after his wife,
Carlota, a Belgian princess by birth. The settlement was also known
as the New Virginia Colony. The virgin queen, Elizabeth I, and the
famously beautiful empress of Mexico were the namesakes for the territories Confederates claimed. Aristocracy justified social hierarchy, land
acquisition, and forced labor.

Maury oversaw the recruitment of new "masters" to settle in Mexico, for which he received an annual salary of five thousand pesos—a
princely payment for the time. The emperor appointed Magruder as
the chief of the Land Office and superintendent of surveys for Carlota.
Magruder hired a group of Confederate engineers to divide the land
into private lots, design public spaces, and plan transportation (including a railroad terminus). Magruder also enlisted recruiters across the
American South and in California. Like their predecessors in Texas
decades before, these agents promised free land and a preservation of
traditional values for those who felt constrained in their war-torn, occupied communities. White colonization in Mexico followed the long-
standing pattern of westward movement across the continent.

If Maury and Magruder inherited Stephen F. Austin's role forty
years earlier as boosters for settling Mexican lands, Shelby was their
Sam Houston—a decorated military figure who defended the rights of
white settlers and encouraged them to build a new society for themselves. Shelby became a lead settler in Carlota, acquiring a large stone
house, surrounded by a twelve-acre plantation for coffee cultivation.
He moved his family, with the personal support of Maximilian, and
soon others followed. Within a year, five hundred similar homesteads
surrounded Shelby's. Compared to other colonization schemes, Confederate exiles settled in Mexico at a very rapid pace.[15]

Shelby used his logistical skills from the military, and his favoritism
from the emperor, to profit from the new arrivals. He operated a wagon
business, transporting people and goods between the railroad terminus
and Carlota. His employees were Confederate army veterans, many of
whom had marched into Mexico with him. A visiting journalist from

the *New York Herald* described Shelby's business: "His wagons are all of Yankee manufacture, are drawn by ten mules each, and every wagon carries a load of six to seven thousand pounds, the freight of which is 300 to 350 dollars."[16]

Colonization preserved Shelby's elite status among Southerners, and it offered opportunities for personal enrichment. During his first half year in Carlota, he prospered from the stream of new recruits. They were sponsored by the Mexican government, and the colony was guarded by French troops. Shelby and other settlers did not have to pay for their land or the services that made their way of life possible. They never would have received a deal like that if they had stayed in the Union-occupied South. Imperial power and ambition, with forced labor, expanded the freedoms of the exiles.

Life in Mexico was promising for Confederate officers, and it attracted many of them. Alexander Watkins Terrell, a judge in Texas with close personal ties to Sam Houston, joined the exile community. Terrell had left his court and enlisted in the Confederate army in 1863. Despite his late entry and his friendship with Houston, who opposed secession, Terrell rapidly rose to brigadier general.

In May 1865, he announced that he would not surrender but move with his soldiers "to seek with arms in their hands, homes which will be denied here." Terrell marched his men along the familiar exiles' route through Austin and San Antonio and into Mexico. He connected with the French forces defending Maximilian and the American colonizers. And like Magruder and Shelby, he offered his services.[17]

Terrell did not travel to Carlota. Instead, he became an imperial spy. His job was not to fight side by side with the French army or build a new colonial settlement. Terrell's new role was to discourage Confederates and other Americans from supporting Juárez's Liberal Reform forces. He used his personal connections to promote Maximilian and undermine any enemies.

Terrell acted secretly to acquire information that helped the emperor's cause. That is where his treacherous intents were most evident. He promised to "obtain accurate information of the plans and purposes of the yankee government at all times." He proposed sneaking back into the United States to conduct espionage for Maximilian. Terrell was explicit that he would side with the emperor even against his own country: "Should war begin between France and the United States, I would be on the ground and would fall on the right flank of the yankee force on the Rio Grande in thirty days with from two to four thousand cavalry and open communications with your forces at Piedras Negras or Monterrey."

Terrell received six months' salary for his treason against the United States. He also extolled Booth's murder of Lincoln, distributing a poem written by another advocate of exile, Alfred Arrington, which claimed the assassin

died for the weal of the world 'neath the heal
Of too many a merciless Nero.[18]

We do not know how much information Terrell acquired for Maximilian. He probably exaggerated his role. His biographer observes that he played a "double game"—like many spies—continuing to help former allies who remained in the United States. Terrell planned that he would return to Texas eventually, and he wanted to preserve a place for himself within the Democratic Party. Although he clearly worked with Maximilian to undermine the United States government after the Civil War, he claimed that he never pledged loyalty to the emperor. That was a lie. Terrell was loyal only to white supremacy, wherever he could find it.[19]

Maximilian pursued an imperial program that shared many goals with Maury, Magruder, Shelby, Terrell, and the other exiles. They were allies of convenience, and they worked closely together for more than a year. Maximilian wanted a kingdom; the exiles wanted to rebuild theirs. They needed each other.

Napoleon III wavered in his commitment to this strange partnership between the installed emperor and the fugitive former slaveholders. When American secretary of state William Seward warned Napoleon III that the United States would send upward of one hundred thousand

Brigadier General Alexander Watkins Terrell.

soldiers to destroy the French forces in Mexico, the French emperor reconsidered. He knew that Union generals Ulysses Grant and Philip Sheridan had requested permission from President Andrew Johnson to pursue the exiles, especially Terrell. Sheridan recounted in his memoirs that he and Grant considered Maximilian's government "a part of the Rebellion itself" and that "putting down secession would never be complete" until the European invaders and Confederate exiles were expelled from their sanctuaries.[20]

The Union commanders understood how Maury, Magruder, Shelby, Terrell, and other Confederate leaders sought to rebuild the Confederacy in Mexico and then bring it back to the American South. They knew that the defeated rebels had not given up. Grant and Sheridan were open about their concerns, and they were serious about military maneuvers across the Rio Grande. The generals were ready for this fight; the smaller French forces in Mexico were no match for them.

In early 1866, Napoleon changed direction, announcing plans to withdraw his soldiers from Mexico. He was not abandoning North America but preoccupied with more immediate threats from Prussia and other European countries. He began to see Mexico as a diversion rather than an opportunity for French interests. The Parisian court was also frustrated that Maximilian had not eliminated the Liberal Reform resistance.

If anything, Juárez's forces had grown stronger after early 1865, with the arrival of more supplies from General Sheridan and other sympathetic commanders north of the border. During the winter of 1866, for example, Sheridan's forces distributed thirty thousand muskets from the Baton Rouge Arsenal in Louisiana to Juárez's soldiers in Mexico. The end of the American Civil War allowed the enormous Union army—now the largest land force in the world—to arm its friends at home and abroad. The French could not keep pace with that.

Sheridan, in particular, viewed the Liberal Reformers as useful allies. He offered them cover, advice, and encouragement, where possible. He also sought to prevent the exodus of more Confederates, denying them access to the largest Southern ports. The U.S. Army closed American borders to rebellious Southerners, but it opened opportunities for Juárez and others who fought against Maximilian. Sheridan only exaggerated slightly when he wrote that "under the influence of such significant and powerful backing" from the Union army, the Liberal Reformers in Mexico grew "so strong that within two years Imperialism had received its death-blow."[21]

The power of the United States government and its commitment to multiracial democracy—represented by the Republicans north of the border and the Liberal Reformers in Mexico—dominated both sides of the Rio Grande Valley. Napoleon III recognized this changed dynamic. In late 1866, he made the final decision to cut his losses in Mexico. He dispatched warships to return the more than twenty thousand French soldiers protecting Maximilian. By March 11, 1867, they had all departed from the port of Veracruz, where they had first arrived five years earlier.

Maximilian refused to leave. He sent his wife to plead for renewed assistance from Napoleon, without success. He collected his remaining loyal soldiers, mostly Mexican conservatives attached to the court, and moved northwest to the city of Querétaro. This was a more defensible position, but Liberal Reform forces captured him after two months of fighting. On June 19, 1867, Juárez ordered Maximilian's execution by firing squad. Maximilian's death was the final blow for Napoleon's North American dreams and the Confederacy's move to Mexico.

The execution of the emperor was a shock to all, both American and French. Secretary of State Seward had tried to prevent it at the last minute, for fear of antagonizing Napoleon III. Juárez, however, wanted to ensure that Maximilian did not live to lead another intervention against him. He also wanted to show the citizens of Mexico and other nations that he had the power to govern the country with a firm hand. Although criticisms of the execution continued, the Liberal Reformers

A supporter of the Liberal Reformers in Mexico, Édouard Manet painted this account of the execution of Maximilian soon after the event. The painting was controversial in France, where Manet lived, because it criticized Napoleon III's intervention in Mexico. *Credit: Édouard Manet*

quickly reestablished their rule over the Mexican Republic, removing the remaining pockets of imperial and conservative resistance. Maximilian had mobilized these groups; his death signaled their imminent demise.

The same was true for the American exiles who had attached themselves to the emperor. Carlota and other colonies collapsed when the French garrisons departed and funding from the emperor evaporated. Before Juárez's forces could reach the settlers, they packed up their belongings and prepared to flee again. Some traveled to Havana, Cuba, which still allowed slavery, but almost all the exiles made their way back to the United States, often on U.S. Navy ships sent to Veracruz to observe the French withdrawal.

The American gunboat *Tacony* carried Shelby, his family, and many of his soldiers-turned-settlers to New Orleans. Terrell and Magruder fled separately to Havana, where they sought additional opportunities for troublemaking. They made their way back to the United States shortly afterward. Maury did not stay in Mexico either. He traveled to London, where he had spent most of the Civil War as an ambassador for the Confederacy. He would return to his native Virginia in 1868.

None of the exiles were tried for treason although each had participated in a rebellion against and then joined forces with an adversary of the United States. On Christmas Day 1868, in the last months of his presidency, Andrew Johnson excused their crimes. Presidential Proclamation 179 (we would call it an *executive order* today) granted: "To all and to every person who, directly or indirectly, participated in the late insurrection or rebellion a full pardon and amnesty for the offense of treason against the United States or of adhering to their enemies during the late civil war, with restoration of all rights, privileges, and immunities under the Constitution and the laws which have been made in pursuance thereof."[22]

Johnson's order was an intentional erasure of history. It silenced discussion of Confederate crimes, denied the claims of victims (especially former slaves), and returned respectability to men who had treasonously rebelled against their country. The exiles were fully restored. Their advocacy for a closed, racially stratified democracy, ruled by white landed elites, was normalized, even valorized. Men like Shelby, Magruder, Terrell, and Maury could claim that they were heroes who bravely fought for their way of life and would continue to do so.

That was President Johnson's purpose: to restore white male dominance in the South after slavery. The Confederacy remained the prevailing image of what democracy should look like for the millions who fought on its behalf. Like Robert E. Lee and so many others, each of the exiles became the subject of heroic accounts that emphasized courage and commitment, downplaying the flight from country and the ignominious association with European imperialists. Popular magazines, particularly the *Confederate Veteran*, chronicled the adventures of the exiles as warriors who modeled the "necessity of white supremacy" in the South. If Booth was the martyr to Confederate hopes, the exiles were living embodiments of how those hopes could survive even after the soldiers had left the battlefields.[23]

The exiles became oracles for white supremacy and a racially stratified democracy. Magruder was an instant success as a traveling lecturer across the country, including the North, where he regaled audiences with stories of bravery, strength, and camaraderie. Like Booth, he performed the role of moral Cassandra against an allegedly degenerate, racially mixed society. He was articulate and handsome. And he gave his audiences permission to feel superior to Republicans, Mexicans, and especially African Americans. His public events reconnected many former Confederate soldiers and sympathizers, creating a vibrant network for resistance to Republican Reconstruction policies.

On February 18, 1871, Magruder died while residing as a celebrated guest of Houston's most opulent hotel, the Hutchins House. He was initially buried in Houston, but in 1876, the state of Texas reburied his body with full honors in the Trinity Episcopal Cemetery in Galveston, where Magruder had defeated Union forces in battle. His coffin was draped with flowers to spell out: "Our Texas Hero."

In 1894, citizens of Texas raised private funds to build a monument to Magruder. At its public dedication, Thomas N. Waul, another former Confederate general, explained the purpose of the monument and the legacy of Magruder's life: "We glory in the rectitude of the cause and exult in the valor and knightly qualities of the hero...as gallant a soldier and as intrepid a hero as ever drew sword in liberty's cause."[24]

Shelby lived longer, and he attracted similar reverence from the defenders of a closed, racially stratified democracy. He returned from Mexico to his family farm in Missouri, where he joined the state's Democratic Party. Shelby became a somewhat mythic figure for leading the allegedly undefeated Iron Brigade of the Confederacy, a symbol of Southern strength and forbearance for many. He was active in various business ventures with other veterans, including railroad construction and mining. In 1893, as a reward for his assistance to the Democratic Party, President Grover Cleveland appointed him U.S. marshal for western Missouri and Kansas City.

The next year, Shelby deployed the federal forces at his command to repress the nationwide strike of the Pullman Company's railroad workers. This was the largest work stoppage of the late nineteenth century, including more than 250,000 workers in twenty-seven states. As always, Shelby sided with the wealthy and the white. He sent U.S. marshals to strike locations, where they beat and arrested the poor men demanding better pay and work conditions. He showed predictable disdain for immigrant laborers, African Americans, and their supporters in government.

Shelby's Confederate military service remained a source of fame for him, even late in life. In 1895, he was appointed honorary commander of the United Confederate Veterans of Missouri, an organization devoted to honoring Southern veterans and promoting their values. There were obviously no African American members of the organization. Two years later, Shelby died, with less public fanfare than Magruder but with widely held regard among Democrats in the North and South.

Terrell imprinted the values Shelby promoted in Texas law. Terrell entered state politics as an outspoken opponent of Republican Reconstruction policies. He did not have the military record of Magruder or Shelby, but he compensated with direct appeals to white supremacy in the South. He served in the Texas Senate from 1876 to 1884, in the Texas House of Representatives from 1891 to 1892, and again from 1903 to 1905. In between, he was, like Shelby, rewarded for his service to the Democratic Party by President Cleveland, traveling to the Ottoman Empire as the U.S. minister plenipotentiary. Terrell became a part of the royal court in Constantinople, much larger and wealthier than Maximilian's brief court in Mexico City. The exile transformed himself into a distinguished ambassador from the country he had earlier fled.

During his years in the Texas Senate and House of Representatives, Terrell consistently supported legislation limiting African American rights. In 1879, he wrote the law that required a poll tax for voting. In later years, he authored the Terrell Election Law, which created primaries where only white voters would have the opportunity to select party candidates for elected office. The racial restrictions remained on the books in Texas until more than a decade after the Second World War.

Terrell also brought his commitment to white supremacy to the University of Texas, where he served as a regent from 1909 to 1911, defending strict restrictions on African American access to the state's premier institution of higher education. When he died in 1912, Terrell was buried in the Texas State Cemetery, reserved for dignitaries. A county of the state, Terrell County, was named after him. The former judge who joined the Confederate rebellion to protect slavery, and then fled to Mexico to resist multiracial democracy, played a central role in writing the rules for Texas's unapologetically racist democracy. Law and order meant protecting power in Texas for the white landed elite.

If Terrell proved his political deftness from Mexico City to Austin, Maury mastered many of the intellectual settings after the Civil War. He returned to the United States in 1868 and joined the faculty at the Virginia Military Institute. Maury took up residence in Lexington, Virginia, near his longtime colleague Robert E. Lee, who became president of Washington College (now Washington and Lee University).

Maury quickly became an academic celebrity, lecturing on navigation, meteorology, and geography across the country. In 1873, he published a widely read book *Physical Geography*, building on his earlier work, *The Physical Geography of the Sea, and Its Meteorology*. Despite his failed foray in Mexican colonization, Maury made himself into a respected scientific voice. Scholars cited his research well into the next century.

Maury's science was not free from his narrow views about society. Both before and after the Civil War, African Americans were conspicuously absent from his observations about the geography of the United States. As he helped to rebuild the intellectual world of the American South, Maury designed it around the landed, white male elites who had long dominated society. He expanded educational and research opportunities, advocating the creation of Virginia Agricultural and Mechanical College (later Virginia Technical University) for example, to strengthen the power and status of those who already had both.

After Maury died in 1873, Southern leaders added his name to numerous university buildings, schools, and ships. In 1929, Richmond erected a statue to Maury—"Pathfinder of the Seas"—on its Confederate-lined Monument Avenue. The statue was only removed in the summer of 2020, following a nationwide effort to eliminate public shrines to white supremacy.

The men who fled the American South after Appomattox were also the men who made the American nation in the next decades. They converted the treachery of their exile into a narrative of courage, loyalty, and commitment. They used their networks to rebuild the institutions of white landed power and resist multiracial challenges. Most of all, they argued that freedom after slavery required the protection of white privilege. That is what they defended on the Civil War battlefields, in the Carlota colony, and back in the American South. Freedom for some meant denying it to others.

They were taking a stand, but not to "live and die in Dixie," although they enthusiastically sang those words. The exiles had proven their willingness to abandon the land that they loved. They had shown their attachment to their privileges and status, above all. Their strongest commitment was to the preservation of their power and the subordination of others, particularly former slaves. In this sense, they never gave up on the goals of the Confederacy.

The Civil War was not really over for the exiles and their many followers. Although they did not take up arms against the United States government again, they never accepted its stated aims and, thus, never accepted their defeat. Indeed, by 1868, they were not defeated men; they were thriving once again.

Upon return to their homes, they continued to fight for a closed society. They used persuasion, subterfuge, coercion, and, quite often, violence to exclude those who demanded a wider, open citizenry as promised by the Thirteenth, Fourteenth, and Fifteenth Amendments to the Constitution. Such demands were getting louder.

As the exiles became a force in American politics, so did former slaves, many of whom had courageously joined the Union cause. These new citizens challenged efforts to resurrect the old Confederacy.

CHAPTER 4

Citizens

Let us not forget that justice to the negro is safety to the nation.
—FREDERICK DOUGLASS[1]

Black men and women had won the Civil War, according to Frederick Douglass. They had achieved freedom from slavery. And they had freed themselves, with the help of Union armies.

The freed slaves were not passively unshackled; they created their own liberation. Their courageous pursuit of justice, against terrible odds, widened the possibilities of freedom for all people. The destruction of slavery placed African Americans at the forefront of efforts to expand the rights of citizens—a role African Americans would continue to pursue into the twenty-first century. As slavery had long defined the limits of American democracy, its destruction shaped the growth of democracy and confronted its stubborn shortcomings. The freed slaves became prophets of new hope, renewed despair, and, above all, continued struggle.

As the Confederate exiles returned to their homes to defend the world of landed white elites, the freed slaves left their plantations, joined the Union army, and fought for a more open, inclusive society. They invested their labor in new institutions to widen participation, and they voted in large numbers. African Americans pushed forcefully and consistently to enlarge the meaning of democracy in the United States. For a few short years, they had the advantage over the defeated but still resistant supporters of white supremacy.

The early years after the Civil War set the pattern for the coming decades. The conflict over the scope of democracy after slavery was, in the famous words of W. E. B. Du Bois, the "problem of the color line." It touched every citizen.[2]

From its start, Douglass saw the revolutionary potential in the Civil War. A former slave himself, he understood that his kinfolk longed for freedom and would fight for it with tenacity, given the opportunity. This "tremendous war," he proclaimed, gave African Americans a long-awaited "place with all other classes of our fellow citizens" battling to destroy, at last, the "insolent, aggressive, and malignant oligarchy" of slavery. Douglass traveled around the Northern states, recruiting young Black men, including his own children, to join the Union army. He predicted that freed slaves in the occupied South would join their ranks too.[3]

Throughout the war, Douglass pressed Abraham Lincoln to give them a chance. Wary of alienating Northerners who continued to reject arming African Americans, President Lincoln initially resisted creating a multiracial military. He feared losing support in border states, including his native Kentucky. Lincoln and his generals had trouble imagining former slaves standing shoulder to shoulder with white men in battle.

After more than two hundred years of slavery, the degradation of Black bodies had implanted assumptions of inferiority and inhumanity deep in the minds of most Americans. To envision former slaves as Union soldiers was a leap beyond where even ardent opponents of slavery could go. The only image of a slave with a weapon that circulated before this time was a nightmare: the rebellious Black man terrorizing white people. That image continued to strike fear in the hearts of white citizens long after the Civil War. Ending bondage for African Americans did not end widespread opposition to giving them guns.

Freed slaves were not automatically equal citizens. In the imaginings of nearly all Northerners, African Americans were not entitled to the same rights and opportunities as others. They were not to be trusted with the weapons of war, even when they shared a Confederate enemy.

The slaves were the subject of the conflict, but few white Americans wanted to empower them to fight it. The same condescension would characterize later American interventions abroad on behalf of suffering people whom the United States sought to save, without empowering them as equals. In the understanding of many white Americans, the emancipation of slaves reinforced their dependence on the alleged superiority of their liberators: without his white saviors, the Black man could not be free.

The course of the Civil War pushed against these racist assumptions. White citizens in Northern states had become increasingly reluctant (sometimes resistant) to enlist in a war that was deadlier and longer lasting than anticipated in 1861. As the war expanded, the manpower needs for the army grew beyond initial expectations, causing hardships in states that contributed the most able-bodied white soldiers. To field a larger fighting force than ever before in American history, Lincoln and his generals had to try the previously unimaginable.

Gradually, the need for more soldiers compelled the president to enlist Black men in the Union army. Thanks to the recruitment efforts of Douglass and others, thousands of free African Americans in the North came forward to volunteer. Politicians, including Lincoln, were happy to keep the white recruitment goals down, especially as public support for the war diminished in large states like New York.

Slaves in Confederate states occupied by the Union army also made their voices heard. They voted with their feet, running to Union lines, fleeing their plantations and masters wherever they could. The escaped slaves were a burden to the army, which had to feed and shelter them. Returning runaways to the Confederate side was unthinkable because the former slaves resisted; they simply would not go. Besides, if forced back to the plantations, they would only contribute to the enemy's strength.

The most practical solution for the Union army—in fact, the only viable option—was to enlist the freed slaves to help defeat the Confederacy. The African Americans in Union custody were a military resource that could support the army with logistics behind battle lines and potentially fight alongside white soldiers in the field. Ignoring this resource would raise the cost of the war and undermine the Union effort. The slaves gave Union leaders, including Lincoln, an unmistakably good option.

The president was a master at turning necessity into virtue and making what had seemed impossible appear sensible. On New Year's Day 1863, Lincoln's Emancipation Proclamation ended slavery in the Confederate states, and it also encouraged the recruitment of former slaves "into the armed service of the United States." In what was a brief military order, the president denied Confederates their slaves and mobilized that labor for the Union.

Lincoln downplayed the significance of this moment, but it changed everything. The Civil War became a war of liberation, where slaves could fight for their freedom, just as Douglass had hoped. They would be empowered as soldiers, escaping and destroying slavery at the same time. They would become the leading edge of freedom in a rapidly changing American democracy.

African Americans from the North and South answered the call. They rapidly increased the fighting power of the Union. They provided a necessary jolt for a distressed, sometimes desperate army. And they gave renewed purpose to the war. They were fighting for the most basic human freedom—a cause that unmasked the tyranny behind the Confederate defense and the harm that would come from anything short of Union victory. Despite continued discomfort with African American soldiers, Northerners were widely inspired by the courage displayed by the new troops.

African Americans started in support roles during the early years of the war, and by the end, African American soldiers fought in segregated units, often commanded by African American officers. Lincoln spoke of the "double advantage of taking so much labor from the insurgent cause, and supplying the places which otherwise must be filled with so many white men." Lincoln continued, "So far as tested, it is difficult to say they are not as good soldiers as any." No president had ever spoken of African Americans with such praise and implied equality.

"These measures have been much discussed in foreign countries," Lincoln observed. Arming Black men in what had been an all-white U.S. Army had few international precedents. It changed the character of the war and what followed. As Douglass predicted, mobilizing African Americans to fight for freedom gave them a stake in the nation and its laws as never before. The blood spilled for the Union in battle was a down payment on citizenship that Black veterans powerfully claimed after the war.[4]

The newly empowered African American soldiers remade the military and, therefore, American society. When Grant accepted Lee's surrender, there were 179,000 Black men wearing Union uniforms across the country. More than 9,000 additional Black men were sailors in the U.S. Navy. Together, they constituted almost 10 percent of what had grown into the largest military force in the world.[5]

Perhaps most frightening for supporters of white rule, more than 20 percent of African American men between ages eighteen and forty-five

179,000 African Americans, many former slaves, served in the Union army. *Source: J. Oldershaw, Hartford, CT*

found their way into the Union army. That included almost 15 percent of the military-age male slave population in the Deep South. White men continued to dominate the ranks of the Union army because their numbers were much larger, and they received better treatment and more promotions, but the enthusiasm of the African American enlistees was unmistakable.[6]

The majority of the African American soldiers had been slaves at the start of the war. Most could not read or write. They knew the cruelties of the system firsthand, and they courageously fought to end it. In their fighting, the former-slaves-turned-soldiers upended perceptions of this population and its role in American society.

Former slaves were a decisive presence during the last battles of the war. In the vicious fighting around Petersburg, Nashville, and Fort Blakeley, among other places, African American soldiers were near the front lines, pushing back enemy advances and subduing large numbers of Confederate troops. For the final siege of Richmond, General Grant's forces included the largest concentration of African American troops in the war. They proudly marched into the Confederate capital in segregated units, alongside their white counterparts, to dismantle the slaveholder government. By this time, nearly every African American soldier in the Union army had experienced combat and a share of the ultimate victory.[7]

The stakes were enormous for the African American soldiers who, if captured, faced near-certain torture and execution by Southerners, enraged that Black men had taken up arms against them. Former slaves understood the risks. In April 1864, Confederate general Nathan Bedford Forrest had ordered the murder of two hundred African American soldiers captured after the fall of Union-held Fort Pillow in Tennessee. One of the surviving white Union soldiers described Forrest's vengeance as "cruelty beyond the pale":

> The men in Gray were there, aroused by passions born of the "peculiar institution" and determined to main[tain] it at all hazards. It seemed to be the last great act in a drama which had been culminating for two hundred and fifty years. It was, in one sense, on their part, a farewell

shot against victims of the institution they loved so well. Without slavery, Fort Pillow would have been impossible. Under no other system could the fiendish elements which entered into the horrible aspects of that affair, have ever been evolved in the hearts of civilized men.

The author praised the white and Black Union soldiers at Fort Pillow for their "heroism and patriotism." The battle increased their hatred of slavery and their respect for the African Americans fighting to force its demise:

> More than two and a half centuries of wrong were, in a certain sense resented by the men who operated our artillery there against the oppressors of their race. The steady roar of these guns while the conflict lasted, seemed to be echoing back through the ages the story of the slave master's rule and tyranny, while at the same time, this ringing speech of artillery was proclaiming in language not to be misunderstood, that the "Kingdom was coming."[8]

The Confederate crimes at Fort Pillow and other battle sites received widespread attention in the Northern press. News also traveled by rumor within the Union army. African American soldiers knew what had happened, and they recognized that General Forrest was not unique in his vengeance toward former slaves. They turned the fearful promise of slaveholder retribution into motivation for renewed effort to defeat their former masters.

African American soldiers frequently reminded one another to "remember Fort Pillow." They were fighting a known devil, and the only alternative to death was Union victory. Lincoln's soothing words of reconciliation had little place in the vernacular of those who had fled from slavery.[9]

The determination of former slaves added the final energy the Union needed in early 1865 to close out the Confederate forces that were on their heels but still deadly. African American soldiers received less pay and fewer rations than their white counterparts, and their casualty rates in battle were higher than others. They learned quickly, endured difficult conditions, and fought with a consistent ferocity. Above all, they were loyal; instances of their desertion from the army, or serious insubordination, were rare.

African American and white soldiers recognized these contributions. One Black officer observed: "The long contended point of negro fighting qualities is now forever settled. They have proven themselves good soldiers, as well as ardent fighters." A white chaplain agreed and echoed sentiments expressed by other white officers: "They have raised themselves and all mankind in the scale of manhood by their bold achievements." The chaplain concluded that the African American soldiers "must of necessity raise the whole community."[10]

The *New York Times* described the evidence of African American military valor as a "transition so extreme and yet so speedy as what our eyes have just beheld." Black soldiers fighting for the Union triggered a "prodigious revolution which the public mind everywhere is experiencing."

That was an exaggeration, but the change in Northern perceptions of African Americans was indeed startling:

> Eight months ago the African race in this city were literally hunted down like wild beasts. They fled for their lives. When caught, they were shot down in cold blood, or stoned to death, or hung to the trees or the lamp-posts. Their houses were pillaged; the asylum which Christian charity had provided for their orphaned children was burned; and there was no limit to the persecution but in the physical impossibility of finding further material on which the mob could wreak its ruthless hate.

The unmistakable contributions of African American soldiers, reported in the *New York Times* and other newspapers, created a new reality.

> How astonishingly has all this been changed! The same men who could not have shown themselves in the most obscure street in the

City without peril of instant death, even though in the most suppliant attitude, now march in solid platoons, with shouldered muskets, slung knapsacks, and buckled cartridge-boxes down through our gayest avenues and our busiest thoroughfares to the pealing strains of martial music, and are everywhere saluted with waving handkerchiefs, with descending flowers, and with the acclamations and plaudits of countless beholders.[11]

Former slaves had become respected free contributors to the Union—its defense, its economy, and its democracy. The army uniform gave them standing they never had before, along with support and gratitude from the white population, which exceeded the limited advocacy of abolitionists in prior decades.

Although the public ovations for the soldiers suggested they had been embraced by white society, they remained excluded in other ways. In addition to the segregation and inferior pay, the Union army was still a white man's army, led overwhelmingly by white officers trained to see African Americans as subordinates, or worse. Like minority athletes in later generations, the soldiers gained improved status and privilege, but they were still seen as racial inferiors. As it commented on their rise, the *New York Times* was one of countless newspapers to treat the Black troops as an exotic group—"tokens of a new epoch."[12]

The appropriate place for African Americans in the army and in society remained uncertain and controversial at the end of the Civil War. No one, however, could mistake that Black men, including former slaves, were now integral to Union power and identity. The Black soldiers had, through their fighting, created the first multiracial institution in the United States. The Union army was racially mixed as never before. That might not have erased the most stubborn prejudices, but it changed the practice of democracy in the victorious North and the occupied South.

The Civil War had rapidly transformed slaves into soldiers, and now they became occupiers—occupiers of their former masters. It was this that had so enraged John Wilkes Booth when he witnessed African Americans in Union army uniforms guarding white Confederate prisoners of war. The tables had turned incredibly fast on the proud plantation gentry, who were now defeated and destitute, at the mercy of African Americans carrying guns, distributing food, and setting the political future for their former masters.

Social change on this scale was unprecedented in the United States or any other modern society. Union supporters in the North had accepted the end of slavery, but they had not adjusted to freed slaves as a key component of law enforcement. The place of African Americans in a free society was contested throughout the North. Lincoln left little guidance, beyond his recognition of African American service in the military and his stated belief that some of them—"the very intelligent" and "those who serve our cause as soldiers"—should gain the right to vote. Lincoln's last words applied to the question of voting in Louisiana; it is not clear that many of his supporters conceived of African Americans voting throughout the nation in 1865.[13]

Southerners resisted former slaves living freely in their communities, and they could not imagine life with armed African American soldiers occupying their towns. This reality after Appomattox felt like a foreign invasion, where the invaders had enlisted the weakest to rule the formerly strong. The disorientation of Southerners expressed itself initially in a refusal to accept and adjust, and an effort to deny what had changed. In a state like Texas, where African American soldiers were rare and Confederate generals remained powerful, citizens tried to ignore how the war had ended, or even that it had ended.

This was more than a political reaction. Slavery was deeply embedded in every part of Southern life—farming, housekeeping, child-rearing, and, of course, sex. White men were dominant because they had African Americans to control. White women were sophisticated and dignified because they ordered African Americans to do the chores and other household tasks they wished to avoid. White supremacy was central to personal identity, wealth, and status. Taking away slavery suffocated traditional Southern society, denying it the oxygen of daily life. Turning slaves into soldiers set that society on fire, making the ballasts of white rule the kindling wood for its rapid disintegration.

Service in the Union army gave African American families public status and economic stability. Note the fine clothes worn by the African American soldier's wife and daughters.

African American soldiers stepped into this postwar conflict zone. They had to navigate many roles. Most importantly, they were still soldiers after the surrender. They received continued pay and provisions from the Union army, as well as orders from Union commanders. Although free of slavery, they were not free of their military obligations. Those who had fled from slavery to the Union army had nowhere else to go; it was their only home.

African American soldiers were largely garrisoned in hostile, poor Southern communities. They remained there as many of the white soldiers returned North. The Black men who had fought their former masters in battle now had to live among them and, in some cases, help them survive. This involved rebuilding homes and distributing limited public relief supplies. The African American soldiers faced continued hatred from Southerners who, in many cases, turned violent. Former slaves possessed more power as soldiers, but they still had to relive the prejudice of the South. They were occupiers and outcasts at the same time.

Union soldiers constituted the primary law enforcement for the federal government. The African American troops were an obvious target for the resentments of local residents who felt imposed upon by Washington. They stood out from the other Union soldiers, and they were often poorly supported by the rest of the army. They were, however, better armed and fed than the destitute civilians around them, which aggravated the indignity for once proud slaveholders.

Southern targeting of African American servicemen often triggered white mob violence. Efforts by soldiers to enforce the law against defiant civilians drew angry crowds, looking to get back at the former slaves who "needed to know their place." White race riots spread throughout the former Confederacy as angry, lawless groups attacked African American soldiers residing in their communities and the civilians who accompanied them. The attackers were initially local groups of angry men who grew into an organized insurgency, especially after the founding of the Ku Klux Klan by Confederate army veterans in the early months of the occupation.

The first Klansmen organized in Pulaski, Tennessee, to resist the presence of freed slaves in their state. In the spring of 1866, the largest white riot since Appomattox occurred in the city of Memphis, west of Pulaski. Major General George Stoneman, the highest-ranking Union officer in Tennessee, commanded the Third United States Colored Heavy Artillery, which consisted of approximately 150 African American soldiers, stationed around Memphis. The city had a larger population of civilian African Americans who were former slaves and families of the soldiers. The growth of this community, and the daily patrols conducted by Black troops to maintain order, triggered open hostility from white residents and the mostly Irish city police. A congressional investigation reported: "Whenever a colored man was arrested for any cause, even the most frivolous, and sometimes without any cause, by the police, the arrest was made in a harsh and brutal manner, it being usual to knock down and beat the arrested party."

Union soldiers often intervened to protect Black residents, but the mistreatment continued: "The police waited with an evident anxiety for the time to arrive when the colored troops should be mustered out of the service, and should have no adequate means of defense." The elected white leaders of Memphis demanded the removal of the Union forces, who were garrisoned, on General Stoneman's order, south of the city, in Fort Pickering.[14]

On April 30, 1866, tensions reached a boiling point when four white policemen attacked a small group of African Americans, beating them with their pistols and arresting at least one of the badly injured victims. The boldness of this attack mobilized African American soldiers and civilians to demand better treatment. The next day, approximately one hundred of them assembled on a main street in Memphis to cheer for the late president, Abraham Lincoln, and call for fairer treatment of former slaves.

Police officers arrived at the scene of the public demonstration, ordering the African Americans to disperse. White men shouted, "Your old father, Abraham Lincoln, is dead and damned!" The police escalated the conflict when they tried to arrest two of the African American demonstrators, despite the absence of any violence or other lawbreaking. The police were outnumbered but heavily armed.

At that point, a group of African American soldiers in the crowd surrounded the police officers and demanded that they leave the targeted Black demonstrators alone. Some witnesses claimed that the soldiers threatened the police. Within minutes, white police officers and African American soldiers started shooting, mostly in the air, to intimidate one another. There were conflicting accounts of who fired first, and there were also conflicting reports of injuries. The outnumbered police retreated from the scene, and the African American soldiers returned to Fort Pickering for the night.

The police were not done. They raised a vigilante group of more than one hundred armed white men. In the words of the congressional investigation, they began "indiscriminate robbery, burning, and slaughter" throughout the African American sections of town. "The voice of this mob was the voice of revenge and threats of vengeance against the colored people. It was in favor of killing all the colored people, or of driving them out, and also of killing or driving out all those who sympathized with them."

Respected local officials, including the sheriff and the state's attorney general, led the mob. The attorney general was part of a group who boasted, after firing their weapons at unarmed residents: "Two damned niggers out of the way." Another city official shouted to the white crowd: "Boys, I want you to go ahead and kill every damned one of the nigger race and burn up the cradle."[15]

It was a racial massacre, perpetrated by murderous white citizens, enraged by the rise of African Americans. They wanted to "clean out" the city of the "invaders" they viewed as subhuman and threatening. The defense of white respectability motivated the most heinous, inhumane, and criminal behavior.[16]

It continued for three horrible days. The ravenous posse of rioting white men, with wives and children cheering on, burned twelve African American schools, four churches, and more than fifty houses. They killed forty-six African Americans, many of whom were only identified as "unknown negro man" and "colored soldier" in the congressional report. Two white men died, both of whom were part of the police forces. Hundreds of African Americans were seriously wounded, and the property damage for the African American community in Memphis was estimated at more than $120,000—an unrecoverable fortune at that time.[17]

Most of the victims were defenseless; the African American soldiers were locked inside Fort Pickering, and General Stoneman would not allow them to return to town, despite repeated requests from the Memphis residents who were under attack. The general only permitted his soldiers to leave the fort on the night of May 2, more than twenty-four hours after the massacre of African Americans had begun. By that time, much of the damage had already been done, and the frenzied white mob was more difficult to control. A local judge demanded that the African American soldiers turn over their arms to the police forces, who were part of the mob. The soldiers refused.

The attacks on soldiers and civilians continued until the fourth day, May 4, when General Stoneman finally issued a public order prohibiting all public assemblies in Memphis. He instituted martial law, pledging to arrest any citizen who joined a mob, armed or unarmed. General Stoneman also offered military protection, belatedly, to African American families. Armed troops patrolled the streets, and the white rioting in Memphis largely ceased.

"It is to be regretted," congressional investigators observed, that General Stoneman "had not at an earlier period of the lawless and murderous proceedings taken the same resolute steps." He understood the hatred of African Americans in Memphis, and he recognized the brutality exhibited by the white mobs on the first night. The general was well informed by African American residents and his own soldiers.[18]

Although there is little evidence he condoned the mob violence, General Stoneman was hesitant to send his African American soldiers to arrest large numbers of white citizens, including prominent leaders of Memphis. In his testimony after the massacre, he explained that he concentrated his forces on protecting government property, particularly Fort Pickering itself. The soldiers were guarding the fort, not the population around it.

General Stoneman recognized that his African American soldiers, who obeyed their orders by most accounts, provoked white residents by the color of their skin, the uniforms they wore, and the weapons they carried. The general told investigators that the hostility of white citizens in Memphis was simply too great and that his forces were too small to counter it.

Little had changed in local white attitudes since the Civil War, and the presence of African American soldiers had only hardened the resolve of residents to resist change. The soldiers interviewed agreed. If anything, former Confederate newspapers encouraged more hate and violence. "The state of feeling in Memphis," congressional investigators concluded, was "very much now as it was before."[19]

None of the white rioters were prosecuted for murder or property damage. Most newspapers justified the "defense" of their community and quite wrongly blamed the African American soldiers for the violence. Essentially, the victims were blamed for the death and destruction heaped upon them by others. The same was true throughout the former Confederacy. There were very few white allies willing to step forward for African Americans.

Occupation marked a new, more personal struggle for power. Despite their losses on the battlefield, many white citizens continued to fight for control over their communities. African Americans, who had contributed to Union victory, still faced deadly resistance to their participation. Although they had the law and the army on their side, it still was not enough.

Congressional investigators and many former slaves agreed that hope for peaceful change under the law was misguided: "Where there is no public opinion to sustain law, but, on the other hand, that public opinion is so overwhelmingly against it, there is no possibility of its being executed." White mob rule still had the upper hand in Memphis and many other places.[20]

The former slaves had little experience with freedom, and they had to figure it out largely for themselves. They received some assistance from other Union soldiers, a small number of courageous local allies, and men and women who traveled to the South to offer help. The

SCENES IN MEMPHIS, TENNESSEE, DURING THE RIOT—SHOOTING DOWN NEGROES ON THE MORNING OF MAY 2, 1866.—[SKETCHED BY A. R. W.]

Depiction of the white mob in Memphis shooting defenseless African American residents. *Source: Harper's Weekly, May 26, 1866*

latter included white and Black teachers, religious figures, and others who participated in various Northern-based aid societies. They were a diverse and loosely organized collection of reformers on the ground.

The reformers worked alongside the Freedmen's Bureau, created by Congress in 1865, with very few resources, to distribute aid. Led by General Oliver Otis Howard, the bureau relied on the Union army and public charity. The generosity of some citizens—especially educators and doctors—was inspiring, but it was woefully inadequate for the extensive needs of four million landless, uneducated, and impoverished former slaves who now had to support themselves as they also confronted attacks from hostile white crowds. The massacre in Memphis illustrated that former slaves were dangerously vulnerable.

By necessity, African Americans continued to look to the Union army. It was limited in its capabilities and often unwilling to challenge mob violence, but the Union army was more present than any other institution to help former slaves. Service in the Union army offered some protection to African American men, access to food, and a small but reliable income for their families. For at least two decades after the Civil War, the Union army remained the largest employer of African Americans in the United States.

It was the first institution to treat Black men as citizens. Though they were given inferior positions, they had rights in the army. They were entitled to decent treatment, due process, and, most of all, protection of their property and person. Although the U.S. Army was racist, and it would remain so for decades, it recognized the worth of African American soldiers. They were respected as contributors to the nation, offered opportunities to advance as officers, and given access to new skills. Ironically, one of the most authoritarian organizations in the United States, the military, was the freest institution for former slaves.

Many African American enlistees wanted land, but the army generally could not provide it. With few exceptions, the federal government did not take land from plantation owners after the war. The Southern Homestead Act of 1866 opened up forty-six million acres of federal lands for private ownership in the former Confederacy, and eventually more land would become available in the Southwest, but African Americans still had limited access because of local restrictions. They often could not get to the land, acquire supplies, or defend their ownership claims in court. The U.S. Army did not protect homesteads for former slaves. Local law enforcement defended white settlers and frequently displaced African Americans.

Henry Adams was one of many former slaves to join the U.S. Army after the Civil War because he could not acquire land. Born into slavery in Georgia in 1843, he gained his freedom in April 1865 in Louisiana. Adams immediately sought to establish himself as a businessman and a landowner, but he confronted thievery, bullying, and murderous violence from former Confederates all around him. "I ran away," he recounted, "the white people did not sympathize with us; they would take all the money that we made on their places when we went to leave; they killed many hundreds of my race."[21]

Adams ran to the army, enlisting in the Eightieth Volunteers in September 1866. He was initially posted with the occupation forces in New Orleans and later served in Shreveport as well. He continued to encounter hostility from the white population, and he did not feel free, but he had some protection. And he could work, where possible, to help African American communities build schools, churches, and businesses. Adams served in the army for three years, promoted to quartermaster sergeant, with primary responsibilities for supplies and logistics.

Literacy was necessary for this rank. Adams remembered the first teacher he had ever had, when he was stationed at Fort Jackson, Louisiana. Most astonishing, the teacher employed by the army for the Black soldiers was a white lady, Mrs. Bentine. Adams recounted: "We had a school for the soldiers, and we had three hours a day to go to the school."

He soaked up the opportunity to become literate, recognizing the power it would give him to navigate society independently and promote his own ambitions. "I learned to read and write a little in one month's time," Adams explained. Then he eagerly "acquired all the rest myself." He was not alone. Southern law had prohibited teaching letters to slaves. Thousands of illiterate former slaves became readers and writers in the army. Some became more literate than their former masters.[22]

Newly literate African Americans gained voice in society as never before; they could now make themselves heard. Frederick Douglass famously recounted how, as a slave, reading and writing "enabled me to utter my thoughts, and to meet the arguments brought forward." He established a name for himself with his words, and he used his words to tear away at slavery. Similarly, Adams and other former slaves who learned to read and write in the army used their words to assert their citizenship as never before. They now had the knowledge to defend themselves and claim their rights in society.[23]

When Adams left the U.S. Army in 1869, he confronted the same white hostility as before, but now he could use his words, as Douglass had, to organize and fight back. He had close ties to other African American soldiers, and they formed "the committee"—a network of former slaves for mutual assistance. With more than five hundred followers, members of the group helped one another with negotiating contracts, collecting wages, and, most importantly, defending property and families. They could now pass messages and pool knowledge to "get what was due them."[24]

Adams and his collaborators anticipated white violence, and they prepared for their self-defense. The committee was the first free African American intelligence network in the South, fueled by experienced, literate former soldiers. They shared information in Louisiana from as far as Virginia, Missouri, Kentucky, and Tennessee. They pooled their skills. They created the sinews for participation in a hostile society. No one was alone; they worked together for their collective survival.

Kinship and race were at the core of the committee and other emerging African American associations across the South. Many of these groups became known as Union Leagues, organized locally, sometimes secretly, to defend the rights of former slaves as citizens. They relied on connections of family and familiarity to build trust in hostile circumstances. Their victimization as Black men and women in a white society brought them together with common interests in self-protection and mutual support.

Adams and other former U.S. Army officers brought their literacy and skills to these kinship communities. They offered leadership as well. Together, and often unseen by white counterparts, the former slaves nurtured alternative networks for survival and prosperity in the South. These networks ran parallel to the traditional, and largely unchanged, institutions of business, policing, and politics in cities like Memphis. African American freedom did not come from individual rights, which were often violated, but from the ability of formerly enslaved men and women to connect, cooperate, and organize.

That was the real revolution—the freedom to be part of a largely autonomous community of similar men and women. Adams became an influential African American figure after he left the army because he furthered the widening and tightening networks among Black kinfolk. He was a community leader, as were many other former soldiers, ministers, and teachers after the Civil War. They experienced citizenship and democracy as part of a distinct community, separate and adjacent to the white South.

Voting was an obvious focus for African Americans. Although Henry Adams later claimed that he was not political, he understood very well that safety for African Americans required government representation. Former slaves would never be free if they were ruled by men who wished to re-enslave them. Voting was the most basic ritual of citizenship, affirming the rights and dignity of the voters. For those who were denied citizenship for so long, voting was like land ownership, a guaranteed stake in the future of society.

Many former slaves were eager to vote, and they exuberantly cast their ballots as soon as they could, despite threats and intimidation. Adams voted for the first time in 1870, soon after he left the army. He helped countless others to vote and advised them on their choices. They had to vote for Republicans, especially African American candidates: "If we voted the Democratic ticket we would have to carry passes from one parish to another and from one state to the other." Freedom for African Americans, Adams persuasively argued, required electing their allies and their own kind. He emerged as an influential voice for Black power at the ballot box.[25]

African American men across the South voted in very large numbers after the Civil War. They had no experience voting, but they agreed with Frederick Douglass, Henry Adams, and many others who emphasized its importance. It was a way of affirming that they were now free. By 1867, almost 90 percent of Black men in the South registered to vote. The former slaves quickly became the largest voting bloc in the former Confederacy and a majority in three states: South Carolina, Mississippi, and Louisiana. They were almost half the voting population in five additional states: Virginia, North Carolina, Alabama, Florida, and Georgia.[26]

Almost overnight, the illiterate, tortured field-workers from the plantations had become citizens with the power to decide who ruled and who did not. This was John Wilkes Booth's nightmare. Seeing lines of men born into a slave system where they had no rights, now voting to elect state leaders, was a sight to behold. Former Confederates were prohibited from voting in some states, and they often boycotted in others, so the change in the voters made it appear that society had turned upside down.

A Northern journalist commented on the determination of the new voters. They made extraordinary efforts to vote, he recounted, "in defiance of fatigue, hardship, hunger, and threats of employers." They had so little, but they organized themselves to create a multiracial democracy at the ballot box: "Few possessed a pair of shoes, yet for hours they stood on line." The journalist praised their "hunger to have the same chances as the white men."[27]

The eagerness to vote was evident in Alabama, where the Clarke County election supervisor recounted: "There must have been present, near one thousand freedmen, many as far as thirty miles from their home, all eager to vote and return." They had only recently broken away from slavery, but African Americans had quickly organized themselves to reach the ballot box.[28]

That was precisely what offended the white citizens of privilege, who had lost control of Southern politics. A wider, multiracial democracy diminished their power. They described the transformation of former slaves into voters as the end of the republic. They had imported a large Black population to their states as chattel, and now the chattel had escaped its chains, threatening to swallow the white masters in a sea of Black citizens. Governor Jonathan Worth of North Carolina called them the "dregs of society." Government by "mere numbers," he exclaimed, meant "undermining civilization." These words would be used again and again in the decade after the Civil War and across the next century and a half—including the elections of 2016 and 2020.[29]

The one thing that both sides could agree on was that democracy was still fundamentally male. Perversely, African American enthusiasm to vote after the Civil War reinforced presumptions that men should control politics. Henry Adams and other former slaves gained legitimacy as voters through their service in the U.S. Army, which proved they could be so much more than slaves. Their experiences and education in the military gave them status and resources to voice their demands. They could assert a right to be represented, and they could put themselves forward as men who had earned leadership roles on the battlefields of the nation. When an African American leader in South Carolina proudly proclaimed, "Now is the black man's day," he meant "man" as much as "black."[30]

Black women made it possible for Black men to lead. In many ways, they bore the heaviest burdens. They provided extensive nursing, sanitary, and other support services for white and Black soldiers in both armies, North and South. After the war, Black women did much of the interpersonal, day-to-day work for freed slave communities, running businesses, passing news among kinship networks, and keeping families fed and secure. Black women served in important roles, often running African American schools and hospitals. They were leaders and administrators as much as teachers and nurses. As Adams and other men organized associations for mutual support and voter mobilization, the wives and daughters carried the messages and moved the people and supplies, often amid great danger.

Sexual assault haunted slave women throughout the South, accompanied by other forms of physical and mental exploitation. Interracial births were common; Frederick Douglass was one of thousands of slaves who never knew the white father who raped his African American slave mother. Interracial children, like Douglass, were always identified as Black, treated as slaves, and ignored—sometimes sold away—by their fathers.

The ubiquity of sexual aggression did not disappear with the end of slavery. White men continued to force themselves on Black women as an expression of dominance. This aggression diminished the stature of African American men, who had few resources to defend their wives and daughters. Violating Black women while their husbands, fathers, and sons helplessly watched displayed white privilege, and Black vulnerability, in its brutalest and most inhumane form. It was an old act of tyranny made new again to boost threatened Confederate masculinity. Degrading both Black women and men, rape was a continuation of slavery by other means.

During the Memphis massacre, for example, as a white mob burned fifty African American homes and killed forty-six African American citizens, white men raped at least five Black women. The examination of these rapes by congressional investigators revealed how the white mob used sexual violence to exact revenge upon the entire African American community and its Republican supporters. The rapists were performing white male supremacy—showing that they could still dominate their community and enforce Black subservience. They used sex as a form of race war.

Congressional investigators recounted the experience of Memphis resident Frances Thompson, a free Black woman:

On Tuesday night seven men, two of whom were policemen, came to her house.... They first demanded that she should get supper for them, which she did. After supper the wretches threw all the provisions that were in the house which had not been consumed out into the bayou. They then laid hold of Frances, hitting her on the side of the face and kicking her. A girl by the name of Lucy Smith, about sixteen years old, living with her, attempted to go out at the window. One of the brutes knocked her down and choked her. They then drew their pistols, and said they would shoot them and fire the house if they did not let them have their way. The woman, Frances Thompson, was then violated by four of the men, and so beaten and bruised that she lay in bed for three days. They then took all the clothes out of the trunk, one hundred dollars in greenbacks belonging to herself, and two hundred dollars belonging to another colored woman, which had been left to take care of her child, besides silk dresses, bed-clothing, etc. They were in the house nearly four hours, and when they left they said they intended "to burn up the last God damned nigger, and drive all the Yankees out of town, and then there would be only some rebel niggers and butternuts left."

The white men who raped Frances Thompson violated the young girl, Lucy Smith, as well. When the white men saw a portrait of a Union officer in the home, they warned: "You niggers have a mighty liking for the damned Yankees, but we will kill you, and you will have no liking for any one of them."[31]

Black women were forced to suffer deep pain and indignity. Black men were reminded of their weakness, their insufficient masculinity. White Republicans who sympathized with the African American population were warned to stay away or they would cause more harm to the Black people they cared about. The experience of Memphis, with African American soldiers forced to watch and then carry on after the horror, was replicated time and again. Men like Henry Adams condemned the violence of their white counterparts, but they could not stop it, and they could not dwell on it either.

To make progress as a people in this violent and racist context, Black men had to step into leadership roles and assert themselves, but they had to act with great care. The legitimacy of former slaves as leaders required them to appeal to a cautious and professional masculinity that reinforced male dominance and did not threaten other males. Former slaves found freedom by affirming their status as men who subordinated women but avoided antagonizing white privilege, where possible.

Voting showed these dynamics at play. African American men used the ballot box to gain a place for themselves in society as full citizens, not as adversaries of the white men who attacked them. They acted to join the voting male citizenry, not deny its legitimacy. With the ratification of the Fifteenth Amendment to the Constitution in 1870, new voters like Henry Adams were affirming rights for all men, not taking anything away from anyone. "We claim exactly the same rights, privileges, and immunities as are enjoyed by white men," a group of African Americans in Alabama explained. "We ask nothing more and will be content with nothing less."[32]

Black voters emphasized representation in politics—the basic foundation of democracy—not expropriation or vengeance. They demanded that all men have a say in choosing their leaders. They claimed no special privilege, just the franchise that other men exercised. And they acted with their bodies, as they had in the war, by showing up in difficult circumstances, making a courageous choice to protect their interests. They seized the moment to change the reality on the ground.

In Mississippi, Black voters created an earthquake. In a state with some of the harshest slave conditions before the Civil War, freed slaves registered and turned out as a majority at the ballot box two years later. They benefited from a large Union army presence in the state, including a sizable contingent of Black soldiers, and an empathetic white commander, General Adelbert Ames. African Americans quickly became a presence, and soon a majority, in local offices, including county supervisors, clerks, justices of the peace, treasurers, and even sheriffs. They also became frequent members of criminal juries. It would have been unthinkable for a single Black man to serve in any of these roles just a few years earlier; now they were predominant.

More than "mere numbers," as former Confederates falsely claimed, the new African American officials represented emerging voices in a multiracial democracy. They acted to bring more fairness to criminal justice. They cooperated with the Freedmen's Bureau and the U.S. Army to build and staff more schools for African American children. They even created some of the first public welfare programs, working with Northern-funded charitable organizations to distribute aid to poor families. Confederate Mississippi was a state that exclusively served white landowners; African American voters put people into office who widened the service of the state to more constituencies, especially former slave communities. They affirmed the citizenship of all men in Mississippi, white and Black, and the obligation of the government to help them.[33]

African American bodies and voices had breached the walls keeping them out of power. They were now in the "room where it happens"—present in the political institutions where they could bargain for reforms with Republicans who needed their support and even some Democrats who saw no alternative. Just as they had changed the Union army from within, now they changed government from within.

Hiram Revels, the first African American appointed to the U.S. Senate, was perhaps the biggest breakthrough. Revels was fortunate to be born free in North Carolina in 1827, the son of a Baptist minister. He also trained as a minister, joining the African Methodist Episcopal (AME) Church, which played a central role in abolitionist efforts before the Civil War and in activities to organize and support freed slaves after Appomattox. During the war, Revels served as a chaplain in the Union army for African American soldiers.

In 1866, Revels settled in Mississippi as a leader of the AME Church in the state. Like Henry Adams and other literate African Americans with army experience, he became involved in politics. In 1868, Black voters elected Revels as an alderman in the riverfront city of Natchez. A year later, Black voters sent Revels to the state's senate. In 1870, the Mississippi legislature chose him to represent the state in the U.S. Senate.

Revels was the first Black senator in the history of the United States, holding the highest federal office of any African American. Revels would serve for a year in Washington, and then another African American, Blanche Bruce, would serve as a senator from Mississippi from 1875 to 1881. The state has not elected an African American senator since then.

Senators were selected by the state legislatures, where African Americans gained seats with their new votes. Perhaps more significantly, in the decade after the Civil War, Black voters directly elected fourteen African American men to the U.S. House of Representatives. Joseph

U.S. senator Hiram Revels. *Credit: Mathew Brady*

Rainey, born to slavery in South Carolina, was the first, sworn in at the Capitol on December 12, 1870. Five other African Americans represented different parts of the same former Confederate state in the seven years after Rainey's election. South Carolina has only elected four African Americans to the House of Representatives (and one senator) in the next century and a half.

Rainey represented his district from the coastal region around Charleston for eight years, and he became a force for his African American constituents. In 1871, Rainey advocated for the Ku Klux Klan Act, which gave the federal government, for the first time, the power to act against states and local communities that denied African Americans the ability to vote, hold elected office, and serve on juries. The act targeted violent white groups, especially the Ku Klux Klan, that attacked Black men and women and their supporters. Congress gave the

Justice Department, backed by the U.S. Army, the power to intervene in the South to provide "equal protection" to all citizens as guaranteed under the Fourteenth Amendment.[34]

Many white Southern elites, like those in Memphis, had largely ignored the constitutional rights of African Americans. Rainey and the four other African Americans in Congress pushed to expand federal powers as part of a series of Enforcement Acts. They prioritized the rights of their voters and sought to reverse the limits on federal action against racist local officials. Speaking from the floor of the House, Rainey demanded: "Tell me nothing of a constitution which fails to shelter beneath its rightful power the people of a country!" He called upon his colleagues in Congress to create a democracy, providing "protection to the humblest citizen, without regard to rank, creed, or color."[35]

U.S. representative Joseph Rainey. *Credit: Mathew Brady*

In the early 1870s, Congress and President Ulysses Grant embraced this multiracial vision as never before. Black voters and their elected representatives made the breakthrough possible. Responding to their pressure, in April 1871, President Grant issued General Order Number 48, authorizing U.S. Army forces, including Black soldiers, to arrest violators of the Ku Klux Klan Act. He charged Attorney General Amos Akerman with prosecuting Southern whites who threatened African Americans, especially around voting. Grant proclaimed that the federal government had a "duty of putting forth all its energies for the protection of its citizens of every race and color."[36]

The president extended Washington's reach deep into the South. He placed the full force of his government behind eliminating armed attackers on African American communities. He largely succeeded in destroying the Klan, one of the most violent groups singled out for attention by Congressman Rainey and other African American elected officials desperate to protect their constituents. Within one year, federal prosecutors indicted more than three thousand Klansmen, a third of whom were convicted and jailed, often by mixed-race juries.

Although Grant's enforcement of the Ku Klux Klan Act did not bring an end to white violence against African Americans, it discouraged former Confederates from displaying their hatred in the open. They now faced stiff penalties and a high likelihood of prosecution, especially if they acted in large groups, as in Memphis and other cities soon after the Civil War. "Peace has come to many places as never before," Frederick Douglass observed. The former slaves and their elected representatives had demanded the federal action that made some progress possible. President Grant sympathized, but he was pushed to action by the diverse voices he now heard from Congress and other elected bodies.[37]

When the Confederate states reentered the Union, they were no longer white republics, dominated by landholding elites. They were now struggling, diverse democracies, with numerous Black voters and leaders. The process of change began with Tennessee in 1866, the first Confederate state readmitted, and it continued through the summer of

1870, when the last Confederate state, Georgia, rejoined. Former slaves fled their plantations, fought in the U.S. Army, voted, and then rewrote the state constitutions in the South. They did not demand restitution for decades of mistreatment but instead sought access to education, economic opportunity, and representation in their communities. They wanted to live with the peace and prosperity of white society.

The decade after the Civil War was a "Second American Revolution" fought in countless local struggles by African Americans to fulfill the promise of the nation's Declaration of Independence: "That all men are created equal; that they are endowed by their Creator with certain unalienable rights; that among these are life, liberty, and the pursuit of happiness." The former slaves made themselves citizens by forcing changes in the law. They suffered repeated attacks and grave harms, and they won. Remarking on the rising influence of African Americans in national and state governments, one Black observer wrote: "The Great Battle is over—victory has been proclaimed."[38]

But this victory was terribly incomplete, and there were still many difficult battles left to fight. Laws changed faster than attitudes and behaviors. Revolution inspired reactionary violence. Citizenship for former slaves threatened the control that white elites wanted in the South. They would not give up power easily. To keep themselves on top, white elites had to hold Black men and women down. And they were determined to do that.

Repression was rooted in habit and tradition. Old institutions and practices of racism lived on, and white leaders in the South used them deliberately. Police forces in Memphis and other cities were common weapons for attacking new citizens. The enforcers of white supremacy had eager crowds behind them, already long experienced in bringing violence against African Americans.

To create a truly multiracial democracy, more than legal change was necessary. African Americans could only do so much. How would the United States transform the basic attitudes and behaviors of white citizens, deeply threatened by the slaves-turned-citizens who challenged their dominance in local communities? How could a democracy built on slavery expunge its racist convictions?

These were the questions that confronted Abraham Lincoln's heirs in Washington, DC. The Republican Party was the party of emancipation, civil rights, and the "Second American Revolution." Republicans had to legislate and implement policies for a new, multiracial democracy. They hoped to turn the dynamic energies of a more diverse society toward economic growth and international expansion that would benefit everyone.

Black men and women pushed the boundaries of American democracy, but they depended on Republican politicians to make the new boundaries stick. This was difficult political work, and the Republicans who followed Lincoln were often hesitant, ill prepared, and even hostile. Although united in their support for the Union, many Republicans were uncertain about what would come next. Their uncertainties and hesitations, especially around the rights of African Americans, would determine the future of American democracy.

CHAPTER 5

Republicans

The Republican Party had started as a regional organization, appealing to white men in Northern states who feared they were losing control of their lives to growing immigrant communities and slave owners. It emerged in small towns in Wisconsin, Illinois, Ohio, and upstate New York. In November 1856, the Springfield, Illinois, *Republican* newspaper captured the emerging sentiment. The editors appealed to "the great middling-interest class": "Those who work with their hands, who live and act independently, who hold the stakes of home and family, of farm and workshop, of education and freedom—these, as a mass, are enrolled in the Republican ranks.... They form the very heart of the nation, as opposed to the two extremes of aristocracy and ignorance."[1]

Early Republicans were small landholders, artisans, and skilled service providers—lawyers, accountants, and medical doctors. They had strong roots in their communities, and they used those local connections for career advancement. They were politically engaged, but they did not think of themselves as powerful elites. And they worshipped in small Protestant congregations that shared a deep skepticism of anyone who worshipped differently, especially Catholics and Jews. Midwestern Protestants were indeed defensive against what they viewed as encroaching moneyed and migrant intrusions on their modest traditions of work and worship in well-ordered, closed communities of families who had lived side by side for a generation.

They were the mirror image of the Confederates. Fears of declining status motivated white men North and South, in opposite directions.

Southern whites who needed slavery to preserve their dominance joined the Confederacy, pushing the Democratic Party to secession. Northern whites who wanted more protection for their families and businesses turned to the Republican Party. It promised a poor-born former Whig, like Abraham Lincoln, the possibility of a country where hardworking white men of modest means could rise and become prosperous landholders. The Republican Party promoted independence and wealth for those who saw little access to either in the Whig or Democratic Parties.[2]

The new political organization drew support initially from disaffected Whigs, especially throughout the Middle West. It attracted a diverse mix of nativists (Know-Nothings), temperance activists, abolitionists, and women's suffragists. The party was largely American-born but skeptical of traditional politicians—particularly urban "machines" that integrated immigrants and shared political favors. It had populist instincts but detested newcomers and angry mobs. It was a collection of ambitious, optimistic, and upwardly mobile men who loved their country but not the people who had run it in recent years.

Lincoln was the most influential early Republican politician. "I was raised to farm work," he recounted. "I was a hired laborer. The hired laborer of yesterday, labors on his own account today; and will hire others to labor for him tomorrow. Advancement—improvement in condition—is the order of things in a society of equals."[3]

This was the promise of "free labor" for Lincoln. "The prudent, penniless beginner in the world, labors for wages a while, saves a surplus with which to buy tools or land, for himself; then labors on his own account another while, and at length hires another new beginner to help him." Lincoln extolled this experience as "the just and generous, and prosperous system, which opens the way for all—gives hope to all, and energy, and progress, and improvement of condition to all."[4]

Breaking from the Whig Party, which was dominated by inherited wealth, Lincoln defined the Republican Party as the champion of free labor: "men, with their families" who "work for themselves, on their farms, in their houses and in their shops, taking the whole product to themselves, and asking no favors of capital on the one hand, nor of hirelings or slaves on the other."[5]

Slavery was the opposite of free labor. Again, Lincoln put it clearly: Slavery "substituted hope, for the rod." It replaced freedom with repression, discouraging hard work and self-improvement. Why would a slave ever try to produce more when all the benefits were taken by his master? Why would a slave ever try to serve the public when he was not allowed access to public resources?

Similarly, why would a slave master invest in his community beyond his plantation, where all his wealth resided in his land and in his slaves? White elites had an interest in exploiting labor and hoarding resources, prohibiting the rise of penniless beginners. Lincoln observed that Southern society had poor roads and schools, even in wealthy counties, because slavery discouraged public development. The system of slavery froze wealth and status in the hands of the slave owners, starving poor whites of access to the opportunities for improvement that Lincoln extolled.

White men were not subjected to slavery, but the existence of the system denied them work, diminished their wages, and degraded the dignity of their labor. The work of the white penniless beginner held little value when a slave master could replace it with a Black body toiling without pay, under the lash. Employers would not compensate poor white working men when they could exploit slaves at much lower cost. Lincoln felt the pain slavery inflicted on free labor personally; he was once the penniless beginner.[6]

The Republican Party opposed the spread of slavery because it harmed working white men. Initially less well known than other party figures, Lincoln gained notoriety between 1858 and 1860 by calling on the federal government to prohibit the spread of slavery into new territories, where Southern elites would otherwise establish their dominance and limit the opportunities for poor white men seeking to make their way. The western frontier would only expand democratic opportunities for ordinary citizens, according to Lincoln, if the Indians were cleared from the land and it was given to "men, with their families" who "work for themselves."

The Dayton, Ohio, *Journal* summarized one of Lincoln's speeches: "The free white men had a right to claim that the new territories into which they and their children might go to seek a livelihood should be preserved free and clear of the incumbrance of slavery, and that no laboring white man should be placed in a position where, by the introduction of slavery into the territories, he would be compelled to toil by the side of a slave."[7]

Lincoln pointed to the model of the Northwest Ordinance, which, at the founding of the country, gave land to white men, prohibited slavery, and encouraged economic development. The free states of Ohio, Indiana, Michigan, Wisconsin, and Lincoln's own Illinois emerged from this arrangement. Lincoln advocated the same model for new states like Kansas and Nebraska, and he warned that if slave interests controlled those states, they would look more like Mississippi and Alabama. The spread of the Deep South into the West would make the continued freedom and prosperity of middle western states more precarious. This was what Lincoln called the "nationalization" of slavery through the injection of "Slave Power" in new territories, promoted by Southern officials and sympathizers in Congress, the Supreme Court, and the presidency.[8]

Before the Civil War, the Republican Party did not oppose the continuation of slavery in the South, nor did it deny that Southerners had a right to the return of their slaves who had fled North. Lincoln went so far as to call his party's positions "conservative." "We must not interfere with the institution of slavery in the states where it exists," he admitted in 1859, but he elaborated, "We must prevent the outspreading of the institution, because neither the Constitution nor general welfare requires us to extend it." This was the purpose of the Republican Party, and it was the basis for Lincoln's successful presidential campaign.[9]

The Republican Party organized around protecting Northern white free labor from the spread of Slave Power. That never changed. The party rejected abolitionism before the Civil War, and when the pressures of the war and fleeing slaves pushed President Lincoln to support emancipation, the party justified this move to defeat the Confederacy.

Humanitarian considerations were not the primary motivation. The Republican Party represented rising white men in the North who did not own slaves. It was not organized for African Americans, even when they entered the party, as newly free men, in large numbers.

Long after Lincoln's death, Republicans consistently opposed Confederate white elites and groups like the Ku Klux Klan, but they did not prioritize the interests of African Americans. The party was anti-slavery and anti-Confederate, but it was never committed strongly to the welfare of former slaves. Lincoln's rhetoric reflected the party as a whole: Although the president spoke eloquently about the damage slavery caused to a free society, he never focused on the experiences of slaves, their needs, or their future. He motivated Northern white voters who cared about how slavery harmed them.

Lincoln never campaigned in the Deep South, and Republican candidates received negligible support from Southern whites. In his two presidential elections, Lincoln did not win a single state south of Missouri; he never came close. President Ulysses Grant made inroads into Southern states only because of African American voters; his opponents continued to monopolize white Southern voters. As more former Confederates voted after 1872, Republican gains in the South evaporated, returning the region to white Democratic rule, as it would remain for the next century.

The Republican Party reached out to Black voters in the former Confederacy through the Freedmen's Bureau and Union Leagues, and it deployed the U.S. Army to defend their right to vote, but it did not support legislation to shift wealth into their hands. A confiscation plan, proposed by Pennsylvania representative Thaddeus Stevens to give land owned by Confederates to former slaves, did not gain support in the party. The same was true for similar proposals to enforce equality in education, business, and recreation. Many Northern Republican voters continued to benefit from white control of agriculture and other commerce in the South tied to wealthy banking and trading interests in New York, Philadelphia, Boston, and other cities.[10]

There was no carpetbagger conspiracy to seize the South's wealth for the North, as some former Confederates alleged. Established business networks crossed regions and benefited from stability, not massive up-heaval. Although Republican voters wanted to limit the political power of former slaveholders, they wished to continue profiting from the cotton, sugar, tobacco, and other items grown in the South. North-ern bankers invested their capital in these industries, and Northern manufacturers used the raw materials to fuel production of high-priced goods for consumption and export. Mississippi cotton was New York fashion after the Civil War as it had been before.

The networks of landowners, producers, and traders remained, and Republican voters wanted to rebuild them as quickly as possible. Removing former Confederate owners and establishing numerous Af-rican American successors, although morally righteous, would have undermined rapid economic reconstruction for Northerners seeking to recoup their costs from the war. Changing land ownership across the former Confederacy would have required much more force, and it would have further damaged what was left of Southern resources. Republicans wanted to make the defeated region a productive part of their existing economic system, not a laboratory for new experiments in farming and commerce. They wanted the profits that flowed North from slavery, now without the slaves.

The very people in the North who sent their boys and spent their money to fight the Confederacy hoped to reestablish economic con-nections after the fighting. If the Republican vision of politics pushed multiracial representation, it did not do the same for wealth, which remained fundamentally white in Republican understandings of capi-talism. Lincoln defended Black voters at the end of his life, but he never envisioned a Southern economy filled with Black businessmen. He and other Republicans could not imagine it, and they had little incentive to take this enormous step. It was easier to leave the defeated white elites in place and to renew business partnerships with them.

Above all, Republicans remained focused on enriching and em-powering white voters in the North. Even with the election of African American officials in the South, these new representatives remained a very small part of the national party. In the years after Lincoln's death, the leading Republican figures were white male congressmen, elected in midwestern and northeastern states. They had little direct connection to the difficult lives of former slaves. After a costly civil war, Republican leaders were most concerned with the welfare of their constituents, and their businesses, not what some derisively called the "struggle over the negro."[11]

President Lincoln's unlikely successor made this balance between multi-racial democracy and Northern economic interests difficult for Republican leaders. At first, it appeared Lincoln and Johnson shared many views. Andrew Johnson was born within two months of his predecessor. Both men grew up in poor families, received little education, and moved frequently at a young age. Lincoln eventually settled in Illinois, Johnson in Tennessee. The two men became prosperous at about the same time, working largely for themselves; a small-town lawyer in Lincoln's case and a small-town tailor in Johnson's. They each entered state politics in the 1830s, served together in the U.S. House of Representatives in the 1840s, and gained national attention for their oratorical skills.

Johnson initially rose faster than Lincoln. He built a loyal following in the Tennessee Democratic Party, which had close ties to farmers and artisans in the state dating back to Andrew Jackson's presidency. Johnson was elected governor and then served as a U.S. senator until the first year of the Civil War. Although he was a slaveholder, and his state joined the Confederacy, Johnson pledged to stand by the Union. He was the only senator from a seceding state to take this courageous position.

"I will not," Johnson told his fellow senators in December 1860, "give up this Government that is now called an experiment, which some are prepared to abandon." Admitting that he had voted against Lincoln and disagreed with Republican opposition to the spread of slavery, Johnson still called upon every citizen "to rally around the altar of our common country, and lay the Constitution upon it as our last libation, and swear by our God, and all that is sacred and holy, that the Constitution shall be saved, and the Union preserved."[12]

Born with little, both Lincoln and Johnson held to the Union as a sacred home for all white men. Despite their limited education, they spoke eloquently for defense of the great American experiment in shared self-governance. Johnson's words were particularly powerful because they came from the most popular elected official in a slave state. Lincoln rewarded Johnson with the military governorship of Tennessee, partially occupied by Union forces in 1862.

Running a difficult reelection campaign two years later, Lincoln looked to Johnson as a figure who could show that the president wanted to bring reconciliation after a long and costly war. Renaming the Republican Party the "National Union Party," Lincoln chose Johnson as his vice presidential running mate. By this time, Johnson had abandoned his defense of slavery, agreeing with the president that emancipation would allow the Union to use former slaves to defeat the Confederacy.

Lincoln and Johnson differed on most other issues. Johnson was a white supremacist who believed that the rights and privileges of democracy should not be shared with former slaves. He referred on multiple occasions to the United States as a "country for white men." In his rambling speech before his swearing in as vice president, he praised how Union forces helped his state break "the yoke of slavery," but he also indicated that he did not see any further role for Congress interfering in the treatment of former slaves. "I desire to proclaim that Tennessee, whose representative I have been, is free." And he meant "free" for white men, not women, who could not vote, and not former slaves, whom he never intended to see as full citizens.[13]

Johnson's remarks were, in fact, quite awkward for the president and the members of Congress assembled in the Capitol for Lincoln's second inauguration in March 1865. The new vice president was visibly drunk, and he seemed out of touch with the growing commitment among Republicans to a multiracial democracy in the South. Johnson was a longtime advocate of prosecuting Confederate leaders for their treason against the Union, but he was not a proponent of Black voting. Some Republicans, including Massachusetts senator Charles Sumner, hoped they could persuade Johnson on this issue; most were thankful he was not president.

President Andrew Johnson. *Credit: Mathew Brady*

The vice president's thinking should not have surprised anyone. He had a long record from his years in Congress. Johnson was a populist who appealed to Southern white men, like himself, who resented the wealthy, elite Southern plantation owners—the men who led the Confederacy and condescended to those without property or education. As an elected official in eastern Tennessee, Johnson represented white families who lived on small hardscrabble parcels of hilly land. Their lives were precarious and filled with backbreaking labor. Some families, like Johnson's, owned slaves, but they could not rely on them to fulfill their needs, as was the case on the grand plantations of the Deep South. For Johnson, the rich landed Tennessee families in Nashville, Memphis, and other areas were the enemy; they hoarded the wealth and privilege that his suffering constituents craved. Johnson railed against the Slave Power elite—the same Confederate leaders Lincoln labeled as "rebels."

Unlike the Republicans who represented Northern white voters with few African American neighbors, Johnson spoke for citizens who lived among large slave populations. Johnson's voters feared that free African Americans would compete with poor white citizens for political voice and economic gain after slavery. Already mistreated by the plantation elite, struggling families in Tennessee could lose the advantage they still possessed over Black laborers if the latter were given the same rights and opportunities. An established white tailor, like Johnson, would likely confront numerous African American tailors appealing to similar customers after the Civil War. Poor white citizens could fall even lower and suffer more deprivation than before.

If Republicans believed Northern whites and Southern Blacks could both benefit from changes after the Civil War, the vice president and his followers envisioned a "zero-sum battle for racial survival." Johnson consistently reminded listeners: "The white race was superior to the black." He promised that even after emancipation, "the relative position of the two races would be the same." Johnson was happy to knock slaveholding elites down a few notches by removing their slaves, but he violently opposed anything that would allow the former slaves to approach the status of poor whites. For that reason, voting, land ownership, and especially labor organizing by African Americans were to be resisted at all costs. Democracy for the destitute white families in Johnson's Tennessee, and many other regions of the South, required continued repression of Black aspirations.[14]

Of course, Johnson was only vice president in early 1865. Republican leaders in Congress who resented Johnson—and some who demanded his removal after his drunken, racist performance at his inauguration—recognized the value he brought to Lincoln as at least a token of Democratic support. Lincoln assured members of Congress that Johnson would have no influence on policy in the last days of the Civil War.

The vice presidency was not a substantial office; like other presidents in the nineteenth century, Lincoln did not consult or even inform his vice president of most decisions—they barely spoke. Johnson was a symbol of the possibilities for national unity, and the less he was seen beyond that, the better.

Lincoln's assassination on April 15, 1865, thrust him unexpectedly into command. Johnson became the first vice president to assume office after the murder of a president. No one had planned for such an event. Johnson was sleeping alone on the night of the attack, unguarded, at the Kirkwood House hotel, about a quarter mile from Ford's Theatre, where he would have been killed by John Wilkes Booth's coconspirator George Atzerodt, had Atzerodt not lost his nerve.

Startled out of bed by news of the president's wounds, Johnson quickly joined the nighttime vigil for Lincoln and then returned to his hotel room. At 11:00 a.m. on April 15, less than four hours after Lincoln's death, the chief justice of the Supreme Court, Salmon Chase, administered the oath of office to the new president. The *New York Times* reported that Johnson was "solemn and dignified," and he expressed a sense of sobering purpose in this difficult moment of transition for the country: "The duties of the office are mine. I will perform them. The consequences are with God. Gentlemen, I shall lean upon you."[15]

The "gentlemen" whom Johnson addressed were Lincoln's cabinet and a small group of Republican senators assembled for the hasty inauguration in the vice president's shabby hotel quarters. They hoped that he would indeed consult with them to begin the hard work of reconstructing the defeated South as part of a growing multiracial democracy. Ill informed of Lincoln's policies, disliked by his predecessor's advisers, and alienated from members of Congress, Johnson was not well prepared for this moment. His emphasis on continuity and cooperation was reassuring.

In his first actions, Johnson reaffirmed his desire to punish the leaders of the Confederacy—promising words for Republican leaders. The new president placed a $100,000 bounty on the head of Jefferson Davis, and he refused to commute the executions of the conspirators behind Lincoln's assassination. Senator Charles Sumner, a vocal Republican exponent of African American rights in the South, was impressed that the new president seemed "very determined" to prevent Confederates from returning to power. The Massachusetts senator thought Johnson might be even tougher on the rebels than Lincoln, who spoke eloquently, but naively in Sumner's view, of reconciliation after the war.[16]

Johnson intended to make the highest Confederate leaders pay for their crimes, but that was all. His instincts remained those of a populist. Johnson's main goal, as always, was to help poor whites in the South, and that involved keeping the former slaves down. Sumner and other senators had little influence on him because Republican voters in the North were not Johnson's voters. The new president had spoken respectfully to those Republicans, but their agreement did not go very deep.

Lincoln's party had made a grave mistake for political expedience in the 1864 election; now they paid a steep price. The Republicans had empowered Johnson, through the vice presidency, to become the virtual dictator of the former Confederate states. He assumed all Lincoln's wartime powers, with the authority to extend those powers over the Southern territories now under military occupation. Lincoln had established the precedent, with the Emancipation Proclamation and many other acts, that the president could force major changes on the ground for military purposes, without consulting Congress or anyone else. Lincoln had acted unilaterally to free the slaves in the Confederacy. Johnson accepted his predecessor's authority to do that, despite his own personal reservations, and he assumed the same powers for himself.

Republicans had created a national executive with the most authoritarian capabilities in American history to that time, which Democrats, especially John Wilkes Booth, had resisted. Now a Democrat wielded the bloated capabilities of the Republican president. It was difficult for Lincoln's party to restrain his successor. They had little time to react after such a shocking, sudden transition.

Congress was not even in session for the first nine months of Johnson's presidency. From April to December 1865, the new president exercised Lincoln's day-to-day control over the country, particularly the occupied South, without any accountability to the legislature. Republicans in Congress had been happy with this arrangement when Lincoln served as president, but now they had few immediate controls over his successor.

Johnson understood the circumstances, and he took full advantage of them. He asserted complete executive authority over the reconstruction of the South. He argued that the Southern states had never really left the Union; they had been hijacked, he claimed, by rebels who were now defeated. Since these were not new territories, they did not fall under Congress's jurisdiction for readmitting states. Johnson asserted, with some justification, that reconstruction after the Civil War was merely law enforcement—the purview of the executive and its designated agencies (including the military), not the legislature.

Sumner and other Republican senators pushed back, but since they were not in session, they could not legislate any restrictions on the president. Johnson moved quickly, beginning with the designation of new governors in former Confederate states. On May 9, 1865, less than a month after Lincoln's assassination, the president extended federal recognition to a new government in Virginia, under a staunch unionist, Francis Pierpont. Johnson ignored Republican pleas to require protections for African American voting rights in this state and other former parts of the Confederacy. Instead, the president emphasized help and reconciliation for white citizens and paid no attention to the needs of freed slaves. He appointed pro-Union figures favored by the Democrats, instead of Republicans committed to political reforms. For Johnson, slave emancipation was the end of change, not the beginning.

On May 29, the president offered full amnesty to citizens of the South who had joined the Confederacy and now wished to return to their family lands and occupations. Johnson aimed his proclamation at the struggling farmers, shopkeepers, and craftsmen who had consistently supported him and other Democrats. He promised to restore their antebellum lives. For the moment, the president exempted the political and military leaders of the Confederacy—including exile figures like Joseph Shelby, John Bankhead Magruder, and Alexander Watkins Terrell—from his declaration of amnesty. Most telling, he excluded large landholders, especially former slaveholders, with property exceeding $20,000 in value.

The presidential stipulations meant that the wealthy and powerful elites of the South, whom Johnson resented, would remain weakened. Poor whites would gain at their expense. Former slaves would remain excluded from most opportunities. Johnson used his pardoning powers to create the common white man's democracy he had long sought.

The governors he appointed around the region did the same. As in Virginia, the president chose loyal defenders of the Union who were also committed to boosting the power of struggling white citizens. They denied that freed slaves deserved anything more than the right to leave their former masters, and some governors even refused that. Johnson's appointed Florida governor, William Marvin, called on African Americans to return to work in the fields and "call your old Master—'Master.' "[17]

That was Johnson's most consistent goal: to make certain that common white men were still masters in the South. He rejected every action that might have helped African Americans. The president ordered the decommissioning of Black soldiers from the Union army. He blocked the efforts of the Freedmen's Bureau to assist former slaves, like Henry Adams, acquire land. Most of all, Johnson amplified Southern fears that African American voters would use their ballots to gain control over public offices and law enforcement. He did everything he could to prevent Black men from voting, and he sometimes encouraged violence with his hateful rhetoric.

Johnson praised open defiance of Republicans advocating for African American rights, condemning them as "cormorants and blood-suckers" who attacked the longtime residents of the South and "have been fattening upon the country." Expelling Northern intruders and keeping freed slaves in their place was essential for peace, the president asserted. He defined these actions as "patriotic"—how good white citizens could "rally round the standard of their country, and swear by their altars and their God" to support a Union of like-minded men.[18]

Although they had lost the war, the states of the former Confederacy rejoined the Union with strict adherence to a closed, whites-only vision of democracy. Each of them moved immediately to enforce laws that would extend the old restrictions on African American freedoms into an era without slavery and prevent full Black citizenship. During the first year of Johnson's presidency, "Black codes" spread throughout the South, giving statutory force to the continued dominance of the former secessionists. White men retained the status they had lost on the battlefield—in the words of one contemporary critic: "getting things back as near to slavery as possible."[19]

The government in Mississippi led the way. Benjamin Humphreys, a brigadier general in the Confederate army, became governor in October 1865 after receiving a pardon from President Johnson. Humphreys accepted the end of slavery in law but not in practice. Even as African Americans were elected to the state legislature, the governor worked with white representatives, still a majority, to pass legislation that prevented African Americans from purchasing land or leaving their former masters' plantations. African American residents of cities and towns now required a "license" from their mayor, permitting them to live in their current location. Those residing in the countryside needed written authorization from the county police. White citizens did not require any of this documentation; they could live wherever they pleased.

The close surveillance of African Americans gave local bosses the ability to coerce former slaves. The Confederates who had owned the plantations continued to use law enforcement to restrict Black men and women. Poor whites actually gained power in this scheme, as many were hired as policemen and sheriffs. African Americans moved from living under the whip to living under close police monitoring; they could not settle anywhere without the permission of powerful white men who, of course, extracted concessions.

The most common of these concessions to white power involved coerced labor. Local bosses forced African Americans to sign uneven contracts, often called "apprenticeships," where they pledged their work to a white landholder for multiple years, in return for meager pay. Former slaves had to sign these contracts in order to find employment, and they often could not read or understand the terms. White citizens could buy out the labor contracts of African Americans, forcing them to move from one employer to another with no say in the matter. They could be traded against their will.

On request by police, African Americans had to show that they were working under a labor contract. Despite the frequent unfairness of these agreements, Black workers could not rescind or amend their commitments. Freed slaves deemed negligent in their work obligations, as judged by local officials, faced heavy fines and imprisonment. And white citizens could punish Black laborers for poor performance, with no explicit legal protections against abuse. The whip was still commonly used to keep African Americans in line.

The new laws expressly prohibited any effort to advocate for African Americans stuck in these slave-like arrangements. Mississippi muzzled public criticism from white and Black residents with heavy fines, imprisonment, or worse. Any effort to organize a protest, or even a meeting among African Americans to examine their work conditions, was prohibited under anti-vagrancy laws. Despite the saturation of weapons among former Confederate citizens, many of which were used to threaten freed slaves, African Americans were unequivocally prevented from defending themselves. They had no gun or knife rights: "No freedman, free Negro, or mulatto not in the military service of the United States government, and not licensed so to do by the board of police of his or her county, shall keep or carry firearms of any kind, or any ammunition, dirk, or Bowie knife." Former Confederates did not believe the First or Second Amendment applied to Black men. That double standard has endured for more than a century.[20]

The Mississippi Black codes enforced a rigid two-class society. The slaves were emancipated but not really free. The new laws empowered wealthy landlords to command cheap and plentiful labor for harvesting their crops and performing other services. The Black codes boosted poor white citizens by protecting their opportunities from African American competition. If the former slaves had to stay on the land, they could not challenge the small-town craftsmen, shopkeepers, and tailors who, like Andrew Johnson, feared a loss of work and position in a more open society. White rights dominated Mississippi democracy, which was what the president and his Southern allies wanted.

South Carolina, North Carolina, Texas, and other former Confederate states echoed Mississippi's laws. South Carolina's Black code, passed in the days before Christmas 1865, called African American workers "servants" and their white employers "masters." It not only required the servants to adhere to unfair contracts and prohibited labor organizing but went so far as to regulate how they spent their nonworking hours: "Servants shall be quiet and orderly in their quarters, at their work, and on the premises; shall extinguish their lights and fires, and retire to rest at seasonable hours." Drunkenness and other unruly behavior were heavily penalized, and any close physical relations between Black men and white women were strictly prohibited.

Most representative of President Johnson's favoritism for poor whites, the South Carolina code limited African American competition with traditional craftsmen, artisans, and shopkeepers. White men, like both Lincoln and Johnson, worked in these occupations without training or public regulation. South Carolina required freed slaves, many of whom had received training on their plantations, to apply for permission to practice their trade. The state created a licensing requirement, with mandatory renewals and heavy fees each year, only for African Americans. Judges in state courts, who were entirely white and usually inexperienced in the trades, determined which Black men could set up business and which could not.

White businessmen, free from all these requirements, would obviously have an advantage. The new law discouraged, and frequently prevented, competition from freed slaves. To force African Americans into labor contracts, the South Carolina law stipulated: "No person of color shall practice any mechanical art or trade unless he shows that he has served an apprenticeship in such trade or art."[21]

Following its southern neighbor, North Carolina was explicit in the double standard it enforced for prosecuting crimes. Under the state's Black code, African Americans were prohibited from testifying in court against white citizens accused of property crimes. This meant that freed slaves could not file charges or bear witness if a former master stole their money or damaged their home. As in other states, African American men were also prohibited from any sexual relations with white women, even if consensual, on penalty of death. White men continued to face little penalty for coerced intercourse with Black women, many of whom were now working under labor contracts for them.[22]

Texas expanded on the model of the Carolinas in enforcing labor contracts for freed slaves, prohibiting African American testimony against white citizens, and outlawing intermarriage or Black male sexual relations with white women. Texas also required separate railroad compartments and schools for white and Black citizens. The state's homestead law denied African Americans access to public lands.

As the Confederate exiles from Mexico returned to Texas and other states, these legal exclusions of African Americans increased in intensity and violence. The Texas Black codes ensured greater opportunity for a growing white settler population, competing with African American and Mexican American families, often subjected to similar repression. The large, diverse, and former Mexican territory was Americanized through enforced white supremacy.

The Black codes imported to Texas from Mississippi, the Carolinas, and other states did that work. They ensured subordinate labor for landowners and a favorable system of justice. The codes helped poor white men rise, and they limited competition. This arrangement was integral to making states like Texas lands of opportunity for men who followed the footsteps of Abraham Lincoln and Andrew Johnson— moving into new territories as Lincoln's penniless beginners, seeking to "work for themselves, on their farms, in their houses and in their shops, taking the whole product to themselves."[23]

President Johnson and the Southern Democrats who wrote the Black codes resisted Republican efforts at multiracial cooperation, but they echoed the dream at the heart of the Republican Party from its founding: "The free white men had a right to claim that the new territories into which they and their children might go to seek a livelihood should be preserved free and clear of the incumbrance of slavery."[24]

This hopeful vision of land for free white men, without slavery, left little space for African Americans or other nonwhite groups. Republican members of Congress were constrained in their efforts to undo the Black codes because they shared similar assumptions about who deserved primary place in American democracy. Andrew Johnson and his allies were cruel and flagrant in their racism, but they were also creatures of the Republican free white vision that had brought Lincoln to the presidency and kept the Union together.

Nine months after they last met at Lincoln's second inauguration, Republicans returned to the newly renovated Capitol in December 1865. They controlled both the U.S. Senate and the House of Representatives because the former Confederate states remained mostly absent. Republicans were determined to push back against President Johnson's advocacy for exclusive white rule in the South. The challenge for members of Congress after the Civil War was building a white man's democracy that still gave more opportunities to African Americans and other groups.

Lincoln's unexpected successor had encouraged white repression by the same men who had lost the war but who were quickly becoming the winners of political change. Republicans wanted to build a democracy where white citizens shared some power, even as they remained dominant. Sharing power, particularly at the ballot box and in the economy, would limit the Democratic Party's control of the region, allowing Republican penetration below the Mason-Dixon Line.

During the first months of 1866, Republicans in the Senate proposed legislation to expand the work of the Freedmen's Bureau and provide new protections for civil rights. The first bill gave the agency more resources to help former slaves and the authority to defend them when attacked or denied basic rights. Members of Congress wanted to empower the Freedmen's Bureau to cooperate with U.S. military forces still stationed in Memphis and other parts of the South. A more active Freedmen's Bureau would ensure that freed slaves were really free, and not re-enslaved by other means.

The second Senate bill went further. It reflected Republican hopes for fairer treatment of African Americans, guaranteeing their ability to work productively and live safely in the United States. The goal was to encourage citizenship, not dependence, among freed slaves. The bill fell short of equal access to land, education, and wealth, but it embraced the basic Republican position that each man—especially Lincoln's penniless beginner—should control his own labor, property, and life.

The legislation promised to "protect all persons in the United States in their civil rights, and furnish the means of their vindication." This was the first civil rights bill in American history since the Bill of Rights. It was the first legislation to use the phrase *civil rights* for African Americans.

The Civil Rights Bill extended foundational rights to Black men and women, and it placed firm restrictions on state governments. The Bill of Rights guaranteed the rights of white citizens against federal power; the Civil Rights Bill protected those rights for white and Black citizens against state governments. The legislation guaranteed equal application of the law to all citizens, regardless of race or previous condition of servitude—a breathtaking commitment that contradicted almost one hundred years of history and the recent state Black codes.

The Civil Rights Bill began by creating birthright citizenship: "All persons born in the United States and not subject to any foreign power" were "citizens of the United States." The only exception allowed in the legislation was for "Indians," the Indigenous peoples subjected to continued removal and violence by the U.S. government after the Civil War. Under this legislation, African Americans and other nonwhite individuals born in the United States were entitled to the rights and protections that American Indians were denied. Former slaves, like all other non-native peoples, had the same rights "in every state and territory" to control their actions and protect their property. The legislation enumerated the content of these rights in detail: "to make and enforce contracts, to sue, to be parties, and give evidence, to inherit, purchase, lease, sell, hold, and convey real and personal property, and to full and equal benefit of all laws and proceedings for the security of person and property, as is enjoyed by white citizens."

That last phrase—"as is enjoyed by white citizens"—was crucial. It denied the two-tiered system of law, landownership, and work that kept freed slaves subjected to the whims of their former masters in much of the South. The legislation prescribed specific federal penalties—a $1,000 fine or imprisonment—for anyone who denied equal application of the law. Federal district attorneys and marshals were given the power to enforce these penalties and require local officials to follow the law. In some circumstances, the U.S. military would step in to ensure compliance.

The real focus of activity in this legislation was the courts. Federal judges were given new powers to supersede the orders of states, counties, and cities that denied African Americans their basic rights. This amounted to a federal nullification of the Black codes: "The jurisdiction in civil and criminal matters hereby conferred on the district and circuit courts of the United States shall be exercised and enforced in conformity with the laws of the United States." Federal judges would be the protectors of former slaves; they would have the authority to punish those who exploited and terrorized vulnerable populations.[25]

That was a heavy burden for the courts, a burden they could not carry. Even with law and Congress on their side, judges had few tools to enforce their rulings. District attorneys and federal marshals were often sympathetic to local communities. Mayors, sheriffs, and police chiefs frequently served the landholders and local toughs determined to keep the former slaves down. The Freedmen's Bureau had limited personnel under arms, and U.S. Army soldiers were in short number across the vast territory of Southern states. As was the case in Memphis during the infamous riot, military commanders were hesitant to interfere in local disputes, often waiting until it was too late.

Republican leaders in Congress recognized these constraints on enforcement. Critics of the Freedmen's Bureau and Civil Rights Bills called for more vigorous enforcement through the creation of a national police force (what would become the Federal Bureau of Investigation a half century later) or a heavier military presence. The vast majority of Republicans, however, rejected these obvious solutions. The party supported equal application of the laws but not the necessary expenditures or direct intervention in the South. They wanted to limit conflict, and they wanted to devote government resources to more profitable programs, especially westward settlement. Republicans relied on the goodwill of Southerners and President Johnson, even though they knew these were false hopes. They deluded themselves into believing that their good intentions were enough to overcome local resistance.

Andrew Johnson contributed to the resistance. The president vetoed both the Freedmen's Bureau and Civil Rights Bills. He directed
his anger at Congress, accusing the legislative branch of overstepping
its bounds. Only the president, he wrote, "is chosen by the people of
all the states." Of course, Johnson had never been elected president by
anyone.

Johnson accused Congress of acting in the interests of Northern Republicans and not the white residents of the South. The cost of financing
the Freedmen's Bureau and the confiscation of land and other resources
from Southern whites, Johnson explained, would harm citizens in the
former Confederate territories, whom he believed the Republicans were
mistreating: "The appointment of an agent for every country and parish will create an immense patronage, and the expense of the numerous
officers and their clerks, to be appointed by the President, will be great
in the beginning, with a tendency steadily to increase. The appropriations asked by the Freedmen's Bureau as now established, for the year
1866, amount to $11,745,000. It may be safely estimated that the cost
to be incurred under the pending bill will require double that amount."
The president also objected that the legislation would "take away land
from its former owners," which he strongly condemned.

Congress was doing far too much for the former slaves, according to Johnson, providing corrupt "patronage," in his view. "The idea
on which the slaves were assisted to freedom was that on becoming
free they would be a self-sustaining population," he explained. "Any
legislation that shall imply that they are not expected to attain a self-
sustaining condition must have a tendency injurious alike to their
character and their prospects." Helping the former slaves, Johnson
argued, would make them dependents, hurt white citizens, and exceed
the obligations of government. Emancipation was enough, and any
additional government aid or protection, the president believed, was
too much.[26]

Johnson went further in vetoing the Civil Rights Bill, which he characterized as a Republican effort to seize control of Southern communities. He echoed Confederate claims that states and local governments

should determine rights based on race. The Constitution, Johnson argued, "guarantees nothing with certainty if it does not insure to the several States the right of making and executing laws in regard to all matters arising within their jurisdiction." The president defended the continued unequal application of the law, and he rejected Congress's power to do anything about it. He condemned the legislative efforts to strengthen federal courts as a particularly aggressive overreach, turning "the State judge into a mere ministerial officer," emasculated by Congress.

This was Johnson's most passionate point. The Republicans were using legislation, he argued, to harm white citizens, favoring Northern interests and freed slaves over them. Republicans were turning the historical order of power in the South upside down rather than accepting the traditions that had long promoted stability and status for so many. The Civil Rights Bill would "establish for the security of the colored race safeguards which go infinitely beyond any that the General Government has ever provided for the white race," Johnson thundered. "In fact," he continued, "the distinction of race and color is by the bill made to operate in favor of the colored and against the white race."

That could not stand. The president warned that Congress's radical program would "resuscitate the spirit of rebellion" among Southerners, "arrest the progress of those influences which are more closely drawing around the States the bonds of union and peace." In the president's telling, the Civil Rights Bill was an act of war on the South, and Johnson had to stop it. He claimed, falsely, that Lincoln would have done the same.[27]

Lincoln had vetoed seven bills during his presidency, but none by asserting such overwhelming presidential authority and preference for a single region. He had exercised far-reaching war powers with the consistent approval of Congress. Few presidents contested the powers of Congress and acted with the same contempt as Johnson. His belligerence echoed Andrew Jackson's war on the Bank of the United States more than thirty years earlier, but President Johnson did not have the popular support of his twice-elected Tennessee predecessor. Johnson's power was derived from Booth's assassination of Lincoln, and he was using that power to thwart Lincoln's party and its congressional majority.

Republican radicals and moderates were outraged. Johnson did more than anyone else to unite the still-new Republican Party—in supporting federal enforcement of political reforms in the South and in opposing him. Members of Congress had hoped to cooperate with Lincoln's successor, but now they recognized that he was worse than incompetent. He was obsessed with preserving a limited, white male democracy in the South. He resented landholding elites, and he used the considerable powers of his office to assist former Confederates. Apart from accepting the end of slavery, Johnson was determined to reverse the Republican victory in the Civil War.

For the first time in American history, members of Congress overrode the president's vetoes, passing the Civil Rights Bill in April 1866, and a revised version of the Freedmen's Bureau Bill in July. This set up a war between the legislature and the executive branch. Congress authorized and funded more muscular federal activities to protect African Americans in the South, but the president still oversaw the implementation of these measures through the U.S. Army and other agencies that reported to him. Although Johnson could no longer govern the South unilaterally, as he had in the months immediately after Lincoln's death, he could obstruct Republican legislation through diversion, noncompliance, and disobedience. He pursued all three tactics, with extensive support from Southern governors and other local officials.

To strengthen the nation's commitment to civil rights, Republicans extended the Civil Rights Bill into a constitutional amendment. Senator Jacob Howard from Michigan explained that he and his colleagues wanted to create more pressure for enforcement, converting the legislation into a core part of constitutional law. Civil rights became permanent and irreversible; this was an enduring, if still incomplete, victory for multiracial democracy. In response to continued presidential and state resistance, Senator Howard announced that Republicans wanted protections for all citizens to extend "beyond the reach of [those] who would pull the whole system up by its roots and destroy it."[28]

By July 1868—two years after Congress overrode Johnson's veto to pass the Civil Rights Bill—the Fourteenth Amendment was ratified by twenty-eight, and soon, thirty states. This included nine former Confederates states that Congress required to accept the amendment, despite opposition from their white voters, before they could rejoin the Union. The states affirmed the rewriting of the Constitution to prohibit slavery under the Thirteenth Amendment, and they now guaranteed citizenship to "all persons" born in their states, as well as "due process of law" and "equal protection of the laws." In unequivocal words, the Fourteenth Amendment ordered that "no state" could "make or enforce any law which shall abridge the privileges or immunities of citizens," including former slaves.[29]

This rewriting of the Constitution did not negate the Southern Black codes, because it did not guarantee the right to vote, work, marry, own property, or live in a particular place—all of which remained parts of local democracy, heavily controlled by the states. Federal courts could, in theory, reject state laws that treated African Americans unequally, but they would not do that until nearly a century later. The power to define "equal protection of the laws" remained with the states and local communities.

Congress showed little will to step into these issues of local interpretation. It rejected the inclusion of specific language about how equality should be defined in practice for voting, work conditions, or lifestyle choices. The details continued to divide the party and expose hesitations. Thaddeus Stevens, Charles Sumner, and other radical Republicans had proposed detailed requirements for equal treatment of all citizens in early drafts of the Fourteenth Amendment, but a majority of Republican senators rejected them, accepting continued second-class status for African Americans, North and South. Although Republican voters wanted the most violent forms of mistreatment in the South reversed, they were not willing to reject discrimination more fully, nor were they ready to invest their limited resources in this endeavor.

Republicans turned to the courts and especially the U.S. Army for the enforcement of basic civil rights. Johnson was commander in chief, but military leaders were bound to the Constitution and laws passed by Congress, not the whims of the president. Federal judges were hesitant to rule where they lacked muscle to make their rulings stick amid hostile local communities. Therefore, the presence of U.S. Army soldiers became crucial for adherence to the law. Without displays of federal force, many Southern communities continued to brutalize former slaves.

Congress passed a series of Reconstruction Acts in 1867 to unchain the army from the president's restrictions on its deployments in the South. The first of these acts, approved on March 2, 1867, was the most important. It took political power from the president-approved governors in the former Confederate states and gave it to the occupying soldiers. Congress divided the region into five military districts, and it required "an officer of the Army" who was sworn to the Constitution to enforce the law and squash local resistance. Each officer would use "sufficient military force" to "protect all persons in their rights of person and property, to suppress insurrection, disorder, and violence, and to punish, or cause to be punished, all disturbers of the public peace and criminals." Congress did not distinguish between white and Black "persons," as the president did, in its charge to the military.

The army would indeed become the needed muscle for the federal courts, empowering "civil tribunals to take jurisdiction of and to try offenders." In the case of local resistance, the army now had the authority to "organize military commissions or tribunals for that purpose." Congress prohibited state and local leaders from challenging military power as they had in Memphis and other violent areas: "All interference under color of State authority with the exercise of military authority under this act, shall be null and void."[30]

The Reconstruction Acts were breathtaking in their transfer of power from civilians to the military. The legislature usurped presidential command, delineating clear guidelines and purposes for soldiers on the ground. The U.S. Army became the Republican Congress's army, enforcing its vision of civil rights.

The Second Reconstruction Act of March 23, 1867, ordered the army to protect African American voters. Local officials were hostile, so Congress told military officers "to cause a registration to be made of male citizens of the United States, twenty-one years of age and upwards." Race was excluded as a qualification for voting. Congress ordered the military to take over registration of African American voters where states refused.

The commanding general in each district would now oversee the elections for fairness and safety, certify the results, and ensure that elected officials attended conventions to write new constitutions for each state. Congress intended for African American voters and elected representatives to play a major role in making law and policy. Military officers could remove individuals from office who were not elected according to federal rules, especially if they impeded the work of newly elected representatives.[31]

Army control of elections enabled an upsurge in African American voting and a transformation in Southern leadership. Soldiers protected the voters and confirmed their choices. The military forced white citizens to honor the voting rights of former slaves. African American men emerged as a powerful voting bloc, electing their own representatives across the South. They participated in conventions that rewrote state constitutions to guarantee their basic rights and eliminate the worst forms of racial tyranny.

Although American society remained deeply unequal, the Civil Rights Bill, the Fourteenth Amendment, and the Reconstruction Acts opened Southern democracy more than ever before. They constituted a truly breathtaking expansion of congressional control and African American freedoms in a few short years. The scope and rapidity of these accomplishments contributed to a backlash, deepening distrust of the federal government, and resentment toward Republicans in the former Confederacy.

The progress of the late 1860s was not the culmination of the Civil War but its continuation. The widely read *Army and Navy Journal* advised soldiers that the conditions in the South were still in a "state of war"—"the same state of war which prevailed at Lee's surrender." Two years after Appomattox, the military took more direct action in the former Confederacy, imposing martial law in numerous states as it confronted an organized white insurgency. The continuing war was about who would control the region—a violent group of white men or a wider mix of races?[32]

Military coercion worked in the South. No other Republican tactic achieved as much in prying former slaves free from the grasp of former slaveholders. No other institution did more to protect African American freedom than the U.S. Army. The Northern white officers who led the occupying forces were not racially enlightened, but they were radicalized by what they observed as a violent and dangerous insurgency of former Confederates. The attacks on African Americans were attacks on the federal authority that Northern soldiers had fought to defend. Army enlistees recognized the resistance to law in the South as a grave national threat, and they saw struggling African American citizens as courageous actors who could bring a better peace to the region and to the country as a whole.

Major General Ulysses S. Grant.

Ulysses Grant, still commanding general of the U.S. Army, shared his soldiers' growing concerns about white insurrection. After Lee's surrender, he initially counseled for military caution in the South, arguing that peace would come from avoiding provocative displays of Northern force. Grant wanted to rely on the honor and goodwill of Southerners, exemplified, in part, by the Confederate commander's retreat from the battlefields. Grant was also sanguine about the limited influence of the defiant but feckless Southern exiles—Shelby, Magruder, Terrell, and others—organizing under Maximilian's doomed rule in Mexico.

The Memphis riots in the spring of 1866 shook Grant's confidence in peaceful change, and the attack on African American reformers in New Orleans that summer pushed him over the edge. New Orleans had reelected its Confederate mayor, John T. Monroe, and its Confederate police chief, Thomas Adams—both of whom advocated violence against freed slaves who challenged white authority. On July 30, 1866, a mob of policemen and civilians had attacked a small gathering of African Americans meeting to discuss political reforms. The white attackers clubbed and stabbed members of the peaceful assembly. When the African Americans in attendance surrendered, they were shot in cold blood. Thirty-four Black men and four white supporters were killed by the mob, and more than one hundred and fifty others suffered serious injuries.

Local journalists blamed Republicans for provoking this massacre, but they could not hide their horror at the vengeful, violent white mob. A reporter for the New Orleans *Picayune* recounted how the peaceful, unarmed African American attendees were "mutilated and literally beaten to death as they sought to escape." It was "one of the most horrid pictures it has ever been our ill fortune to witness." That was saying a lot after all the battlefield deaths of prior years.[33]

Grant received a report from the same trusted officer he sent to secure the Southern border against Maximilian's exile army. Major General Philip Sheridan rode from Texas to New Orleans and sent his first assessment to Grant on August 1. He criticized the African American assembly for acting as "political agitators," but he strongly condemned the mayor for using violence "in a manner so unnecessary and atrocious as to compel me to say that it was murder."[34]

The next day, Sheridan shared a damning verdict:

The more information I obtain of the affair of the 30th, in this city, the more revolting it becomes. It was no riot; it was an absolute massacre by the police, which was not excelled in murderous cruelty by that of Fort Pillow. It was a murder which the Mayor and police of the city perpetrated without the shadow of a necessity; furthermore, I believe it was premeditated, and every indication points to this. I recommend the removing of this bad man. I believe it would be hailed with the sincerest gratification of two-thirds of the population of the city. There has been a feeling of insecurity on the part of the people here on account of this man, which is now so much increased that the safety of life and property does not rest with the civil authorities, but with the military.[35]

Sheridan's dispatch conveyed a new urgency to Grant. Comparing the New Orleans massacre to Fort Pillow—the Confederate army's murder of surrendering Union soldiers two years earlier—opened an unhealed wound. Sheridan was unequivocal that the U.S. Army had to step in and remove traitorous local officials. This included the mayor of New Orleans—a "bad man"—whom President Johnson had pardoned and encouraged.

Depiction of police and white civilians attacking a peaceful African American assembly in New Orleans. *Credit: Theodore Russel Davis*

Grant took Sheridan's advice to heart. He defied the president and declared martial law in New Orleans. The U.S. Army seized control of the city; Sheridan's forces offered protection to African American residents.

This was just the beginning. Grant lent his prestige to Republicans in Congress calling for more direct military rule of the South. He wrote his old colleague and commissioner of the Freedmen's Bureau, General Oliver Otis Howard, explaining that the governments and courts in the South "afford no security to life or property" for African Americans. Grant helped to bring Howard's accounting of state crimes against former slaves to the attention of congressmen.[36]

The Reconstruction Acts approved Grant's assertion of power. Congress gave him the authority he needed to put the military in charge throughout the South, despite objections from President Johnson. In many ways, Grant collaborated with Republicans to cut the president off from his constitutional role as commander in chief. Congress went so far as to prohibit Johnson from giving direct orders to any of the generals; Congress required that he go through his secretary of war, as Lincoln never had. Stanton consistently blocked the president.

Grant became the Republican substitute for an isolated and illegitimate chief executive. Neither Grant nor Johnson had been elected president before 1868, but the former was a beloved figure in the Republican North for his battlefield victories. He was also highly regarded by African Americans in the South as a liberator from slavery. Southern Democrats reviled Grant, and they condemned his usurpation of the commander in chief's authority. That condemnation of Grant, however, only justified his extension of military power against insurrectionaries throughout the region.

Following Grant's orders, General Sheridan removed the mayor of New Orleans from office, along with the state's attorney general. Soon after, he deposed the governor, magistrates, judges, sheriffs, and police chiefs in the state who had promoted violence. The U.S. Army took over the government of Louisiana. Sheridan did the same in Texas, including the removal of Governor James Webb Throckmorton.

When Southern Democrats and President Johnson accused Sheridan of launching a coup, Grant ignored his commander in chief again and promised Sheridan: "I shall do all I can to sustain you." President Johnson did, in fact, remove Sheridan, but Grant blocked former Confederate officials from taking power. He supported more direct military action to arrest and punish local advocates of violence. By the end of 1867, Grant had made himself the most powerful figure in the South, the most consistent defender of federal law against white resistance.[37]

Through a new institution, the Military Supervisory Government, Grant coordinated the five military districts created by Congress to govern the South. Asserting the superiority of "war powers" over local authority, military officers enforced equal protection for all citizens under the law. They desegregated New Orleans trolley cars, made employers renegotiate unfair labor contracts, and helped citizens to purchase land and settle in new homes. In many towns, soldiers stepped in to protect African Americans against violence perpetrated by police officers and white mobs. Military courts superseded civilian courts, offering Black men and women fair trials and prosecuting white criminals when local justice was not possible. In Virginia, for example, the U.S. Army created thirty military courts, ordering civilian judges and police officers to follow federal law. Justice for former slaves came from the men in uniform who tried to correct the biases of the traditional men in robes.

The number of U.S. Army soldiers in the South declined during 1867 and 1868 from twenty-three thousand to fewer than twenty thousand, but the former Confederacy received the lion's share of the military's attention. More than 40 percent of the total force was stationed in the region. To accommodate the increasing demands on troops in a vast territory, Grant built additional military outposts, with fewer soldiers in each location. He spread out his forces to increase their reach. The goal was simple: to make the army's presence more ubiquitous while keeping total numbers manageable.

In Mississippi, for example, the army tripled its posts, moving into more of the poor and rural parts of the state. Similar patterns of base-building occurred in Florida, Louisiana, and Arkansas, among other states. The new military posts were often ragged and haphazard, and the soldiers on duty were short on resources. They developed, however, an appreciation for the needs of African Americans and a respect for the challenges they faced. The bases became sanctuaries where Black families could flee for protection, learn skills, and build partnerships. The military was not free of racism, but the bases offered spaces where the Civil Rights Bill and the Fourteenth Amendment were respected, and African Americans could feel safe.

The outposts nurtured economic opportunities for struggling families. In Baton Rouge, Louisiana, African Americans lived and farmed land within base walls. In many locations, Black men and women provided food, cleaning, and other services, receiving a decent wage and better treatment than elsewhere. The bases also became community gathering locations, where African Americans could organize for political participation and self-defense.[38]

The U.S. Army could not remake the former Confederacy—an occupation force never can. The soldiers who policed the South had their greatest effect in providing some safety for new citizens to enter the economy and politics. The army encouraged the emergence of free labor for African Americans—the core of Republican Party ideology and the opposite of the coerced labor that white overseers sought to enforce through contract and violence after emancipation.

The military gave African Americans a chance. Like other Republicans, Grant was not creating a truly equal society but one that was open to new actors and fairer in its application of the law. He wanted the South to look more like the North—with free male wage earners, diverse family landholdings, and peaceful adherence to federal law.

That is how Black men like Hiram Revels and Joseph Rainey were able to get elected to state and federal office, participate in the rewriting of state constitutions, and support vibrant African American schools and businesses. They gained a rising voice from their courage, and the army protected them from hostile neighbors. The partnerships first forged between white officers and former slaves on numerous battlefields now extended into countless Southern communities.

White citizens held tightly to the exclusionary politics of the Democratic Party, and their violent organizations grew, but the army pushed them back to create some security for Black men and women. Like the United States as a whole, the South witnessed the rise of more diversity and more exclusion at the same time.

American democracy alternated like a seesaw between these positions. The Republicans had more weight on their side, but their opponents remained firmly in place too. General Ulysses Grant had succeeded Lincoln as the most powerful Republican, but President Andrew Johnson, like John Wilkes Booth, still commanded the local support to constrain Republican ambitions.

Although the Republican Party won the military battles of the Civil War, the fight over the meaning of America continued. That fight would trigger the first impeachment of a president.

CHAPTER 6
Impeachment

The presidency can protect and threaten democracy at the same time. The president speaks for the American people as the only representative elected by the nation as a whole. The president has personal control over the machinery of a powerful government and is insulated from direct accountability for four years. It is very difficult, perhaps impossible, to punish a sitting president for breaking the law.

Alexander Hamilton defended the creation of this "energetic executive." The Constitution charged the president to defend the country against foreign attacks, ensure the steady execution of the laws, protect property, and secure "liberty against the enterprises and assaults of ambition, of faction, and of anarchy." Drawing on the experiences of disunity under the Articles of Confederation, Hamilton warned: "A feeble executive implies a feeble execution of the government."[1]

But too much energy in the executive is also dangerous. From the founding to the present, observers have warned that presidential power can inspire abuse, even dictatorship. This was precisely the claim that supporters of the Confederacy, including John Wilkes Booth, made about what they perceived as Abraham Lincoln's excessive use of wartime powers. The president destroyed their homes, freed their slaves, and occupied their communities, with very few limits on his authority. At the end of his life, Lincoln seemed ready to give the freed slaves voting rights. That felt like the act of a tyrant to Southerners.

Hamilton had promised that the Constitution would rein in extraordinary war-making powers, forcing a president like Lincoln to observe limits from Congress, the courts, and the people. Presidents had to face the voters every four years, and Hamilton was confident that Americans would not reelect a chief executive who had abused his powers. A president defeated in reelection would lose all authority, becoming an "ordinary" citizen again. He would be subjected to criminal prosecution in federal and state courts for corruption and other illegalities. Hamilton believed that prospect would deter wrongdoing in office.[2]

If it didn't, if the president committed what the founders called "high crimes and misdemeanors," then there was the recourse of impeachment, a political process invented to allow Congress to declare that the president was so derelict in his duties and so threatening to the republic that he must leave office before the end of his elected term. A majority in the House of Representatives and two-thirds of all senators had to agree on this drastic route.

Impeaching and convicting a president sets a very high bar, but it requires fewer votes than the two-thirds necessary in *both* the House of Representatives and the Senate to override a veto of legislation. If a president is so often at odds with Congress that the legislature frequently reverses his vetoes, then he can expect to face impeachment as well. Presidents therefore have a strong incentive to cooperate with Congress, even when the opposing party is in the majority.

During the first seventy-five years of the republic, presidents respected this logic. They rarely vetoed legislation and only did so when they knew that they had enough support in Congress to prevent a reversal or worse. Even Andrew Jackson, who condemned his legislative opponents and received a formal censure from Congress, exercised his veto powers knowing that his opponents did not have enough votes to override or impeach him. President Jackson had consistent supporters in the legislature, and they made it possible for him to serve two terms without impeachment.

Andrew Johnson occupied a much more precarious position. He had never been elected president, and he confronted a Congress dominated by Northern Republicans, who became increasingly hostile to him. His repeated vetoes of the Civil Rights, Freedmen's Bureau, and other bills antagonized large Republican majorities in the House of Representatives and the Senate. Members of Congress not only reversed these vetoes, they took ever-more desperate action to disempower the defiant president. They questioned his opposition to legislation, along with his reluctance to execute the law. Members of Congress believed that Johnson encouraged federal, state, and local groups to deny basic rights to citizens, especially former slaves. Presidential defiance was, according to Senator Charles Sumner, the "consideration which makes ardent representatives say that he must be removed."[3]

The Northern press echoed Sumner, with language condemning Johnson's alleged violation of his presidential duties. The *Atlantic Monthly* called him a "demagogue and autocrat": "insincere as well as stubborn, cunning as well as unreasonable, vain as well as ill-tempered, greedy of popularity as well as arbitrary in disposition, veering in his mind as well as fixed in his will." The *New York Tribune* was even more scathing, explaining that Johnson had "dragged the robes of his office through the purlieus and filth of treason." The editors did not hold back. They characterized Johnson and his appointees as "the worst men that ever crawled like filthy reptiles at the footstool of power."[4]

This was rough stuff. Andrew Johnson was not simply at odds with Congress; he was at war with Congress. He challenged not just the legislation passed by the first branch of the U.S. government but its right to have its legislation enforced by the executive, as the Constitution requires. When he refused to recognize the civil rights of citizens, guaranteed by a bill Congress passed over his veto, he denied the legislature its power to make the laws. To most members of Congress, this was an act of treason, a violation of the president's oath. To Johnson, his actions affirmed his role representing the whole American population. As he and his supporters understood their circumstances, Johnson was sheltering a region of the country that was devastated by war, underrepresented in Congress, and now subjected to Northern vengeance. A defiant Johnson presidency was not dictatorial from this perspective but protective of local democracy in the Southern states.

Johnson and his supporters turned the Republican defense of Lincoln on its head. Lincoln had used extraordinary presidential powers to save the Union and free the slaves. His successor claimed the same right to preserve what he saw as the essentials of the Union— particularly white supremacy. If Lincoln could use his power to protect African Americans, why couldn't Johnson do the same to protect white landholders? Congress had ceded lawmaking supremacy to Lincoln during the Civil War; his successor did not recognize their right to take it back. Johnson claimed that the president, not Congress, was the primary representative and protector for citizens. He was Hamilton's "energetic executive."

For the first time, Congress turned to impeachment. The emerging debate centered on whether and how Congress could limit the president's transgressions. The president claimed continued war powers; Congress believed he was misusing those powers. The president asserted that he represented citizens ignored by a Congress controlled by Northern Republicans. Members of Congress contended that the president subverted the national majority. Both sides argued for democracy but with radically different interpretations of what constituted legitimate authority.

This debate was, of course, personal. Senators like Charles Sumner wanted to remove the man they viewed as a drunk usurper in the Executive Mansion. President Johnson resented how Sumner and others questioned his authority, diminishing him in comparison to Lincoln.

The opponents of presidential power had become its defenders; the advocates of an energetic executive were now its opponents. The real question was: Democracy for whom? A multiracial community, including former slaves? Or a democracy for white residents of the South who had recently lost so much? Congress and the president were surrogates for these opposing positions, as Lincoln and Booth were three years earlier.

During the Civil War, Republicans in Congress remade the federal court system to reduce the dominance of Southern influences at all levels. On the eve of the conflict, the nation had nine federal circuits, which administered local and appellate court cases in federal law across their respective regions. In most instances, the judges appointed in each circuit came from the states in that circuit. The same was true for the U.S. Supreme Court, which had nine justices, one coming from and overseeing each circuit. (The U.S. Constitution does not specify the number of justices on the highest court.)

The judicial circuits were not equal in population or territory. Five of the nine were composed entirely of slave states. Defenders of this system justified the regional imbalance by tradition and transportation needs, but it was yet another example, like the pre–Civil War Senate, of how Southerners manipulated federal institutions to protect white male landholders. The presence of so many judicial circuits in the South meant that powerful figures in the region were ensured that "men of their kind" would judge them and ultimately rule in their favor. The guarantee of a majority on the Supreme Court, with at least five justices coming from the Southern circuits, gave slaveholders the protections they needed. Decisions like *Dred Scott v. Sandford* in 1857, which ruled that African Americans were not entitled to citizenship under the U.S. Constitution, were the consistent result.

Lincoln and his Republican allies would not allow this pattern to continue. Instead of ignoring the federal court system, as some advocated, they undertook to change it rapidly. In July 1862, Republicans in Congress passed a judiciary act, which consolidated the five slave state circuits into three. The remaining six circuits were redrawn to give greater representation to the northern parts of the country, especially the free states west of the Mississippi River that had been largely excluded.

The next year Congress went a step further, creating a new circuit for the states of California and Oregon combined. The Tenth Circuit Act of 1863 also added a tenth Supreme Court justice. With a required quorum of only six justices present to hear cases, the highest court could now act without the votes or even the presence of the three justices from the Southern states. In only two years, Republicans had broken the Southern stranglehold on the American justice system and replaced it with their own dominance.

Although he barely served more than one term as president, Abraham Lincoln appointed five justices to the Supreme Court—half of the full bench. Four of Lincoln's nominees, especially Chief Justice Salmon Chase, were loyal Republicans from the party's heartland in Ohio, Illinois, and Iowa. Stephen Johnson Field, who occupied the new tenth seat on the U.S. Supreme Court, was a Democrat, but Lincoln nominated him because he was loyal to the Union and had served as chief justice for California's supreme court. Field, like his Republican counterparts, was neither a slaveholder nor a friend of the Confederacy.

When Andrew Johnson replaced Lincoln, Republicans reversed course. In July 1866, Congress passed a new act that reduced the number of federal circuits to nine again, leaving only one circuit composed mainly of former slave states. Judges from states outside the former Confederacy would now dominate eight of the nine circuits.

Congress also reduced the intended size of the Supreme Court to seven, prohibiting President Johnson from appointing any replacements after the death or retirement of current Supreme Court justices. Judge John Catron, a Democrat from Tennessee, died at the end of May 1865, but Congress's new legislation left his seat unfilled. There remained only one judge from the region, James Wayne of Georgia—a Democrat, originally nominated by President Andrew Jackson. Wayne's death in 1867 left the Supreme Court without a single Southern justice.

Republicans had taken full control of the courts, initially by expanding their size, now by reducing them. Congress used its statutory power to prevent Andrew Johnson from appointing Southern Democrats to federal judgeships, even as it had done precisely the opposite for Abraham Lincoln. When Ulysses Grant, a Republican, succeeded Johnson as president in March 1869, Congress passed an act that expanded the Supreme Court to nine again, allowing the new president to nominate another Republican justice, Joseph P. Bradley from New Jersey.

No Southerner would serve on the Supreme Court until 1877, when Grant's successor, Rutherford B. Hayes, nominated John Marshall Harlan, a Republican from Kentucky and a civil rights supporter. No Southern Democrat would serve on the Supreme Court until 1888, more than a quarter century after the start of the Civil War.[5]

Lincoln, and later Grant, benefited from Congress's maneuvers; Johnson did not. Through the federal courts, Republicans clawed back the wartime powers they had given to Lincoln. They redesigned the judicial system to diminish Johnson's legal powers, cornering him behind a hostile Congress and Supreme Court. The Reconstruction Acts of 1867 added to the president's isolation, limiting his day-to-day command of the armed forces occupying the South. Republicans monopolized all the legislative, judicial, and military positions in the country, and they worked in concert against Johnson and his white allies in the former Confederacy.

Johnson fought back the only way he could, by empowering the Southern states and undermining the other branches of the federal government, wherever possible, often through noncompliance with the law. The president used his pardoning power for this purpose, returning former Confederate leaders to positions as governors, mayors, marshals, sheriffs, and state judges. He appointed Southern Democrats widely, and he removed Republican officeholders where he had that power.

As Republicans used the institutions of the federal government to protect former slaves and restrict white masters, Johnson felt more dependent than ever on the latter. Republicans seized federal power to expand democracy; Johnson tried to reduce that federal power. He was the first commander in chief to work against the government that he led. He felt he had no choice if he wished to protect white rule. Republicans in Congress concluded that they had to remove him for the sake of a wider, more inclusive democracy.

Johnson's impeachment was not about the Constitution. Neither he nor his opponents were driven by the text or the evolving meaning of the nation's founding document. The Thirteenth Amendment had ended slavery in 1865, and the Fourteenth Amendment promised birthright citizenship and equal protection in 1868. Those were the laws of the land. What really mattered in regard to impeachment was whether the president had to enforce these laws vigorously, or if he could resist and ignore them, as Johnson did.

Article II of the Constitution states: "The executive power shall be vested in a president," but it is unclear what that means. The subsequent sections describe leadership of the military, pardoning powers, treaty-making, and appointments. The most direct statement of presidential responsibility comes near the end of the article, in Section 3: "He shall take care that the laws be faithfully executed." Congress makes the laws under the Constitution; the president ensures that they are enforced.

But what constituted presidential enforcement? Was the president obligated to put his full energy into congressional legislation he deemed unjust? Was the president prohibited from supporting state laws and officials who challenged federal law? "The Framers of the Constitution have left us," one leading scholar observed, "a legacy not only of certainties but of questions."[6]

No president before Johnson confronted single-party dominance of the federal government driving changes that challenged his deepest values. Congressional opposition to presidents was common, but never as overwhelming and hostile to presidential authority as in the years after Lincoln's death.

The impeachment clause of the Constitution, which immediately follows the sentence on faithful execution of the laws, calls for the removal of the president for "treason, bribery, or other high crimes and misdemeanors." The impeachment clause says nothing about removal of the president for failure to enforce congressional legislation or Supreme Court rulings. Andrew Jackson had infamously made this point three decades earlier when he ignored the Supreme Court's ruling protecting American Indian sovereignty, *Worcester v. Georgia*.

The debate about impeachment became a debate about which part of government, Congress or the executive branch, protected democracy and which was a source of tyranny. The Republicans obviously had the better legal and historical argument; Johnson and the Southern Democrats had the weight of tradition on their side. No president had ever been removed from office for failing to execute the law. And until at least the middle of the twentieth century, no federal official was removed for defending white supremacy. Johnson's defiance of civil rights was, in some sad ways, faithful to the repeated roles of presidents in American history, before and after. He was unlawful and respectful of legal traditions at the same time—and that made his impeachment both necessary and deeply problematic.

The final battle between Congress and the president began in the summer of 1867 when Johnson took advantage of the legislature's recess to remove Edwin Stanton from his position as secretary of war. Initially appointed by Lincoln, Stanton had overseen the army during the Civil War and the years after. He had directed the manhunt for John Wilkes Booth and the other conspirators. He had also supported Republican efforts to protect African Americans in the South, despite President Johnson's opposition. The Reconstruction Acts gave the secretary of war important powers in governing the five military districts carved from the former Confederacy. Johnson desperately wanted a presidential loyalist in that position.

Republicans anticipated Johnson's move to replace Stanton by passing the Tenure of Office Act, over the president's veto, on March 2,

Edwin Stanton, secretary of war for presidents Abraham
Lincoln and Andrew Johnson. *Credit: Mathew Brady*

1867. This legislation prohibited the president from removing Senate-confirmed cabinet members (the secretaries of state, treasury, war, navy, interior; the attorney general; and postmaster general) without the "advice and consent of the Senate." It further enabled the Senate to reverse dismissals that occurred during its recess. The Constitution gave Congress the power to reject cabinet appointments it did not like; now Congress claimed the power to prevent cabinet dismissals it did not approve. The president had lost control of his most important executive authority—the ability to choose the leaders of federal agencies.[7]

Johnson resisted what he and others interpreted as an overstep of Congress's constitutional powers. How could any executive function without control over the cabinet? Why did Congress grant Lincoln so much executive authority but now strip it all back from Johnson? What about separation of powers?

The president had a strong case, but he initially tried to get his way without a full-on challenge to the Tenure of Office Act. On August 12, 1867, he sent a letter to Stanton announcing: "You are hereby suspended from the office as secretary of war, and will cease to exercise any and all functions pertaining to the same." Johnson wished to make Grant the new secretary, which would have the added benefit of removing the general from his day-to-day duties in the South. The president ordered Grant to follow Stanton's dismissal with the removal of two highly regarded army officers, known for their disciplined enforcement of federal laws in the former Confederate states: Generals Philip Sheridan and Daniel Sickles.[8]

Republicans saw these moves for what they were: presidential sabotage of Reconstruction legislation. When Congress returned to session, it pushed back. On January 13, 1868, the Senate voted to rescind Stanton's suspension, returning him to the War Department and Grant to his role as commanding general of the army. The Senate's action followed the letter of the Tenure of Office Act, but the president now refused to accept these terms. He wrote to Grant, instructing him "not to obey any order from the War Department," unless explicitly confirmed by the president. Grant understood that he was legally bound to follow the civilian chain of command from Stanton, who was his superior as the reinstated secretary of war. He also recognized that Johnson's actions were unhinged and contemptuous of Congress. Grant wrote to the president that, contrary to his demands, he would follow the "practice under the law and customs of the department."[9]

Johnson continued to pressure Grant, but the general refused in more explicit terms and with an eye to protecting his own hard-won reputation. (Grant was well aware of his political future as a possible Republican candidate for president.) In an angry letter that the general penned in early February 1868, he wrote his commander in chief: "I can but regard this whole matter, from the beginning to the end, as an attempt to involve me in the resistance of law, for which you hesitated to assume the responsibility in orders, and thus to destroy my character before the country."[10]

The general's resistance further antagonized Johnson, especially when Congress published their angry correspondence. Lincoln had exercised direct command over his generals during the Civil War, issuing personal demands to them (frequently by telegraph) and firing them, most notably General George McClellan, with little advice from the War Department or Congress. Johnson wanted the same personal control over the military, but he would never have that while Stanton, Grant, and their Republican allies stood in his way. The president needed a loyal secretary of war to protect his personal authority.

Exasperated and desperate, on February 21, 1868, Johnson ignored the Tenure of Office Act and fired Stanton without the consent of Congress. The president arranged to replace the highly regarded cabinet official with a friendly military administrator, General Lorenzo Thomas, who had clashed frequently with Stanton. To rub salt in Republican wounds, Johnson also tried to appoint the disgraced Union general and Democratic presidential candidate George McClellan as his minister to Great Britain. When he learned of these provocative moves, Secretary of the Navy Gideon Welles, a supporter of Johnson, commented to his diary: "The President is vigorous and active, but too late, and has attempted too much at once."[11]

Stanton saw the weakness in Johnson's attack. He rejected what he regarded as an illegal order to resign, and he refused to leave the War

Department. The next day, he ordered the arrest of General Thomas for his part in this scheme. Republicans in both houses of Congress expressed their immediate support for Stanton. The Senate passed a resolution condemning Johnson's effort to purge his cabinet. Numerous senators sent letters to Stanton, urging him to stay on. Senator Sumner scribbled a short and direct message: "Stick."[12]

Representative Thaddeus Stevens called for immediate action in the House. He renounced his colleagues who had counseled for "moderation" as Johnson continued to defy Congress and undermine legislation. This pattern had continued for almost three years, with ever-more presidential recalcitrance. Ill and weary of age, the seventy-five-year-old Republican stalwart from Pennsylvania was determined to remove the president who stunted the promise of multiracial democracy. Stevens reminded his colleagues: "Didn't I tell you so? If you don't kill the beast, it will kill you."[13]

Although reluctant in the past, Stevens's colleagues were now ready to kill the beast. Within hours of the president's attempt to fire Stanton, Representative John Covode, a longtime advocate of civil rights, also from Pennsylvania, proposed a motion in the House to impeach the president. It passed three days later with overwhelming but clearly partisan support: 126–47. All but two of the Republicans present in the House voted for impeachment; every Democrat present voted against.

The resolution did not include specific charges, which followed later. House Republicans expressed their firm belief that Johnson had committed "high crimes and misdemeanors," and they devoted themselves to firing him, instead of Stanton. The war between Republicans and the president had reached a breaking point.

Johnson was on the defensive, especially with a Republican-controlled Congress organized against him. He was, however, resigned to accept a fight with his adversaries as the necessary and unavoidable path to recovering his executive authority. He hoped to pressure members of Congress through the voters in the South who supported him and those in the North who were wary of radical plans for African American inclusion. Johnson understood that white supremacy retained broad appeal, even in some Republican strongholds. The Civil War had shifted from military battlefields to a public trial of the president—the first in American history.

House Republicans tried to make the fight about more than African American rights, emphasizing law and democratic accountability. They wrote eleven detailed articles of impeachment, many of which were repetitive, emphasizing various parts of the Tenure of Office Act and other pieces of legislation that they insisted the president had violated with malice. Article 10 made the broadest charge, that Johnson had acted "to excite the odium and resentment of all the good people of the United States against Congress and the laws by it duly and constitutionally enacted."[14]

Article 11, written by Thaddeus Stevens, was the most direct. It explained that Johnson had acted "in disregard of the requirements of the Constitution that he should take care that the laws be faithfully executed." The article also accused the president of dereliction in his duties and conspiracy against the government. The House of Representatives charged Johnson with "attempting to devise and contrive means" to "prevent the execution" of the law—the very definition of criminal conspiracy.[15]

The trial of an impeached president was not a criminal proceeding. The fifty-four senators, selected for office by the elected legislatures in twenty-seven states (most of the Southern states had not yet been readmitted to the Union), acted as the jurors. The Constitution required that they take a special oath for this purpose. The chief justice of the Supreme Court, who was also a highly partisan Republican, Salmon Chase, presided over the trial. The standard for conviction and removal of the president was not guilt beyond a reasonable doubt or even a preponderance of evidence. The senators did not have to stick to the federal criminal code, which would apply to a traditional indictment of citizens, including elected officials, in a court of law. The Senate trial conformed to none of these rules.

The Constitution is clear that the role of senators as jurors in an impeachment trial "shall not extend further than to removal from office, and disqualification to hold and enjoy any office of honor." These decisions do not substitute for "indictment, trial, judgement and punishment, according to law." The Senate had to determine whether the first impeached president committed "treason, bribery, or other high crimes and misdemeanors" and whether those transgressions merited his removal from office. Judgment depended on how the senators weighed the evidence and the opinions surrounding the charges.[16]

The evidence presented at the president's trial varied greatly in form and quality. The trial was inherently political, involving assessments of legitimate and illegitimate uses of power, which inevitably brought out partisan judgments.

Republicans controlled the Senate, where they held their largest majority ever, with forty-two of fifty-four seats in the chamber. If they stuck together, they easily had the necessary votes to convict Johnson. But the politics of the trial made that difficult. Shared hatred of the president did not translate easily into agreement on what to do next.

Since Andrew Johnson did not have a vice president, the president pro tempore of the Senate, Benjamin Wade from Ohio, would replace him if removed. This was the line of succession, legislated by Congress in 1792. Wade was a controversial and outspoken Republican stalwart who demanded more federal enforcement of civil rights in the South and stronger efforts to pursue racial and economic equality in the North. He went so far as to argue for African American voting in Ohio, as well as in the former Confederacy. His consistency won him approval from radicals, but it cost him support in his home state. In 1867, he lost his bid for governor of Ohio to a more moderate Republican, Rutherford B. Hayes.

On the eve of Johnson's impeachment, Wade returned to the Senate with renewed energy to push against what he derided as the cowardice of many fellow Republicans. He spoke out on behalf of poorly paid workers and expressed support for women's suffrage. Wade championed efforts to break down the prejudices "between the man that labors and him that doesn't." He threatened that if Republican "dullheads can't see this, the women will, and will act accordingly."[17]

Wade allied with Charles Sumner in the Senate and Thaddeus Stevens in the House, but other members of his party resented his dogmatism. They viewed him as uncompromising and irresponsible. He alienated many voters, as well as cautious colleagues. Lyman Trumbull and William Pitt Fessenden, two of the most influential "moderate" Republicans in the Senate, found Wade insufferable. They viewed him as a threat to the future electability of their party.

Although core Republican voters resented Andrew Johnson's defense of Southern planters, they shared some of his fears of radicals, like Wade, upending the status quo. The pressure to temper Wade was strong within his own party. The prospect of him becoming president, if Johnson were convicted, frightened both Republicans and Democrats.

The shadow of a possible Wade presidency hung ominously over the impeachment proceedings. "It seems," the *New York Times* observed, "that this personal feeling is so bitter that some of the interested parties contemplate a proposition for the election of a new presiding officer." Wade remained president pro tempore in the Senate because his Republican supporters were as loyal as his Republican opponents were antagonistic. "Better counsels will doubtless prevail," the newspaper predicted, but that was not assured.[18]

President Johnson's trial opened on March 5, 1868, with a large crowd of observers packed into the ornate Senate chamber. Charles Dickens, who was touring the United States at the time, commented that the impeachment had become national entertainment. The famous English author lamented that the debates in Congress "instantly emptied our great gallery here last night, and paralyzed the theatres in the midst of a rush of good business."[19]

Each day, thousands of citizens went to witness the debates at the Capitol. Many thousands more followed detailed, and often salacious, newspaper coverage. The *New York Times* described the anticipation surrounding the usually quiet Senate setting: "The galleries were full long before noon, and an extra force of police stopped the anxious spectators at the head of their stair-cases, and kept them in tedious waiting for their turn, the turn being that when some tired out or disgusted listener relinquished his or her seat, then one person, and one person only, was allowed to pass the batons and buttons of the policemen to the inside of the galleries. The morning hour dragged heavily, for people handsome for the impeachment."[20]

For the first time in U.S. history, the Senate served as a court of impeachment for President Andrew Johnson. *Credit: Theodore Russel Davis*

The Senate chamber looked different. Between the raised dais and wooden desks of the senators, chairs were assembled for members of the House of Representatives and the president's counsel. It was unprecedented for members of the House of Representatives to occupy seats in the chamber and speak to the Senate. The seven men chosen for this task were the House managers: over the course of the trial, they would make the case for conviction of the president. The trial began with their reading of the articles of impeachment, and their speeches in elaboration.

Senators expected the president to answer the charges personally, and Johnson was inclined to do that. He relished the opportunity to condemn his accusers face-to-face. On the advice of his counsel, however, the president chose to submit a written response, after a requested delay, on March 23.

In a rambling and repetitive statement, Johnson rejected all charges, defending the constitutional powers of the presidency. He denied allegations of his malice or his desire to subvert the law. Instead, Johnson claimed that he was executing the laws, as he understood them, and he also asserted "freedom of opinion and freedom of speech" in his "political relations" with other branches of government. Johnson argued that his defense of white supremacy, in defiance of Congress, was perfectly appropriate. He asserted that his actions followed precedent, and Republicans were recklessly overstepping their constitutional bounds, harassing and repressing the president.[21]

The dueling positions from the proponents of conviction and the defenders of the president were predictable. These were well-rehearsed arguments, and they each held some truth. President Johnson had tried to subvert congressional legislation, and he had encouraged others, particularly in the Southern states, to do the same. But Republicans in Congress were taking stronger action than ever before to limit the president's powers over almost every aspect of policy. Congress constrained his ability to command the military, and it prohibited him from firing cabinet officials. Now Congress was asserting the right to remove a president rather than waiting for the voters to decide. Would this become a precedent for Congress to purge future presidents who challenged the majority party? Would any president be able to perform his duties independently again?

The trial dragged on for more than two months, with continued public fascination and frequent recesses for backroom negotiations. The drama surrounded some of the speeches but most especially the witnesses. The House managers and the president's lawyers called numerous officials to testify, including secretary of war–designate Lorenzo Thomas and Civil War hero General William Tecumseh Sherman. The testimonies confirmed what everyone knew: that Johnson wanted to fire members of his administration who worked closely with congressional Republicans. The president had a personal agenda, and he believed he was under siege.

General Sherman made it clear that although President Johnson's actions were irregular, they still allowed for the competent management of the military and other executive agencies. The debate was not about Johnson's intentions but whether he undermined the lawful functioning of the federal government as the House managers claimed. The president's incompetence was largely accepted; the question was if his actions merited removal. Would such a drastic and unprecedented remedy improve the country? Would it repair America's divided democracy?

These questions raised doubts in many observers who hated Johnson but feared the destruction of the presidency by an indignant Congress. Johnson's removal would surely embolden the most radical impulses in the Republican congressional delegation, led by the man who would become president, Senator Benjamin Wade. Increased conflict with Southern leaders seemed likely, and men like Wade looked to deploy additional force in the region. More warfare, not less, would follow.

The removal of the president would also diminish the domestic and international stature of the nation's commander in chief. The *New York Times* echoed this growing concern among Northern voters. The newspaper had consistently condemned President Johnson's intransigence, and it initially supported impeachment, but the course of the trial shifted its position: "If Mr. Johnson is removed in the way proposed, no President will hereafter hold his place when a majority of the House and two-thirds of the Senate belong to the opposite party."[22]

As the trial continued, Republican moderates voiced these fears. Senator William Pitt Fessenden, the powerful cochair of the Joint Committee on Reconstruction, accused members of his party of "acting like fools, and hurrying us to destruction."[23]

Fessenden feared that the impeachment trial amounted to a Republican demand to control the presidency without waiting for a vote by the people. The voters would get to choose a new president just six months after Johnson's trial, in November 1868. Would the benefits of forced removal before the election outweigh the costs to orderly democratic processes and separation of powers? Fessenden increasingly thought not.

Senator James Grimes, another Republican moderate, agreed with Fessenden. He warned his fellow partisans against self-righteous actions that would "destroy the harmonious working of the Constitution for the sake of getting rid of an unacceptable president." Earlier Grimes had explained that years of executive "misrule" were preferable to the "shock of impeachment" and its aftermath with a radical figure, like Senator Benjamin Wade, taking the presidency from its present holder.[24]

Grimes, like Fessenden, was not defending Johnson; he was protecting the moderate elements of the Republican Party from a power grab by those who wished to build a multiracial democracy with all speed. Grimes and Fessenden reflected the second thoughts of their voters. They were patriotic defenders of the Union and consistent opponents of violent repression in the South, but they were also cautious believers in continued white control over change in the country. At its core, the Republican Party favored free labor, managed by leaders who prevented too much change too fast. Ending slavery was already a radical leap; mainstream Republicans were hesitant to unseat a president and empower the strongest supporters of African American equality so soon after emancipation.

The trial of Andrew Johnson made the intemperate president appear moderate and safe in comparison to what might follow his removal. He was the devil everyone knew. Johnson encouraged this perception by staying mostly silent in public during the long trial as his opponents raged against him. His absence from the proceedings was an advantage.

Johnson also made personal appeals to moderate Republican senators, promising to avoid actions that would further antagonize Congress. During a private meeting with Senator Grimes, the president pledged that in exchange for votes to acquit, he would refrain from any new "rash act" or "indiscretion," and he "would consult with and listen to the advice of his Cabinet." If he survived impeachment, Johnson would offer the cautious moderation that some senators craved.[25]

To prove his seriousness, the president withdrew his original secretary of war–designate, Lorenzo Thomas. Following his meeting with Grimes, Johnson nominated General John Schofield. A decorated Civil War commander and graduate of West Point, Schofield had served as the military governor of Virginia, where he facilitated African American voting in the state. He was respected by congressional Republicans for his independence and commitment to the law. Johnson had previously criticized the "radicalism" of Schofield, which made his nomination a meaningful concession to Republicans and a sign the president was committed to cooperating with Congress after impeachment.[26]

Grimes shared Johnson's promises of more congenial behavior with other Republican moderates. Senators Fessenden and Trumbull were especially receptive. With Grimes, they formed an emerging Republican opposition to removal of the president in the second month of his trial. To stay in office, the president needed seven Republicans to join all twelve Senate Democrats in voting against conviction. Grimes, Fessenden, and Trumbull began to build a coalition of Republicans that would soon come close to that number. There were forty-two Republicans in the Senate at the time, representing very diverse states, all of which were dominated by white voters. Finding the handful necessary to back the moderate position became possible once these respected figures stepped forward to express their doubts about convicting Johnson.

The resistance to removal from the moderates divided the Republican Party across the country. The Iowa *Daily State Register* demanded Grimes's immediate resignation for collaborating with the presidential enemy. Senator Sumner accused Fessenden, Trumbull, and their followers of searching for an "excuse" to place their personal interests above the party's "great cause." Sumner also called out what he perceived as the "vindictive hate" of these party leaders for the multiracial advocacy of Benjamin Wade, Thaddeus Stevens, Sumner, and other radicals. To Republicans intent on expanding democracy and removing a president who defied their authority, the moderates had become apologists for the worst of white supremacy.[27]

The old divisions on slavery within the Republican Party were now manifest in divisions over how far Congress could go to enforce racial justice. Major figures like Fessenden and Trumbull still preferred inaction to decisive change. They were more comfortable with an incompetent and resistant white president than a more inclusive democracy with diverse political actors, including former slaves. Just as Republican moderates rejected abolition before 1862, they resisted rapid civil rights advances after Lincoln's death. Impeachment was an unflattering mirror of the party.

The sharpness of Republican divisions meant the vote on President Johnson's conviction was controversial and unpredictable. The first roll call in the Senate occurred on May 16, 1868. The days before involved backroom maneuvers and personal arm-twisting. Johnson's defenders were particularly active, promising patronage and other favors in return for votes to acquit the president.

The most notorious case was Edmund Ross, a Republican senator from Kansas. The governor initially appointed Ross to the Senate in July 1866, after his predecessor was exposed for accepting bribes and killed himself. Ross ascended quickly, only to participate in the same corrupt politics. Perry Fuller, the wealthy frontier trader who had bribed the previous senator, continued as before with Ross. In 1867, he paid members of the state legislature $42,000—a small fortune at the time—to keep Ross in his Senate seat. Johnson's defenders knew Ross was a bought man, and they knew they could appeal to him through his patrons.[28]

Senator Edmund Ross cast the deciding vote against President Andrew Johnson's conviction and removal from office. He was bribed by the president. *Credit: Mathew Brady*

The deal was quite simple, negotiated on the eve of the Senate vote. President Johnson promised Fuller that he would appoint him to a lucrative federal position in return for Ross's vote to acquit. On the morning of the Senate vote, Fuller instructed Ross how to vote in return for his continued support, including cash. Ross had previously announced that he would vote to convict the president, but he abruptly shifted his position.[29]

Ross skipped the morning caucus meeting of Senate Republicans and then nervously entered the crowded chamber shortly before voting started at 12:30 p.m. Chief Justice Salmon Chase, presiding over the trial, called the Senate roll. When he came to Ross, near the end of the alphabetized roster, it was clear that his vote would determine whether the charge of impeachment had the required thirty-six votes—two-thirds of the fifty-four senators at the time. Ross fidgeted at his desk and then rose to the chief justice's question: "Is Andrew Johnson, president of the United States, guilty or not guilty of high misdemeanors as charged in this article [article 11 of the House impeachment charges]?"

"Not guilty!" Ross exclaimed.

Gasps were heard across the floor of the Senate and the spectators' gallery. The Republicans could not collect enough votes in their own party to convict the president who defied their legislative authority. They could not slay his defense of white supremacy. A despondent Thaddeus Stevens exclaimed: "The country is going to the devil."[30]

It was very close. The final vote on May 16 was thirty-five guilty, nineteen not guilty—just one vote short of the two-thirds required for conviction. The votes remained unchanged as the Senate voted on the remaining articles of impeachment. Although the vast majority of senators chose to remove the president, seven Republicans cooperated with the Democratic minority to keep Johnson in office.

The president promptly appointed Ross's benefactor, Percy Fuller, collector of revenue in the Port of New Orleans. Fuller used this position to steal $3 million, for which he was later arrested and, of course, defended by Ross. The Kansas senator procured other lucrative appointments for his friends, including the powerful state superintendency of Indian lands and the surveyor general for the territory. A member of the president's staff remembered that after impeachment, Ross "was at the White House a good deal" for "appointments in Kansas." Johnson continued to pay out on his bribes until his last days in office.[31]

Andrew Johnson survived the first presidential impeachment in American history, but just barely. He was damaged by the organized public attacks on his integrity from the majority of elected officials. He was isolated even from his supporters in the South, who recognized that he had less than a year remaining in his presidency and would never get elected to another term. Republican opposition to his policies would remain as strong as ever, and he was now dependent on a number of moderates who had voted to keep him in office, even as they still supported basic Reconstruction reforms, especially the right of African Americans to vote in the South. Ross and other Republicans exploited the president's remaining powers for their purposes. They kept him boxed in so he could do little harm.

Impeachment failed to convict, but it succeeded in diminishing Johnson. After a near-death experience, his swagger was gone. His weaknesses were evident.

The weaknesses of the American democratic system were also on display. The Civil War had migrated from the battlefields to the two-mile strip of land connecting the Executive Mansion and the Capitol. The separation of powers between the executive and the legislature—a cornerstone of the Constitution—created a fiery stalemate when the two branches could not agree on the most basic of all questions: What kind of democracy would the United States have? And who decided?

President Johnson refused to accept the laws made by a Republican majority in Congress. The fatal flaw of the Constitution was that it offered little recourse. Congress could not enforce the laws itself, although it tried through General Ulysses Grant, but that raised additional concerns about the lawful use of military power at home. Congress also tried to control the composition of the Supreme Court, but the court had limited means for enforcing its decisions. The president could not change the laws himself, although he tried, but his role was necessary to make the laws stick. He is *the* federal law enforcer in America's democratic system.

Impeachment is the only avenue the Constitution offers to remove an unlawful president, other than balloting every four years. Impeachment takes the power of election temporarily away from the people and allows Congress to choose who is president. That is why it has never worked, even when a president is so obviously derelict in his duties. For Congress to convict a president, a supermajority of its members must tell their voters that their ballots for president were meaningless.

Andrew Johnson was never elected president, but he was the vice president on the ticket with Abraham Lincoln that won a big popular victory in 1864. For Republicans to negate that vote, members of Lincoln's party would have to challenge the wisdom of his voters, who were also their own. The hesitance of moderate Republican leaders in 1868 reflected this political reality.

John Wilkes Booth understood the working of American democracy better than Alexander Hamilton. Hamilton's "energetic executive" did not unify the country, and he did not improve the execution of the law. Just the opposite. Booth killed Lincoln because he recognized that a different executive could protect the interests of white landholders in the South and limit the reach of federal authority. Booth did not anticipate that Andrew Johnson would become such a president—he conspired to kill him too—but he intuited how the presidency could be used to keep democracy smaller and more limited to serve white men.

That is what Andrew Johnson did. As Republicans pushed to expand democracy, Johnson pushed back to constrain, exclude, and reverse. He provoked hatred in the cause of poor white Southerners, and the civil war between the branches of government carried on.

African American citizens were caught in the middle: attacked by the president's Democratic supporters, defended but still subordinate in the efforts of congressional Republicans. Although the status of former slaves was at the center of debate, they were hardly present in the decision-making institutions. Their voices were rarely heard on either side. The impeachment of Andrew Johnson proved that they had little influence on who ruled and how. African Americans neither impeached nor acquitted the president. They had to watch, strive, and suffer.

Andrew Johnson's presidency ended as it started: with conflict and uncertainty about what would come next. American democracy remained riven with divisions over basic questions about inclusion and power. Republicans and Democrats had little faith they could convince one another. The battle lines hardened, and both sides fought more viciously to capture control of Congress and the presidency. In the months after impeachment, white and Black Republican voters would turn to General Ulysses Grant, as they had before, to save some elements of multiracial democracy.

CHAPTER 7

Will to Power

Every fight has its moment of clarity when the combatants recognize the essentials of the conflict and what it will take for one side to triumph over the other. In his second meeting with Robert E. Lee, a day after the surrender at Appomattox, Ulysses Grant recorded the Confederate general's prophecy: Lee "said to me that the South was a big country and that we might have to march over it three or four times before the war entirely ended."[1]

The next phase of the battle for the future was not about arms or territory but the hearts and minds of citizens. Who would have the will and determination to force change on the other side? Grant understood that although Confederate leaders had surrendered, they still had an advantage in the stubbornness of their commitment to their cause. Northern citizens possessed more power but perhaps less will to use that power in the South.

Grant asked Lee to speak out in favor of accepting Northern authority, but Lee refused. He claimed he could not take that position as a military figure who placed himself above politics. That was a calculated dodge. Lee encouraged the separation of the battlefields from the larger struggle by dividing the military reality from the mission.

Loss in battle against a larger Union was inevitable, but the Confederate cause could continue by other means, and it did. In some ways, it was renewed by the martyrdoms of Lee's soldiers and John Wilkes Booth. Republican attacks on President Andrew Johnson made him a perceived victim too. Reverence for the sacrifices of these men sustained the image of a noble South.

Ulysses Grant, the emblem of the Union army, was the first American president elected after Lee's surrender. Grant was not prepared to impose a military solution on the South. The human and financial costs of continued fighting were too high for Northerners, who wished to return to their homes. They "were tired of the war" and "tired of piling up a debt which would be a further mortgage upon their homes." Union supporters wanted stability and opportunity, not continued bloodshed to stamp out resistance.[2]

Grant saw no alternative to accepting a withdrawal from the battlefields while keeping modest Union forces in the South and hoping for the best. Grant advocated "the course that would be the least humiliating to the people who had been in rebellion." He stuck to this position even as he enforced civil rights laws and suppressed resistance from former Confederates. Grant still preferred to persuade rather than compel. Better than almost anyone, he understood the costs and limits of force.[3]

Northern fatigue and indifference were Grant's greatest challenges. Inaugurated as president in March 1869, he struggled to balance the need for continued force in the South with the pressures from that region and the North to limit costs and humiliations, especially for white citizens. "Let us have peace," Grant promised as a presidential candidate, but "peace" could not be an excuse to turn away from Southern Reconstruction, as Democrats wanted, or double down on military enforcement, as radical Republicans demanded.

Pragmatic by temperament, Grant sought a pathway to multiracial democracy that avoided white humiliation. He was elected president for this reason. The majority of his voters—white Republican men from the North and West—wanted to reverse the excesses of racial repression, but they did not want more war. The promise of even moderate federal reforms pushed against violent local resistance, leaving little space for the basic protections Grant hoped to achieve for former slaves, who were often his most loyal supporters.

The vast majority of white citizens in the former Confederacy held tight to a Democratic Party that refused all steps to empower former slaves, especially at the ballot box. Soon after Grant's election, a leading Texas newspaper alleged that federal soldiers protecting African American citizens in the South were a "radical tool" for "tyrannical rule." More blood would be spilled, the newspaper warned, if Grant did not back down. Peace was only possible by abandoning federal reforms and allowing white supremacy to thrive.[4]

Grant recognized that securing the rights of Black Southerners would require more federal force, not less, even as he continued to promise national harmony and a return to normal life in the North. Like Lincoln after his first election, President Grant had to reconcile peaceful hopes with wartime realities. Unlike Lincoln, Grant had to lead voters who had paid the heavy costs of war for nearly a decade.

President Johnson had strengthened Southern resistance; President Grant needed to find a way to bolster Northern determination without doing too much to frighten his tired voters into a full retreat. Civil War divisions remained and were perhaps hardening, but the conflict was about who had more will to keep fighting, not who had more money or guns.

It took a thoughtful, experienced military commander to see the conflict for what it was. It took a skilled politician to succeed in such complex circumstances. Grant was more of the former than the latter.

His inaugural address displayed his strengths and his weaknesses. Abandoning the aspirational poetry of Lincoln, Grant spoke in simple and direct prose. Observing that the country was still struggling with the divisions of the "great rebellion," he admitted: "Many questions will come before it for settlement in the next four years which preceding administrations have never had to deal with. In meeting these it is desirable that they should be approached calmly, without prejudice, hate, or sectional pride, remembering that the greatest good to the greatest number is the object to be attained."

In contrast to Andrew Johnson, Grant promised "all laws will be faithfully executed, whether they meet my approval or not." He defended African American voting rights, pledging support for the ratification of the Fifteenth Amendment to protect them. And Grant called for the "security of person, property, and free religious and political opinion in every part of our common country, without regard to local prejudice."

He insisted on the equal and universal enforcement of laws protecting these rights: "Laws are to govern all alike—those opposed as well as those who favor them." These commitments were powerful because they reflected Grant's experience fighting rebels and lawbreakers. Listeners in March 1869 believed him.

But the new president's ability to create what he called a "happy union," just months after Johnson's acrimonious impeachment, was less evident. His inaugural speech was noticeably negligent in its politics. When he spoke of policy, Grant emphasized paying debts, protecting the value of money, and cooperating with foreign nations. He offered few details and little inspiration for how he would bring citizens together. There were no "mystic chords of memory" or invocations to "bind up the nation's wounds," as Lincoln memorably summoned his listeners in his inaugural statements.

Grant acknowledged the divisions over the future course of American democracy, but as at Appomattox, he accepted the reality and hoped for the best. He spoke honestly to listeners; he did not seek to move them. And maybe he knew that he couldn't.[5]

President Ulysses S. Grant in the civilian attire he wore in his new role. *Credit: Mathew Brady*

African American voting in the South was nonnegotiable for Grant. He commented in his memoirs that although he doubted the capability of many former slaves to choose elected leaders, his Union army experiences convinced him that the federal government had to protect the right of African American men to vote. They had fought courageously in battle, participated actively in the writing of state constitutions, and campaigned effectively for the election of state and federal representatives, including many individuals from their own communities. The African American presence in local governments was essential to rebuild Southern society and prevent the continued repression that provoked violence. Grant had personally witnessed the crucial roles played by African Americans as teachers, farmers, businessmen, and political leaders in suffering communities. Former slaves, now free men and women, were the fuel for Reconstruction.

Grant believed that other Republicans shared his perspective, despite their continued concerns about African American "ignorance." "As to myself," Grant recounted, "while strongly favoring the course that would be the least humiliating to the people who had been in the rebellion, I had gradually worked up to the point where, with the majority of the people, I favored immediate enfranchisement."[6]

This was still a radical position in 1869. African American voting was unthinkable at the start of the war, and it remained a largely taboo subject in the weeks after Appomattox. At the time of Lincoln's assassination, Grant and most Republicans probably shared Booth's discomfort with the idea of Black men electing leaders. This had never happened before, even in the sections of the North most opposed to slavery. The Republican Party platform in 1868 uncomfortably argued that although freed slaves had earned a right to vote in the former Confederacy, the conditions in the North were different: "The question of suffrage in all the loyal states properly belongs to the people of those states."[7]

Republicans needed African American votes in the South, where they had few white voters, but the prospects of Black votes in the North unsettled their core of white supporters. Former Confederates were quick to hammer at this hypocrisy: The advocates of a multiracial electorate for the South still adhered to a limited electorate in their own communities. White supremacy was less flagrant but still real in the Republican heartland.

What moved Grant and so many of the key figures in the party was the necessity of getting Southern Blacks to the voting booth. Without that, Republicans could not win elections in the region, or perhaps nationally. In the 1868 presidential election, Grant won the national popular vote by about three hundred thousand—less than the total number of African American voters in the South. To protect these voters, the Republicans needed stronger federal restrictions on state efforts at suppression, including violent intimidation.

The most direct solution was to put African American voting in the Constitution, and that required an amendment. Northern states would feel uncomfortable pressure to enfranchise their African American citizens, but the amendment could be written to give them some flexibility. Connecting the voting rights of citizens North and South negated the strong objection that one region was treating the other unfairly; the same rules would apply to the whole country. African Americans pushed for this very outcome, and their extensive turnout in the 1868 elections made constitutional enfranchisement difficult to resist, especially for those who needed their votes.

Republican members of Congress acted before Grant was inaugurated. They did not pass a universal guarantee for male suffrage in the United States but instead a narrow prohibition on race exclusion at the ballot box, as frequently practiced in the South. The text of the proposed Fifteenth Amendment was simple: "The right of citizens of the United States to vote shall not be denied or abridged by the United States or by any State on account of race, color, or previous condition of servitude." The proposed amendment gave Congress the power to enforce its provisions.

Not a single Democrat in the House or the Senate voted for the amendment; it relied exclusively on Republicans in both chambers for the two-thirds approval before going to the states for ratification. Hesitant Republicans had avoided a bold expansion of voting rights for all citizens. Women remained excluded. And states could still restrict voting for men on nonracial grounds, including possession of a criminal record, lack of proof of residence, and unpaid taxes—tactics still used two centuries later.

These loopholes allowed states to continue limiting who voted, but the amendment created a powerful constitutional prohibition on exclusion by race. The amendment made voting law multiracial as it had never been before. One African American religious leader called it "the final seal of God in the condemnation of American slavery." Frederick Douglass exclaimed: "I seem myself to be living in a new world. The sun does not shine as it used to."[8]

Grant placed his presidency behind the ratification of the amendment. He advocated for it not as a continuation of the conflict between North and South but as a final step to complete the aims of the war and forge a new foundation for the country. The amendment would not penalize former Confederates, most of whom had regained their right to vote by 1870 with the return of the secessionist states to the Union. The amendment widened the electorate without any necessary burdens on Northern citizens. If anything, it increased their potential influence through the African American citizens who were likely to vote Republican for a long time to come. The Fifteenth Amendment increased the participation of Black voters. Their participation would promote white Republican interests, with little cost.

Some states, dominated by white legislators, held out against the amendment, including Tennessee, Kentucky, Maryland, and Delaware—all states with large African American populations who could gain voting access. California and Oregon also rejected the amendment, fearful that it would give voting power to their large Chinese populations. The Southern states with African American representation in their state legislatures ratified the amendment rapidly as did the remaining Northern and western states. With the support of the president, Congress required the former Confederate states still seeking readmission to the Union—Texas, Georgia, Mississippi, and Virginia—to accept the amendment as well. Thirty states ratified the text within one year, more than the three-fourths required to change the Constitution.

On March 30, 1870, it became the law of the land. Grant sent a triumphal proclamation to Congress announcing: "The fifteenth amendment to the Constitution completes the greatest civil change and constitutes the most important event that has occurred since the nation came into life."

Referring to the four million former slaves, who were now citizens and voters, the president described the amendment as "a measure of grander importance than any other one act of the kind from the foundation of our free Government to the present day." This was hyperbolic but also serious. The president recognized the significance of a multiracial electorate. The Thirteenth Amendment expunged slavery from the Constitution, and now the Fifteenth Amendment guaranteed African Americans the right to choose the nation's leaders, including the president.

Addressing continued Republican hesitations, Grant called on Congress to not only enforce the law but help "encourage popular education throughout the country, and upon the people everywhere to see to it that all who possess and exercise political rights shall have the opportunity to acquire the knowledge which will make their share in the Government a blessing and not a danger." This was a return to Lincoln's emphasis on preparing people for democracy through public schools and universities—both in short supply in the South. The Freedmen's Bureau and the U.S. Army remained the primary federal institutions for giving former slaves and other citizens the support they needed, despite local restrictions.

Grant articulated the shared anxiety, North and South, that African Americans might not be ready to vote. Even as he praised the creation of a multiracial electorate, he echoed white supremacist attitudes: "Institutions like ours, in which all power is derived directly from the people, must depend mainly upon their intelligence, patriotism, and industry. I call the attention, therefore, of the newly enfranchised race to the importance of their striving in every honorable manner to make themselves worthy of their new privilege."

The president drew a sharp contrast with "the race more favored heretofore by our laws," which did not need to prove its worthiness to vote. The Fifteenth Amendment reduced the legal barriers to African

American male suffrage based on race, but it allowed for many other barriers that did not explicitly focus on the color of a man's skin. "Intelligence," as Grant himself implied, was a judgment that would allow state officials to exclude the allegedly unprepared. The president also mentioned "industry"—the subjective evidence that a potential African American or other minority voter participated in work deemed appropriate. And "patriotism," was, of course, the most problematic. If the Constitution did not protect the voting rights of dissenters, then civil rights activists were susceptible to exclusion for their challenges to dominant authorities, especially former Confederates in the South. Public efforts to defend the voting rights of vulnerable groups, a form of protest labeled as "unpatriotic" in many places, became an excuse for denying those rights.[9]

This was precisely the experience of the years after 1870. Grant's words pointed to the reality of continued restriction, long embedded in Republican support for voting by some but not all African Americans (and women and various immigrant groups). The Fifteenth Amendment allowed many more exclusions, even as it eliminated the most obvious one.

A few months removed from the heady days around ratification, Frederick Douglass recognized this sad reality. He reconsidered his exultation about "living in a new world," describing the "hardships and wrongs which continue to be the lot of the colored people." He attributed the stubborn conditions of subordination to attitudes that ran much deeper than a surrender or a change of law.

Speaking to both Southern Democrats and Northern Republicans, Douglass explained that African Americans "wear a complexion which two hundred and fifty years of slavery taught the great mass of American people to hate, and which the Fifteenth Amendment has not yet taught the American people to love." The reverse of what Grant had said at ratification was true: The former slaves were "worthy" of voting—they had struggled mightily to leave the plantation and live in a democracy. Many white opponents were still not ready to accept that change, although it was written into the Constitution. If anything, they used the amendment to inspire other available means of voter repression.[10]

The Ku Klux Klan, a collection of Confederates who first organized in Tennessee after Lee's surrender, turned the Fifteenth Amendment into a rallying cry for racial violence. If African American men could now elect the leaders in a community, then these new voters had to be eliminated for white men to retain their control. Former slaves not only threatened the accumulated wealth of landholders, they now had the Constitution on their side. Vigilante violence, going beyond the law to protect the community, became the hallmark of the Klan and other white supremacist groups throughout the South. Grant's inauguration lent their advocacy for what scholars would later call "ethnic cleansing" a wider and more enthusiastic following.

The months around the ratification of the Fifteenth Amendment were the most violent in the South since Appomattox. Although the notorious Confederate general Nathan Bedford Forrest resigned in 1869 from his post as the first Grand Wizard of the Ku Klux Klan, the white terrorist group metastasized into a regional insurgency. In state after state, cells emerged of white men, often wealthy and respected, who adopted the Klan's fraternal rituals, including graveyard gatherings and nighttime rides with white-hooded costumes. These antics were designed to bond the participants and frighten those excluded from the organization's secrets. They aimed to strike fear in African American voters and their supporters.

By 1870, Klan-inspired groups shadowed near every Southern community, from South Carolina and Georgia to Texas and Mississippi. They organized around local "dens" of conspirators, usually led by Confederate army veterans. As was the case during the Memphis Massacre four years earlier, the murderous violence of the Klan was widely endorsed by elected Democrats—they either denied its severity or called it "self-defense." When identified publicly, Klansmen were rarely prosecuted for their violence but often praised for their actions. Southern sheriffs, mayors, and powerful landholders participated in what were violent festivals of hate that boosted their careers. Klan brutality allowed former slave masters to perform as strong rulers again.

Drawing of two Ku Klux Klansmen with their white
hoods and weapons. *Source: Harper's Weekly, December
19, 1868*

Abram Colby, a former slave who had been elected to Georgia's state
legislature, was one of hundreds to suffer Klan violence. He recounted how
a mob of "first class men"—"one is a lawyer, one a doctor, and some are
farmers"—viciously attacked him. On October 29, 1869, the Klansmen
"broke my door open, took me out of my bed and took me to the woods
and whipped me three hours or more and left me in the woods for dead."

The Klan's message was clear: "They said to me, 'Do you think
you will ever vote another damned radical ticket?'" Colby expected
they would kill him anyway, so he answered honestly: "'If there was
an election tomorrow, I would vote the radical ticket.' They set in and
whipped me a thousand licks more" with "sticks and with straps that
had buckles on the ends of them."

Fifty-two years old at the time, Colby had experienced the bru-
talities of slavery, but the whipping that night—four years after slavery
ended—extinguished his will to resist white authority. The Klansmen
had "broken something inside." He was not only fearful for his own
life but for his family: "My little daughter came out and begged them
not to carry me away. They drew up a gun and actually frightened her
to death. She never got over it until she died [a few months later]."[11]

Colby never ran for office again. The Klansmen who attacked him,
and whom he identified, were not prosecuted. This story was repeated
many times over in Georgia. White officials and journalists blamed the
Black victims for the violence, calling them "agitators" and "liars."[12]

In North Carolina, the Klan not only spread fear, they took over the
state government. They targeted Wyatt Outlaw, one of the most prominent African American organizers in the state. Like thousands of other
Black men, Outlaw had joined the Union army and fought to end
slavery. After the surrender, he helped to found a branch of the Loyal
Republican League, which encouraged voting in Alamance County,
wedged between Greensboro and Raleigh. Outlaw was also the first
trustee of the African Methodist Episcopal Church in the community
of Graham, where he was elected town commissioner. He had a personal connection to the state's Republican governor, William Holden,
who was despised by the Klan.

Klan terror in the region motivated Outlaw to participate in a series
of armed police patrols, designed by the county government to protect
residents from harassment and worse. The patrols included a mix of
white and Black citizens. On at least one occasion, Outlaw's group dis-
persed a mob of white-hooded night riders seeking trouble.

Klan leaders did not take well to police power exercised by a Black
man, especially one who was so effective at bringing African Americans
out to vote. On February 26, 1870, they sent a posse of one hundred
hooded white men to break into Outlaw's home on the main street in
Graham. They pulled him from his bed as his three children and his
mother watched in horror.

Outlaw never returned home. The rabid mob beat the kidnapped man, dragged him through the town streets, and then hung him from a tree in front of the county courthouse. That still wasn't enough. The Klansmen mutilated his limp, bruised corpse, and they attached a note for all to read: "Beware you guilty both white and black."[13]

In murdering a powerful opponent, the Klan sent a chilling message to all supporters of African American rights. One of the murderers later explained that Outlaw was hung "because he was a politician": "He had been a leader of negroes; and been elected once." Another assailant commented that Outlaw was "blustering around," causing trouble by agitating people to vote. He was too "mouthy"—a criticism frequently leveled at politically active African Americans. The Klansmen who killed Outlaw made certain to slash his mouth as they hung his body.[14]

Outlaw's fate was not unique. The Klan killed other African Americans and Republicans in North Carolina. In May 1870, they murdered a white state senator, John W. Stephens, for his support of the Freedmen's Bureau, the Union League, and African American suffrage. To show their power, a group of Klansmen stabbed Stephens in a back room of the Caswell County Courthouse, where they left his body to demonstrate that the law could not protect Stephens or other defenders of African American voters.

These murderous tactics paid dividends a few months later when Klan-supported candidates dominated state elections. White and Black Republicans were frightened away from the polls. Democratic defenders of white supremacy benefited from the Klan and other groups that helped to bring out loyal voters. In November 1870, the Republican Party lost control of the state legislature in North Carolina; the new Democratic majority included numerous Klan members and sympathizers.

Governor Holden declared that the state faced an organized insurgency, bent on seizing control of the entire government. He ordered state militia units to arrest violent Klansmen, and he requested federal military assistance. The Klan, however, evaded prosecution thanks to sympathetic state judges who repeatedly released arrested conspirators.

The Klan widened its appeal during the crackdown as more white men were drawn to it.

In 1871, violence against African Americans and other Republicans increased throughout North Carolina. The new Democratic legislature impeached and removed Governor Holden from office. He was the first governor in American history to suffer this fate. Holden's successor, Tod Caldwell, was also a Republican, but he was careful to avoid challenging the Klan. White men in sheets continued to intimidate citizens and suppress Black votes. Through terror, white supremacists essentially nullified the Fourteenth and Fifteenth Amendments in North Carolina.

The situation in South Carolina was even worse. The heart of cotton country, the state made a difficult transition from slave plantations to tenant farming. In the northwest corner of the state (the "up-country"), the African American population was especially active in politics. Former slaves organized themselves to negotiate for fairer tenancy agreements with their former masters, so that they could keep more of what they grew as free men and women. In addition, they organized in Union Leagues to vote and nominate candidates for office. To protect themselves against heavily armed white men, African Americans in the up-country created their own militias, with small weapons stockpiles.

The image of armed Black men voting for their own representatives triggered fears that white landholders were losing control of their communities. One wealthy planter complained that the former slaves were too politically involved, "leaving fodder and cotton to take care of itself." This respected gentleman from York County expressed the common concern that African American independence threatened the "respectable crop" sustaining white families.[15]

The Ku Klux Klan played upon these anxieties. By the end of 1870, the organization had embedded itself in nine South Carolina counties so deeply that it supplanted local government. Klansmen riding at night patrolled the roads, they broke up Union League meetings, and they confiscated weapons from Black militias. They threatened African Americans with whippings—evoking a return to slavery—if they refused to work under the unfair labor contracts their former masters imposed.

In Spartanburg County alone, federal investigations documented more than two hundred whippings. In York County, the estimate reached as high as six hundred whippings. Public punishment imposed by white mobs forced African Americans to comply with white landed interests. The Klan was so influential in the communities that there was virtually no response from law enforcement, many of whom had joined the Klan themselves. African American families resorted to sleeping in the woods, hiding out from the night riders in white hoods who terrorized their homes.[16]

The Klan used its power in the up-country to brutalize and control the former slave population in personal, sadistic ways. Hooded night riders often targeted African American families, using sexual violence to assert white male dominance, humiliate Black women, and emasculate Black men. Rapes of African American women, perpetrated by white men, were not illegal in South Carolina.

Klansmen took advantage of this horrible bias in the law. In the spring of 1870, they raided the home of Sam Simmons, a Black Republican in York County, and his wife, Harriet Simril. They terrorized this family on at least three separate occasions. On the first visit, they shouted at Sam, forced him out of the house, and then beat him. The Klansmen demanded that he support Democratic candidates, which he refused to do: "He told them he would rather quit all politics, if that was the way they was going to do to him."

Sam's defiance encouraged the Klan to escalate. They returned on another night, this time with a larger posse. The hooded men called for Sam, who was hiding in the woods. They forced their way into the house, spit in Harriet's face, threw dirt in her eyes, and ate her food— including five pies she had stored in her cupboard. Harriet recounted what happened next: "After a while they took me out of doors and told me all they wanted was my old man to join the Democratic ticket; if he joined the Democratic ticket they have no more to do with him; and after they had got me out of doors, they dragged me in to the big road, and they ravished me out there."

Harriet identified the three men who raped her: Ches McCollum, Tom McCollum, and "big Jim Harper." They were never prosecuted, and they returned again. Harriet now hid in the woods with her husband. The Klansmen burned her house to the ground, making it clear that they would repeat their attacks if the family, and its neighbors, still supported Republicans.

Harriet and her husband could not resist, especially without assistance from law enforcement. They continued to hide from the Klan— they "got out of the way of them." That meant avoiding politics. The Klan did not convert Sam to the Democratic Party, but they scared him into quiescence. He probably never voted again.[17]

African American men and women were not the Klan's only targets in South Carolina. The hooded terrorists vented their rage against white Republicans with similar ferocity. They aimed to degrade supporters of Black suffrage, showing that they were no longer true white men of the South. The Klan wanted to depict multiracial advocacy as race mixing, and they sought to scar those who participated in it as lost "mongrels," no longer pure.

Night riders enacted this punishment on William Champion, a white election official who protected Black voters. A posse of Klansmen shot into his home, then blindfolded and abducted him. They took him to a field where they whipped him repeatedly until he nearly passed out.

That wasn't enough. The Klansmen wanted to show how his support for African American suffrage degraded his race and made him less of a white man. They forced him to kiss the buttocks and vaginal area of a Black woman also in their captivity. Then they made Champion kiss her Black husband's buttocks. After that, the Klansmen forced Champion and the Black woman to have sexual intercourse, in public. The night of horrors finished with the hooded posse demanding that Champion whip the Black woman's husband.[18]

William Champion's terrible ordeal, like Harriet Simril's, was not unique. It was repeated hundreds of times in up-country South Carolina after the ratification of the Fifteenth Amendment. The prevalence of this violence did more than intimidate Republicans; it dehumanized them. Black and white citizens had to accept a strictly enforced color line that excluded African Americans and their white supporters from political participation. Constitutional rights meant little as vicious terrorists roamed the countryside.

The atrocities in South Carolina, and the efforts at resistance by African Americans, drew President Grant's urgent attention. He had witnessed the brutality of the Civil War firsthand, and he understood the depths of white supremacy in the South. He was, however, stunned by the flagrant lawlessness of the Ku Klux Klan. Grant received accounts from newspapers, local politicians, and citizens who wrote to him, pleading for help.

C. F. Jones, a clergyman from Spartanburg County, was one of many to write the president. Jones owned a farm with numerous African American tenants who worked the land. He described how his land was "invaded by a gang of disguised ruffians, who went from house [to house], dragging the inmates out, beating them, firing pistols at them."

Jones continued: "A bullet has since been extracted from the head of one—another aged, upright, Christian man, was slaughtered, in his own yard, while begging them to spare him. I applied to the nearest trial justice. He could do nothing." Jones explained that he and other good citizens "are left totally helpless, under a reign of terror. If we knew the murderer, and were to denounce him to the authorities our lives would be forfeited." Jones closed with an admission of his own vulnerability: "Please not to publish my name, or I might suffer."[19]

Grant was moved by these personal letters. He often read them to his cabinet, so much so that some of his advisers, particularly Secretary of State Hamilton Fish, felt that he was distracted from other policy matters. For Grant, the rampages of the Klan in South Carolina became a priority. White mobs attacked the authority of civil government and the Constitution. They also challenged Grant's position as the primary enforcer of the nation's law.

Grant responded forcefully, recognizing that he was now at war with the Ku Klux Klan. He ordered the U.S. Army to move one thousand soldiers into the up-country. On March 24, 1871, he announced that these forces would protect citizens against "domestic violence" and "enforce the due execution of the laws." Grant issued a "command" for the members of the Klan and other "unlawful combinations" to "disperse and retire peaceably to their respective abodes within twenty days."[20]

The Klan did not back down. Nighttime raids on African American families and the homes of white sympathizers continued. General Lewis Merrill, the general commanding soldiers in York County, found evidence of Klan spies infiltrating his camp. Mayors, sheriffs, and other local authorities continued to shield Klansmen and help them to evade U.S. Army arrests. During the summer of 1871, Merrill reported to Grant that violent white supremacists continued to resist—there were as many as two thousand Klansmen in the region (double the number of soldiers) and thousands of additional sympathizers.

The president lobbied Congress for more direct powers in South Carolina and other states defying federal law. The Ku Klux Klan Act, passed by Republicans in the House and Senate and signed by Grant on April 20, 1871, gave the federal government the legal authority to prosecute state officials and private individuals for violations of civil rights, especially the Fourteenth and Fifteenth Amendments to the Constitution. The act was transformative because it meant that Klansmen could no longer count on sympathetic municipal and state law enforcement to shield them from punishment.

The Justice Department, created a year earlier by Congress to staff federal law enforcement around the country, took the lead in sending lawyers to South Carolina and other states, where they charged Klansmen with civil rights crimes and brought them to trial in federal courts. Attorney General Amos Akerman made the prosecution of domestic terrorists a priority, and he worked closely with the U.S. Army to incarcerate them. Within a year, Akerman secured more than three thousand federal indictments and six hundred convictions of Klansmen.

Grant understood that the federal government had to take on this burden. By the end of his first term in office, there were two systems of justice in the United States: a state system that was blatantly white supremacist, especially in the South, and a federal system that aspired to be inclusive of everyone. African Americans could testify in federal courts but not many state courts. Judges and juries in federal courts convicted vigilantes; state courts rarely did, for at least the next century.

The president used his office to bolster federal efforts. In October 1871, he placed the nine counties of South Carolina's up-country under martial law. He also suspended the writ of habeas corpus in those territories. These executive orders allowed U.S. Army soldiers and federal marshals to initiate curfews against night riding, confiscate weapons, arrest suspects, and remove local officials. Citizens charged with Klan activities could not appeal for their release until after trial in a military or federal court. Through the army and the Justice Department, Grant reoccupied the South Carolina up-country. He sent the full force of the federal government to crush the Ku Klux Klan there.

It worked. By late 1872, the men in hoods were less prevalent in South Carolina and many other states. Justice Department lawyers fanned out throughout the former Confederacy, and federal courts convicted known Klansmen. More than one thousand were convicted in total—enough to scare others into hiding. The U.S. Army did not have the resources to police every community closely, but its Southern presence gave protection to Black and white Republicans. Federal lawyers and soldiers put the white terrorists on the defensive.

The elections in November 1872 were the freest in American history to that time and for many decades after. Seven hundred thousand more citizens voted than four years earlier, including a large number of African Americans in the South. Three hundred and twenty Black legislators were elected to state and federal offices—a number not reached again for more than a century. Grant easily gained reelection to the presidency, winning a number of former Confederate states: Virginia, North Carolina, South Carolina, Alabama, Mississippi, Arkansas, Louisiana, and Florida—all states where Republicans were deeply unpopular among white voters. Federal enforcement of the Fifteenth Amendment, and the crushing of the Klan, allowed African American citizens to cast their ballots as never before. They elected men who would use the powers of government to protect them.[21]

The president's successes hardened resistance. White Southern leaders accused Grant of invading their communities again. A prominent Mississippi newspaper condemned the "mongrel administration" imposed on ordinary citizens who were trying to protect their land and their families against a federal force of "blood suckers." Democrats accused the Republicans of stealing the 1872 election by buying off and over-counting Black voters. This became a common accusation, voiced repeatedly for the next century and a half. Southern whites claimed that Grant was using federal resources to favor African Americans and other minorities as replacements for the traditional men in charge. After losing high-turnout elections in 1872, false claims about "election fraud" gained wide currency among anxious white citizens across the region.[22]

They also gained a following in the North. Moderate Republicans, including Senator Lyman Trumbull of Illinois and Representative James Garfield of Ohio, believed the federal government was doing too much for the former slaves. Although they rejected the belligerent rhetoric of many Southerners, they argued that the costs of federal enforcement were too high.

Garfield complained that Congress was neglecting important opportunities to invest in economic development through railways and other lucrative projects—many of which lined the pockets of wealthy business barons. Garfield wanted to grow industry, not continue fighting the Civil War. The Ohio congressman and future president believed that Grant was distracted by the turmoil in the South. Garfield observed that Grant was "very anxious the Congress shall do nothing else, but legislate concerning the Ku Klux Klan."[23]

Leading Northern Republicans wanted to move on. The fight in the South was no longer their fight now that the Union was secured, slavery abolished, and Republicans firmly in control of Congress. Where the federal government should get involved, they believed, was in securing the land and finance for business, not pouring more resources into the never-ending struggle to shove reform down the throats of a resistant South. Garfield and others embraced the "states' rights" arguments of former Confederates because it served their priorities, which did not include suffering African Americans.

Both Garfield and Trumbull accused Grant of overstepping his constitutional bounds, reprising Abraham Lincoln's wartime control of state governments, which they claimed only prolonged the war and its deprivations. A faction of Republicans, led by Senator Trumbull and Missouri senator Carl Schurz, split off from Grant's party to form their own "Liberal Republican" opposition. Close allies of Lincoln, they now believed that Grant was extending federal power in peacetime beyond where the first Republican president ever would have gone. They emphasized Lincoln's call for reconciliation, and they condemned Grant for continuing to probe into the deeper sources of conflict.

Liberal Republicans were a growing faction of white Republicans who had favored civil rights but now opposed federal intervention in the South. They sought an illusory compromise that would bring white supremacists around to accepting African American participation in their communities. This mythic and unrealistic hope for voluntary change was convenient for white citizens who were secure in their own rights. They sincerely wanted to improve the lives of former slaves beyond their home states but without having to pay to do so.

In the fall of 1872, Horace Greeley took up the cause of an illusory compromise. Greeley was the cantankerous publisher of the *New York Tribune* and a longtime opponent of slavery, but he opposed Grant's interventions in the South. Greeley ran for president as both the Liberal Republican candidate and a Democratic Party ally, hoping to forge a bond between the two groups.

His candidacy, and the Liberal Republican movement as a whole, only encouraged opposition to the necessary enforcement of federal laws. The Klan used Liberal Republicanism as a cover for continuing their attacks on African Americans while blaming the national government for the violence. The night riding of hooded men was not a major problem, Klan apologists contended, until Grant brought attention to it and tried to stop it.

Greeley and his Liberal Republican–Democratic coalition lost the 1872 election badly, but they did win six Southern and border states, and almost three million votes. They provided an off-ramp for moderate voters who were tired of conflict. Through his campaign, Greeley encouraged those who had supported Lincoln's war on slavery to retreat from the war on white terror.

The retreat had begun, even as Grant's administration took the necessary steps to crush the Klan. The public will outside the South to continue difficult enforcement efforts was clearly falling. Resistance in the former Confederacy, however, remained strong, bolstered by renewed anger at the U.S. Army soldiers marching through South Carolina and other states. Resistance also grew within Grant's cabinet, where Secretary of State Fish and Secretary of the Interior Columbus Delano—both close collaborators with Northern business leaders—pushed for more attention to economic needs. They viewed the Klan as a distraction.

Fish and Delano, working with railroad titans Collis Huntington and Jay Gould, conspired to undermine Grant's enforcement efforts. They targeted the most important prosecutor of the Klan, Attorney General Akerman. Fish and Delano criticized the aggressive work of the Justice Department, they demeaned Akerman, and they organized public opposition to him. Huntington and Gould lobbied the president and members of Congress to remove the attorney general.

Grant was loyal to his advisers, and he had high regard for Akerman. A lawyer from Georgia and a former Confederate army soldier, Akerman had converted to a passionate defender of civil rights. He led an effective group of lawyers working throughout the South—which made him a villain in many eyes. He also insisted on bringing the stories of white terror against African Americans to Northern audiences. Respectable citizens in New York, Boston, and Philadelphia should not be able to hide behind other priorities and escape what Akerman called the "simple narration" of brutality down south.

Akerman's passionate integrity was his downfall. The more the attorney general accomplished in exposing and prosecuting the Klan, the more he generated opposition among powerful figures. By late 1871, the pressure on Grant from his party, his cabinet, and his business allies was too great to ignore. Hoping to preserve the support of these groups for his administration and its continued law enforcement in the South, the president realized that he had to sacrifice Akerman. He needed to show the powerful critics of the attorney general that he was responsive. A quieter, less controversial figure in that role—Oregon senator George Williams—would give Grant some needed cover from his detractors.

On December 12, the president reluctantly wrote to Akerman. Grant's personal anguish, and his frustration with the pressures upon him, shaped his words: "Circumstances convince me that a change in the office which you now hold is advisable, consulting the best interests of the government, and I therefore ask your resignation." Grant followed that regretful language with a clear endorsement for Akerman's work: "I wish to express my approbation of the zeal, integrity and industry which you have shown in the performance of all your duties."[24]

Akerman offered his resignation the next day. The attorney general expressed his continued admiration for Grant and their shared goals. Akerman understood the political circumstances of the moment, and he fell on his sword. He and the president hoped that his departure would appease Northern opponents of continuing Justice Department prosecutions in the South.

Akerman was not optimistic. He wrote to Benjamin Conley, the Republican governor of Georgia who would soon be pushed out of office as well. Akerman lamented that for Northern Republicans "such atrocities as Klu-Kluxery do not hold their attention." Audiences in New York, Boston, and Philadelphia were "active and full of what is called progress," which meant they were intent on running "away from the past." Of course, violent white supremacy was not past, as much as tired Northerners wished it so.[25]

With Republican opponents of federal enforcement coalescing, Grant had to fight his own party, as well as the Democrats. After winning a convincing electoral victory in 1872, he was marooned between Southern resistance and Northern indifference. He admitted as much in his second inaugural address, where he recounted his consistent service to his country "since the eventful firing upon Fort Sumter." He bemoaned that since entering the presidency, he had been "the subject of abuse and slander scarcely ever equaled in political history."

Lincoln had faced worse, including assassination, but he did not express the same vulnerability in his more famous second inaugural address. Lincoln felt firm support from the Republican Party in 1865; Grant did not eight years later.

The general-turned-president promised to bring the violence to an end, at last: "My efforts in the future will be directed to the restoration of good feeling between the different sections of our common country." Grant called out the lawbreaking and mistreatment of African Americans in the South, and he reaffirmed his commitment to prosecuting violent attackers: "The effects of the late civil strife have been to free the slave and make him a citizen. Yet he is not possessed of the civil rights which citizenship should carry with it. This is wrong, and should be corrected. To this correction I stand committed, so far as Executive influence can avail."

Grant was careful to argue that he opposed permanent federal intervention in the South: "The States lately at war with the General Government are now happily rehabilitated, and no Executive control is exercised in any one of them that would not be exercised in any other State under like circumstances." His speech conveyed a sense that he was ready to move on, to look beyond continued racial strife.

As a whole, Grant's speech echoed his Liberal Republican critics. The president promoted new markets and economic growth as alternatives to conflict. He gave special place to "the construction of cheap routes of transit throughout the land, to the end that the products of all may find a market and leave a living remuneration to the producer." This was the language of the railroad moguls and the business titans who were emerging as dominant political influences. They had pushed to remove a zealous attorney general, and now they defined the agenda for a reelected president.[26]

The Civil War had allowed businesses to grow across the North and West, as they supplied the army and then rebuilt the country. By 1872, the railroads, factories, and banks dominated the Republican Party, not the small-town professionals and shopkeepers of Lincoln's time. Expanding capitalism now mattered more than defending the multiracial democracy Grant had fought to create.

Grant's second term was shaped by these forces. One of the country's keenest observers sensed this shift. Just months after Grant's second inauguration, Mark Twain and his coauthor, Charles Dudley Warner, coined the phrase *Gilded Age*. Their very mediocre novel gained wide and enduring attention because it offered a sobering "tale of today," especially for citizens lacking access to the promised wealth of a more industrial society.[27]

Those left behind included landed white families in the South, who clung to the Democratic Party, which defended their status against perceived rivals. African Americans in the South (as well as American Indians, immigrants, and women) were also left behind. The Republican Party, which once reached out to many of these groups, paid less attention than before. The white men who spilled blood for the Union were drawn to gold rather than national purpose, Twain chastised. Lincoln's Republican Party of free labor transformed into a party of wealthy industry one decade later.

Grant recognized this problem, but during his second term, he could do little about it. The popular determination to defend white privilege in the South and the increasing eagerness to get rich in the North suffocated remaining sentiments for racial justice. Grant could no longer motivate his own troops.

If Southern wealth remained tied to the old plantation lands, Northern riches were in the new businesses, especially the railroads. In the years after Appomattox, the United States entered a railroad-building spree, with new lines saturating east–west routes around the Great Lakes and the midsection of the country. Between 1865 and 1873, the railroads doubled their tracks, reaching more than seventy thousand miles at the time of Grant's second inauguration. The completion of the first transcontinental line in 1869 symbolized the emergence of a railroad-dominated national economy, and it was just the beginning. The years from 1870 to 1872 witnessed more laying of track than at any time before in American history. When Republican leaders, including Grant, thought about economic growth, they focused on the railroads.[28]

The railroads were chartered by federal and state governments, which provided the land for their routes. The governments often procured the land by force from groups living on it. The U.S. Army played a leading role in the western plains, clearing American Indians for the railroads to build through those territories. The workers on the railroads, particularly imported Chinese laborers, were policed by state and federal officials to ensure timely construction.

Despite their reliance on government aid, the railroads were run for profit. They required extensive financing through the sales of shares in their operations (stock) and the contracting of loans from banks and other investors (bonds). To manage their complex operations—laying track, fueling railcars, selling tickets, scheduling trains, and more—railroads developed hierarchical bureaucracies with managers of various kinds. Their organization approximated, in some ways, the army. Unlike the military, however, the railroads had boards of directors and executives who ran the business for lucrative compensation. The railroads were the first major American corporations, mixing government support, bureaucracy, and capital to enrich their largest investors.

They looked big and impressive, but they had weak foundations. The wealth generated by the railroads was largely speculative, based on anticipated revenue from shipping contracts and ticket sales. The promoters built the lines and expected people to come, but they often didn't. By 1873, the railroad carrying capacity in the United States far exceeded demand. The railroads were heavily in debt, and they relied on additional investments to cover their costs. The boom had become a bubble.

On September 18, 1873, the bubble burst. Jay Cooke & Company, one of the largest banks investing in the railroads, could no longer pay out the bonds it had issued. Cooke had tirelessly borrowed to finance the Northern Pacific Railroad, and he could not raise enough new money to cover his older debts coming due. Cooke suspended his bank's activities in New York, triggering a bank run across the country. Citizens worried about their own savings deposited in banks that invested in the railroads. Would their banks close too?

Stocks of railroads and other businesses crashed as people sold madly, trying to recoup cash wherever they could. They depleted their bank accounts, hoarding their savings at home, and forcing more banks to shut their doors. On September 20, the New York Stock Exchange suspended its activities.

The hopes for prosperity in Northern Republican circles had risen fast with the growth of the railroads, and they crashed hard as the industry suffered from too much rapid building and investment. Although Grant was not a direct recipient of railroad bribes, many of those around him—including his first vice president, Schuyler Colfax—had received payments from the men and banks promoting the new lines. It became clear that the promises of profit were exaggerated and often dishonest. Powerful Republican Party leaders contributed to the disinformation because it benefited them personally.

The concentration of power and wealth around leading Republicans triggered widespread suffering after what contemporaries called the Panic of 1873. It was really more of a depression—in many ways deeper than the Great Depression a half century later. Twenty-five railroads stopped paying creditors in the weeks after the September crash. Seventy-one more railroads went into arrears the next year. Railroad stocks plummeted, eventually by 60 percent. As the railroads went into bankruptcy, their bankers closed their doors too, followed by the other businesses that relied on the railroads and banks. There were more than five thousand bankruptcies in the last months of 1873.

Millions of once-prosperous Americans lost their jobs, particularly in cities like New York, where unemployment was estimated at 25 percent soon after the crash. As incomes declined and new investments ceased, prices for industrial and farm products plummeted. Factories laid off their workers, and farmers had trouble selling their crops. The gains many communities had made in the years since Appomattox were wiped out, and for the next decade, many families who had dutifully served the Union cause found themselves living worse than they had before the Civil War. There was no war dividend for them. The same was true for families suffering in the poorer Southern states.[29]

The economic collapse decisively shifted Republican priorities. The party could no longer promise easy prosperity. It could not justify expenditures on civil rights in the South either. Business leaders in the North focused intently on trying to rebuild their fortunes, turning to the federal government for help. They demanded that the Treasury increase the supply of money and, where possible, purchase their products. Farmers also wanted more access to money, which motivated their calls for "free silver" as a supplement to the limited gold holdings used for much of the nation's finances.

The economic urgency of 1873 and subsequent years killed whatever Republican will remained for the burdens of enforcing multiracial democracy in the South. If Grant confronted resistance from many party leaders after his reelection, a year later, he faced a united opposition. The attention of white Republican voters, still the vast majority of the party, narrowed to their needs outside the South. Civil rights remained in the party platform but not in its daily concerns. Under attack for the economic collapse on his watch, and the evidence of corruption among those close to him, Grant disengaged. He had few major initiatives in his second term. He was largely silent on civil rights.

Southern Democrats were not silent. They turned the economic depression into a justification for renewed attacks on African Americans. If resources were short, Southern Democrats wanted to make certain that white men were in charge of distributing them. They argued that the Republican promises of prosperity through multiracial democracy had proven hollow. With falling cotton and other crop prices, white farmers needed to hold their labor costs down, which meant keeping African Americans on their land at low wages. With the economy contracting, white tradesmen wanted to eliminate competition from African Americans and other groups. Deprivation became a justification for racial exclusion and violence.

The Ku Klux Klan did not officially reemerge, but organized violence against African Americans picked up rapidly. In April 1873, a white militia in central Louisiana massacred more than one hundred African American Republicans as they struggled to defend local elected officials from attack. The heavily armed white mob was organized by a former Confederate army lieutenant, who had been elected sheriff, Christopher Columbus Nash. He and his followers proclaimed that they would never allow Black Republicans to rule in the state.

The town of Colfax in Louisiana's Grant Parish—named for the president and his first vice president—had a large former slave population, many of whom served in the Union army. They owned local land, ran a town school, and elected African Americans to office. The residents understood the hostility around them, so they organized their own Black militia to defend their community.

The local militia held off various attackers for three weeks, using the town courthouse as a fortification. They even dug trenches around the building to impede hostile groups. On Easter Sunday, April 13, 1873, Nash and his posse of 140 white men brought a cannon into town, which they used to bombard the courthouse. Once they breached its wall, Nash and his men set the building on fire.

The African American defenders, including elected officials, surrendered, running from the burning courthouse carrying white flags. Nash's posse assembled the African American victims and then killed them in cold blood. Some were shot, some had their throats slit, others were hung from trees. One of the victims who survived by playing dead recounted overhearing an attacker shout that "he did not come 400 miles to kill niggers for nothing." A member of the white posse remembered that one of his collaborators "lined them up and his old gun went off.... [H]e killed all five of them with two shots. Then it was like popcorn in a skillet."[30]

Colonel Thomas W. DeKlyne, the Union officer sent to restore order in Colfax, recounted the scene:

> About one-third of a mile below the courthouse we came upon a party of colored men and women carrying away a wounded colored man upon a sled. At a little distance in the field were the dead bodies of two colored men. About two hundred yards nearer the courthouse were three dead bodies of colored men, and from that point to the courthouse and its vicinity the ground was thickly strewn with dead.... Many were shot in

On April 13, 1873, a posse of 140 white men attacked the African American community of Colfax, Louisiana. They overthrew the local government and killed African American citizens in cold blood: "Many were shot in the back at the head and neck; one man still lay with his hands clasped in supplication." *Source: Harper's Weekly, May 10, 1873*

the back at the head and neck; one man still lay with his hands clasped in supplication; the face of another was completely flattened by blows from a gun, the broken stock of a double barreled shotgun being on the ground near him; another had been cut across the stomach with a knife after being shot; and almost all had from three to a dozen wounds. Many of them had their brains literally blown out.[31]

This was a massacre perpetrated in the United States, in plain sight—"the bloodiest single act of carnage" in the decade since Appomattox. It was a violent coup against a local Black government, designed to keep white men in control of the state through murder. News from Colfax terrorized African Americans and their supporters throughout the South. The same could happen to them; the Colfax murderers surely had many followers. Northern Republicans largely ignored these events.[32]

Three of the white perpetrators were convicted by federal authorities, but their convictions were reversed when the U.S. Supreme Court ruled, in *U.S. v. Cruikshank*, that the federal government did not have jurisdiction to charge these men for what were, in the court's eyes, state crimes. Of course, the Louisiana courts, like other state courts, refused to punish white men who attacked Black citizens, even when the evidence of brutality was so overwhelming.

In a stunning manipulation of history, Democrats turned Colfax into a heroic defense of white rule against "rioting" African Americans. According to this false narrative, the Black population in central Louisiana was trying to steal control of government from good citizens, threatening them with violence. The anniversaries of the massacre inspired orgies of repeated violence against African Americans by white militias.

On the forty-eighth anniversary, April 13, 1921, the white residents of Colfax unveiled a marble obelisk in the town's cemetery, honoring the white men who perpetrated the massacre. The monument singled out the three white vigilantes who died in the violence, with no mention of the more than one hundred innocent Black victims. The monument was dedicated: "In Loving Remembrance, Erected To the Memory of The Heroes.... Who Fell in the Colfax Riot Fighting for White Supremacy."[33]

Thirty years later, the town added a plaque at the site of the massacre, with the words *Colfax Riot* in large print. A description followed: "On this site occurred the Colfax Riot in which three white men and 150 negroes were slain. This event on April 13, 1873, marked the end of carpetbag misrule in the South." The plaque and the cemetery monument have lasted into the twenty-first century.[34]

"Carpetbag misrule" referred to President Grant, the U.S. Army, and Republican officials who defended civil rights in the South. Grant was slow to respond in public, but he moved more military force into Louisiana as the state witnessed increasing violence against African Americans—provoked by the massacre in Colfax and the complicity of local law enforcement. Over the next year, Grant deployed five thousand federal troops to combat white militias and protect Republican officials. He dispatched General Philip Sheridan to put down the sources of insurrection in Louisiana. Sheridan dutifully reported that before his arrival, and since Appomattox, more than two thousand African Americans had been killed by white militias in Louisiana. And the numbers continued to grow.[35]

The president angrily wrote to the Senate, describing the "butchery of citizens" in Colfax and other parts of the state. He explained that white militias displayed "blood-thirstiness and barbarity," which was "hardly surpassed by any acts of savage warfare"—a very strong statement coming from someone who had seen as much war as Grant. The president reported that he had reluctantly deployed military forces in Louisiana, as he had earlier in South Carolina, to restore law and order.

Grant's account was clear about the brutality but restrained in response. He accepted that federal forces could not stay long in Louisiana, even as the violence continued. In contrast to his earlier actions against the Ku Klux Klan, Grant now had to accept that most Americans, including his voters, believed federal troops in the South were "unnecessary and irritating," and perhaps harmful to larger national goals after the recent economic collapse. The African American deaths at Colfax motivated fewer voters than the desire to limit interventions in the white South.[36]

The November 1874 congressional elections brought this sad realization home to Grant and other Republicans. Democratic candidates won more races than at any time since the start of the Civil War. They gained nine seats in the Senate, reducing the Republican majority below the two-thirds necessary to overturn presidential vetoes. Most shocking, the Democrats picked up ninety-three seats in the House of Representatives, a new majority and the second-largest electoral swing in U.S. history. The election ended more than a decade of Republican dominance.

Democratic victories were centered in the South, but the party also picked up voters in the North and West. It appealed to white men, including many immigrants, who believed that the Republican Party had lost touch with their needs. Voter restrictions and intimidation, especially in the former Confederacy, kept thousands of African Americans from the polls. The turnout among white voters in all regions grew, and it remained high for the coming decades. The 1872 election was the high-water mark for multiracial voting; by 1874, the electorate was whitening, thanks to Southern violence and white mobilization.

With the Democrats on the rise and in control of the House, President Grant had to curtail his already reduced civil rights agenda. His opponents in Congress blocked his efforts at every turn. In March 1875, Congress passed a long-sought act to ban racial discrimination in public accommodations and transportation, but the legislature removed all provisions for enforcement, making it a dead letter before it became law. Congress moved decisively to cut expenditures by the military and the Justice Department in the South.

Grant was hemmed in by both Democrats and Republicans. He looked weak in the face of rising violence and continued economic difficulties. His last two years were the most miserable of his presidential experience. The man who defeated Robert E. Lee and crushed the Ku Klux Klan left office as a figure of disrepute, remembered for the scandals of his associates and his failed enforcement of civil rights. For proponents of multiracial democracy, Grant did too little. For defenders of white supremacy, he meddled too much.

President Grant's last days in office illustrated that the country was far from the peace he had promised. Although he inherited a deeply divided society, he initially led a federal government unified behind the Republican Party and its commitment to enforcing the Constitution. Grant tried to execute the laws faithfully, but the widening resistance to these efforts quickly divided the government. The United States had less consensus around race and democracy during Grant's final year than it had when he accepted Robert E. Lee's surrender a decade earlier.

Defenders of white supremacy remained steadfast in their determination to protect their positions and their privileges, as Lee had warned at Appomattox. Grant refused to march over the country "three or four times" then and was unable to do so later.

Grant's early successes contributed to the decline of his presidency. Evidence of progress on civil rights convinced many Republicans that sacrifices were no longer necessary and that they did not need to continue fighting. They could focus instead on getting rich in new industries. Grant proved to be a leader of integrity, despite the corruption around him, but he lacked the political skills to motivate his own supporters to keep up the fight. Grant's Republicans staggered through his second term still committed to a multiracial democracy but hesitant, uncertain, and limited in their willingness to commit resources to the cause. Although they had more money and guns than the Democrats, they chose not to use them.

The white supremacists used everything they had. They not only willed the war to continue despite their disadvantageous position, they challenged the North to decide if it had the passion and the grit to take on the stubborn South. By the end of Grant's diminished presidency, the North lacked both qualities. The election of Grant's successor would show how much the Democrats gained and the Republicans lost from the consistent defiance of former Confederates.

CHAPTER 8

Contested Election

In November 1876, Americans voted for a president, but they failed to elect one. This was not an unusual occurrence. In 1800 and 1824, Thomas Jefferson and John Quincy Adams each became president after inconclusive voting. Like many later presidents, neither of them was elected by a majority of voting citizens.

Jefferson failed to win more electoral votes than Aaron Burr. The selection of the next president went to the House of Representatives, where it took thirty-six separate rounds of balloting to name Jefferson president-elect on February 17, 1801—months after voting finished across the country. Jefferson's belated triumph occurred amid rumors of violence from his supporters and fears that the country would not, in fact, have a president. The abstention on the thirty-sixth congressional ballot by the lone representative from Delaware, James Bayard, was the last-minute shift that turned the eight state delegations supporting Jefferson's presidency into the necessary majority in the House of Representatives. This was less of a democratic election than a desperate effort to get someone in the presidency and move on.

The election of John Quincy Adams displayed similar dysfunction. In late 1824, the highly regarded but frequently disliked scion of a prior president received fewer electoral and popular votes than the revered military hero Andrew Jackson. There is no doubt that Jackson had more supporters. The election, however, went to the House of Representatives again. Speaker of the House Henry Clay pressured a number of key congressmen to support Adams over Jackson, and on February 9, 1825, the state delegations voted to make Adams president-elect. Clay became his secretary of state. Congressional horse-trading, not votes by citizens, determined the next commander in chief.

Andrew Jackson called this a "corrupt bargain," and he condemned the undemocratic way that presidents were appointed, not elected. He later proposed a constitutional amendment to replace the electoral college with a national popular vote. Without the passage of this amendment, the votes of citizens mattered primarily in promoting candidates, not putting them in office. Restrictions on voting, the allocation of presidential electors in different states, and the negotiations in Congress created a wide gap between the voters and the elected leader. The people did not choose the president. Far from it.

That is not how democracy is supposed to work, and it is not what the framers of the Constitution expected. They wanted a consensus figure chosen, like George Washington, but a divided country frequently could not identify such a figure. The convoluted American system of elections made national divisions worse, and it made the selection of a president arbitrary and contentious.

The 1876 election was, perhaps, the most arbitrary and contentious of American elections ever. President Ulysses Grant considered running for a third term, but just four years after his overwhelming reelection and one decade after his triumph at Appomattox, he had become a widely unpopular figure. Republicans blamed him for poor leadership during the economic panic of 1873. Democrats accused him of filling his administration with bribe-takers and "negro-lovers."

Stung by these attacks, especially from within his own party, Grant announced that he would not seek reelection again, "unless it should come under such circumstances as to make it an imperative duty." Most Republicans greeted Grant's statement with relief. They needed a new leader to help the party overcome current controversies, offering citizens a hopeful vision of economic growth and national unity. But they did not know who that figure would be.[1]

In its short existence, the Republican Party had been dominated by two giants: Lincoln and Grant. All potential successors were dwarfed by their long shadows. The war, Andrew Johnson's impeachment, and other continuing conflicts had tarnished the reputations of most politicians. No one could claim to rise above the contending factions within the Republican Party as, in their best moments, Lincoln and Grant had.

Frederick Douglass voiced this concern as a loyal Republican, anxious about the future commitment of the party to African American citizens. He agreed that it was time for Grant to move on: he "has spoken the right word at the right time." Yet Douglass observed: "There are many great and good men in the land; but to whom among them all, has the order of events given greater power to serve the country than to President Grant?" Douglass closed his letter by recounting that Grant "has been the shelter and savior of my people in the hour of supreme danger and naturally enough we feel great concern as to who is to come in his stead."[2]

Douglass was not alone. Numerous Republicans, Black and white, worried for the future of the party and the country.

The Democrats were more optimistic about Grant's departure, but they also faced an uncertain future. Democrats could not win the presidency with solid opposition from white and Black voters in the most populous Northern states. Republicans had a strong advantage, but it remained precarious so long as they could not get their African American supporters to the polls in the South, and they confronted fatigue and disillusion from many Northern white voters. The Civil War had divided the country between the parties, and the continuing conflict over African American participation kept them as polarized as ever.

The Republican Party had briefly become a national party when African Americans in the South voted in large numbers between 1868 and 1872. After that, when federal enforcement of voting laws receded, the Civil War pattern returned. Democrats represented a solid white South, and Republicans controlled much of the North. Western voters were somewhat unpredictable, but their numbers remained small. The Mason-Dixon Line was still the key border that defined American politics.

The framers of the Constitution had worked to open up these borders, replacing state-based factions with a national system governed by consensus. That was why they created a presidency in the first place—to transcend party and region. Yet as the nation approached the centennial of its Declaration of Independence, party and region meant more than ever. The Fourteenth Amendment guaranteed equal protection under the law to all, but what that meant in practice varied enormously, depending on where you lived. Frederick Douglass delivered public lectures advocating for African American rights throughout the North; white militias lynched men like him in the South. You could not mistake one part of the country for the other.

The election of 1876 was a continuation of the Civil War, fought in the streets, voting booths, and legislatures of the states. The election manifested the divergent multiracial and white supremacist visions of American democracy. It exacerbated divisions and resentments. There is no evidence any significant group of voters changed their minds. (That rarely happens in elections.) Neither party offered new or exciting ideas. The creativity came in finding ways to attack the other side and spread fear.

The election was a gritty, dirty battle to see which side could bring out its voters and keep its adversaries away. Speaking of voters as soldiers mobilized for combat, New York senator Roscoe Conkling rejected the need for "proselytes" to persuade people. He emphasized getting every party member to show up and do his duty at the polls: "We do need the entire Republican vote, and this means work and attention in every school district in the State."[3]

Party efforts worked. In the decades after Appomattox, Americans were "partisan, loyal, and regular." More citizens voted than ever before in 1876—above 80 percent of eligible voters!—although thousands of African Americans and all women were denied the ballot. Once people voted, the real battle became who counted the votes and who determined the winner.[4]

Although voters were predictable, election outcomes were uncertain because they were so close. It mattered more who voted when and where, not how many people voted in total. Individual decisions at key moments had an enduring impact, but no one—including the candidates—controlled the course of events. The election was more mass warfare than mass democracy. It set a model for future elections in a democracy where, ironically, the people voted in large numbers but did not choose their president.

President Rutherford B. Hayes. *Credit: Mathew Brady*

For Republican Party leaders, it made sense for Ohio to choose the president, as it did repeatedly during the next half century. The state reached north to the rapidly industrializing shores of Lake Erie and south to the hilly bluegrass of Kentucky. It had burgeoning urban centers, like Cleveland and Cincinnati, and vast agricultural sections in the west and south of the state. With the third-largest population of any state in 1876, and twenty-two electoral votes, the state was a big prize that Republicans often won, but one that Democrats could win too. To hold the presidency, Republicans had to hold Ohio.

The best way to ensure victory in Ohio was, of course, to run a presidential candidate from the state—a "favorite son." Even though Grant had spent most of his adult years in Illinois, he benefited from his connection by birth to Ohio. The state became more vital to Republican chances after Grant's election, especially as Democrats made inroads in New York and other large Northern states closely tied to Confederate economic interests.

For this reason, the party nominated the state's popular governor, Rutherford B. Hayes, as its presidential candidate in June 1876. Born in the small central Ohio town of Delaware on October 4, 1822, Hayes grew up in very modest circumstances. His father had died before his birth, so he and his sister were raised by a single mother. Hayes attended local schools, a Methodist seminary, and then Kenyon College. He only left Ohio briefly as a young man to get a law degree from Harvard University. Upon his return in 1845, he began a prosperous career as a lawyer in Fremont and then Cincinnati. Hayes was highly regarded for his defense of accused criminals, including runaway slaves. Initially a Whig, he became involved in Republican Party politics on the eve of the Civil War.

Although he was thirty-eight at the outbreak of hostilities, Hayes volunteered for battlefield service in the Union army. He began as a major in the Twenty-Third Ohio Volunteers, where he served alongside another future governor and president, William McKinley. By all accounts, Hayes fought with skill and valor, suffering four separate wounds in various battles. He remained in the Union army for the duration of the war, finishing as a brigadier general, with a final promotion to major general for his outstanding service.

Based on his war record, the Republican Party nominated Hayes for a seat in Congress in 1864 while he was still in the army. He won his first election without campaigning and began his service in Washington in December 1865 during the first tumultuous year of Andrew Johnson's presidency. Hayes ran for the more powerful position of Ohio governor two years later, which he won, and was reelected in 1869. He retired in 1872, largely to focus on his family's precarious finances, but then returned to the governor's office four years later, defeating the Democratic incumbent, William Allen.

Hayes was the most popular Republican in Ohio. His emergence from retirement was part of the Republican plan to hold on to the presidency after Grant. As governor again, Hayes was positioned to run for the nation's highest office. He was a Union war hero, a consistent advocate of civil rights, a proponent of business growth, and a man rooted in farming communities. He was free of personal corruption, and he surrounded himself with moderates, not firebrands.

Although he defended equal protection under the law and voting rights for Black citizens, Hayes was not eager to bring federal enforcement to the South. Hayes promised to restore economic prosperity and move cautiously on building a more inclusive democracy. As governor, he advocated for the ratification of the Fifteenth Amendment, giving African American men the right to vote in Ohio for the first time. He separated himself from radicals, like Ohio senator Benjamin Wade, who advocated more extensive land and labor reforms as well as women's suffrage. Hayes led his state by steering between diverse economic interests and deep racial divisions. Those experiences made the governorship of Ohio a persuasive starting point for the presidency.

Hayes was not the most inspiring candidate; he lacked Lincoln's eloquence and Grant's gravitas. He was, however, the most credible figure for Republicans, who wanted someone to appeal to businessmen, farmers, and professionals across the North and West. He was one of "them"—not an insider to the terrible battles around Congress and the presidency since Appomattox. "Both parties are injured by what is going on at Washington," Hayes wrote. "Both are, therefore, more and more disposed to look for candidates outside that atmosphere." With precious little time in the nation's capital, the Ohio governor and war hero was the perfect "outsider" for the Republican Party.[5]

The Democrats chose a Washington "outsider" too: New York governor Samuel Tilden. As Ohio was crucial for Republican prospects in 1876, winning New York was absolutely essential for the party of the Confederacy. Their reliable base in the South was not large enough, and the Empire State's thirty-five electoral votes were the biggest prize—enough to bring the Democrats close to victory.

Tilden had deep roots in the state. He was born on February 9, 1814, in the Hudson Valley town of New Lebanon, straddling the New York border with western Massachusetts. His father, a local businessman who sold a popular cannabis-based medicine, Tilden's Extract, was a friend of former president and Democratic Party leader Martin Van Buren.

Following Van Buren, Tilden opposed slavery and abolition at the same time. Like many residents of New York State, these Democrats

Samuel Tilden, governor of New York. *Source: Frank Fowler*

recognized the crime of racial servitude, but they accepted what Tilden called a "higher type of mankind" in European immigrants to the United States. Racial equality was impossible, in Tilden's eyes, and he joined other Democrats in supporting the rights of white men in the South to govern their communities as they wished.[6]

Working initially as a corporate lawyer for railroads and banks, Tilden amassed a huge personal fortune. He condemned Republican efforts to limit the spread of slavery as a threat to an American economic system that worked quite well, at least for people like him. Tilden espoused what he called "the master-wisdom of governing little and leaving as much as possible to localities and to individuals."[7]

He opposed Lincoln's election and did not serve in the Union army. After Appomattox, Tilden praised Andrew Johnson for his efforts to "speedily restore the people of the revolted States to their true relations to the Union" and "heal the bleeding wounds." Like most Northern Democrats, Tilden accepted the end of slavery but opposed any civil rights efforts beyond that.[8]

He joined Southerners in accusing the federal government of favoring the freed slaves over suffering white citizens. "Having triumphed" in the fight to hold the Union together, Tilden warned of the "opposite dangers" from a militarized federal government in the hands of aggressive Republicans: "Those dangers come to us in acts of illegal military violence committed in times of peace; in the usurpation by the soldiery of a power to decide the membership of our legislative assemblies, whose right to judge exclusively in such cases has ever been guarded with peculiar jealousy by our race." He called on Democrats, North and South, to resist this "tyranny" and restore "civil liberty and the personal rights of individuals" through the authority of white state legislatures.[9]

Tilden took over as the chairman of the Democratic Party's state committee in New York in 1865, and for the next decade, he became the new Martin Van Buren of the party—another wizard of organization. He rebuilt the party, expanded its reach, and fielded candidates who successfully challenged the waning influence of William Henry Seward and other prominent Republicans in the state. By 1875, he helped to elect Democratic majorities in both houses of the New York legislature. He also boosted himself into the governor's office.

Immediately, Tilden and his supporters prepared for his presidential campaign. With strong support in New York, New Jersey, and the solid Democratic South, Tilden looked like he could attain the nation's highest office. The New York governor had an extensive team of campaign surrogates and a powerful fundraising operation. He also devoted large sums from his personal fortune to campaign literature and other materials.

The Democratic platform was clear and appealing to those who wanted to curtail enforcement of civil rights. The party declared that the Thirteenth, Fourteenth, and Fifteenth Amendments to the Constitution, now ratified, were the "final settlement of the controversies that engendered civil war." Mission accomplished. Further actions by the national government constituted "a corrupt centralism" that supported "the rapacity of carpet-bag tyrannies." The Democratic Party could not turn back time for the Confederacy, but it could free white supremacists to rule with less federal interference.[10]

Tilden had gained fame for taking on the corruption of the city "bosses" in New York, particularly William "Boss" Tweed and his ring of extortionists running Tammany Hall. Tilden gathered evidence against them and forced them to shut down their operations, at least temporarily, in 1875. He promised to do the same for the alleged corruption of Republican politicians.

Democratic efforts to prohibit multiracial participation in 1876 meant more violence, not less. During the presidential campaign, Democratic supporters increased their attacks on Republican voters, especially African Americans in the South. Violence was a mechanism for mobilizing partisans to come out for their side and a tool for intimidating adversaries to stay home.

On July 8, just months before the election, one of the most notorious acts of racial violence occurred in the South Carolina town of Hamburg, east of the Savannah River and the Georgia border. Seventy white men with rifles, calling themselves Red Shirts, entered Hamburg and attacked a local group of African American Republicans. The victims were residents of the town who had organized their own militia to maintain order in their community and encourage political participation. Their only threat to the white men who attacked them was their very existence as an alternative source of authority to the landowners (former slave masters) in the region. Asserting white control and Black subordination, one of the vigilante leaders exclaimed: "By God, I want [the Black militia's] guns, and I'll be God damned if I ain't going to have them."[11]

The white riflemen fired on the cornered African Americans. The militant posse captured thirty of the besieged citizens who sought to escape. In the next few minutes, the rifleman called out the names of the captives they knew and killed them in cold blood—seven in total. They told some of the others to run but shot at them as they fled. The attackers then left the scene of the massacre to celebrate and extoll their defense of Democratic power.

The attackers might have worn red shirts instead of white sheets, but they had the same mission as their predecessors in the Ku Klux Klan. They were probably the same hooligans who had terrorized their African American neighbors in previous years. Their goal was to enforce the authority of the Democratic Party and discourage any Republican organizing or resistance. They sought to "awaken" fellow white men to rise up for their party. Tough, manly citizens were expected to join the posse. Marching together as a militant group, identifying threatening African American voters, and bringing violence upon them was a community-building exercise for white men. They were eager to come out for Tilden and other Democrats who would protect their privileges.

Benjamin "Pitchfork" Tillman organized white mobs to attack African Americans in South Carolina. He later became governor and then senator. He lost his left eye due to a cranial tumor that kept him out of combat in the Civil War. *Credit: Bain News Service*

No one trumpeted for Democratic political violence louder than Benjamin "Pitchfork" Tillman. The future Democratic governor and senator from South Carolina exemplified how the Democratic Party mobilized its supporters and smothered its enemies by brute force. Tillman was one of the proud, bragging riflemen who attacked the African American Republicans in Hamburg. Although he was too sickly to serve in the Confederate army and lost an eye from a cranial tumor, he made his name as an aggressive bully. After he admitted to participation in the Hamburg massacre, his support among white South Carolinians grew.

Tillman became a Democratic hero in the state. Throughout his long career, extending more than four decades, he openly advocated for a blood war against Black voters and their Republican allies. Tillman was crystal clear about his resistance to federal authority, and he attracted a devoted following from hundreds of thousands of white citizens who fought to defeat—and, if necessary, kill—those who would limit their power. Tillman and his supporters reviled Republicans for attempting to bring the races together.

Tillman participated personally in the violence, making it central to his rise as a Democrat. After Hamburg, he organized other white men to ride through nearby towns, terrorizing African Americans and Republicans. In September, Tillman participated in another massacre in Aiken County, where one thousand white men killed thirty African Americans. Only the arrival of U.S. Army soldiers stopped the violence, temporarily.

When citizens started voting in 1876, Tillman made himself a poll manager in his hometown of Edgefield. He harassed Republican voters, "whooping and holloing," as one later recalled. Tillman aimed his pistol at African American citizens whom he hoped to keep away from the ballot box. Robert Chandler, a Black Republican, testified: "Benny Tillman said they had been the rulers of Carolina and they intended to rule it." Only Democratic votes were legitimate in his view.[12]

Yet Democrats did not have a monopoly on intimidation and coercion in the 1876 election. Republican partisans made their presence felt at polling sites too. They bribed potential supporters, including recent immigrants. They bullied obvious opponents. Like the Democrats, the Republicans gave their voters preprinted ballots, which they watched them deposit in ballot boxes, accompanied by a meal and ample drinks, courtesy of the party. Voting was rarely secret, and it wasn't free.

But the violence of the Democrats was on a different level. Throughout the 1876 campaign, as in prior years, the party of the Confederacy used brute force to keep African Americans and others from the polls. Their attacks on Black voters invigorated Democratic supporters.

Although the number of voters in the 1876 election reached a historical high, it still excluded hundreds of thousands of potential voters who, quite literally, feared for their lives if they approached the polls. As white voter turnout skyrocketed, African Americans stayed home. This was a distinct advantage for the Democrats in 1876, and it turned Grant's large lead from 1872 into a narrow pathway for Hayes.

In Columbus, Ohio, with his family, Hayes went to bed on Election Night believing he might have lost. "A cold but dry day," he recorded in his personal diary. "I still think Democratic chances the best. But it is not possible to form a confident opinion." He seemed resolved to accept defeat and return to a blissful retirement with his wife and children.

Hayes had a dark vision of what his defeat would mean for the country: "If we lose, the South will be the greatest sufferer. Their misfortune will be far greater than ours." Hayes went to sleep worrying that under President Tilden "the South will drift towards chaos again."[13]

The next morning did not bring clarity about who had won the election. The returns showed that Democrats had more votes in New York, New Jersey, Connecticut, Delaware, Maryland, and Indiana. And they looked strong in their Southern heartland. Tilden had at least 184 of the necessary 185 electoral votes for victory.

Republicans had to run the table on the remaining states to win. Hayes recounted in his diary how Republican stalwarts still anticipated victory: "A shouting multitude rushed to my house and called me out with rousing cheers." Hayes was honest with the crowd: "In the very close political contest, which is just drawing to a close, it is impossible, at so early a time, to obtain the result."[14]

Tilden was also restrained. Although most newspapers declared him the next president, he did not echo that claim. True to form, he held frequent conferences with party officials in the hours and days after the voting. His campaign team worried that the remaining states where the vote was close—Florida, Louisiana, and South Carolina—all had Republican leaders who were obviously inclined to favor Hayes.

As expected, the Republican governors in the three states called their returns for Hayes, but Democrats offered different totals for Tilden. With the returns so tight, each side had its own count. The high number of voters and the close results meant that the two parties did not agree on the math—"finding" or rejecting a few hundred votes shifted victory from one side to the other. The numbers kept changing as new ballots emerged and suspicious ballots were rejected by one side or the other. There was no impartial vote-counting authority—no one who could offer a set of returns free of partisanship.

Oregon also posed a dilemma. Hayes had clearly won the majority of the votes in that state, but the Republicans had designated a postmaster as one of their three state electors. The Constitution prohibited anyone who held a federal post of "trust or profit" from serving as an elector, and that appeared to rule out U.S. postal employees. The Democratic governor of Oregon, La Fayette Grover, sought to appoint a Democratic elector in place of the Republican postmaster. If he did this, then Tilden would get the one additional electoral vote necessary to reach 185 and the presidency. He was so close—"a hair's breadth," one of his anxious associates commented.[15]

Tilden had many paths to victory; he only needed one of Florida, Louisiana, or South Carolina or the replacement elector in Oregon. But each path had roadblocks and uncertainties. Hayes needed everything to break his way, and he remained pessimistic. Five days after the election, both candidates were deeply uncertain about the outcome. Although Tilden clearly had more total votes across the country, especially with his victory in New York (the most populous state), no one really knew who had won more electoral votes. And that was what mattered.

Both candidates deserve credit for sharing their uncertainty about the outcome and rejecting the urge to pretend it away. Neither actually declared himself the winner, just as neither conceded. Hayes and Tilden were honest in their beliefs that they each had a strong claim to be president, and they were also honest in their admissions that the election system had failed. Hayes was quite explicit in his diary: "All thoughtful people are brought to consider the imperfect machinery provided for electing the President." One week after the election, he and Tilden stared at the possibility that the country had not elected a president, despite the enormous number of votes.[16]

Grant was still president, and his role grew in the selection of his successor. Voting locations in Florida, Louisiana, and South Carolina were often far from the state capitals, where official results were tabulated. The final count in each state required the physical transfer of ballot boxes, often by train. As Republicans and Democrats argued over who received more votes in each state, rumors circulated of planned efforts to interfere with the transfer of the ballots. Each state had a designated board of canvassers charged to oversee the final vote count, and concerns for the safety of those officials quickly emerged. They received threats to their lives, and each side tried to intimidate them to count the ballots as one party preferred.

On November 10—three days after Election Day—Grant wrote two orders to his old comrade in arms General William Tecumseh Sherman, now commanding general of the U.S. Army. The first order sent more federal forces to Louisiana and Florida, removing some from South Carolina, where Grant had increased the army presence due to preelection violence. The president wanted federal soldiers to "insure quiet and a peaceable [count] of the ballots actually cast." The last phrase revealed that Grant was concerned about citizens destroying or adding ballots to change the outcomes. He had already received accounts from Republican sources of Democrats undertaking both actions.[17]

Grant's second order charged the army to combat electoral fraud. The president tasked federal soldiers to guarantee "that the proper and legal Boards of Canvassers are unmolested in their duties." Grant continued, "Should there be any grounds of suspicion of fraudulent counting on either side, it should be reported and denounced at once." The president was determined that the country should not "have the result tainted by the suspicion of illegal or false returns."[18]

Newspapers across the country published Grant's orders, and they provoked an immediate firestorm. Republicans thanked the president for preserving electoral integrity, and they sent numerous accounts of alleged fraud, especially efforts to prohibit and nullify African American votes. Concerned about Democratic vigilantes around New Orleans, Grant wrote to Lieutenant General Philip Sheridan, who still commanded army forces in the region, ordering him to "go in person" to the city, as he had done in previous moments of white supremacist violence.[19]

Democratic leaders perceived Grant's orders as yet another act of presidential tyranny. He was sending the generals who had burned and occupied the South back into their communities. He was using federal soldiers again to limit the independence of the states and to get his chosen candidate into office. The ghost of John Wilkes Booth emerged in a series of detailed, bone-chilling death threats against Grant, spelled out in a flood of ferocious letters sent to his office—more than ever before in his presidency.

"I want to give you notice that your days are short in this world," one self-described "outlaw" wrote the president. "There is three of us to do the Job. You must and shall die. We can afford to hang to Save the Country."[20]

Grant and Sherman remembered Lincoln's assassination. They took the threats seriously, moving four companies of soldiers, in Sherman's description, "to make safe the most important personages and property necessarily here at the Capitol."[21]

Grant did more than move soldiers. He also moved key Republicans. The president wrote to leading party figures, asking them to travel to the disputed states. Many were part of Hayes's "Ohio mafia," including Representative James Garfield and Senator John Sherman (brother of General Sherman). Their role was to watch the counts carefully, report back to Grant and Hayes, and add pressure, wherever possible, to get a favorable outcome for the Republicans.

Garfield would play a particularly important role as a confidant of both Grant and Hayes. He recounted in his diary that the president "urged me very strongly to go to New Orleans, both for the sake of doing what I could to calm the public agitation and witness the canvass of the Electoral votes so as to be ready to debate the case in the House on assembling of Congress."[22]

Less than a week after the votes were cast, Grant and Garfield anticipated that Congress, not the people or the states, would have to decide who was the next president. They were determined to make sure it was Hayes. If Democrats had not prevented thousands of African Americans from reaching the polls, the disputed states and others in the South would surely have gone for Hayes as they had gone for Grant four years earlier. Repeated Democratic voting also artificially boosted Tilden's numbers. Benjamin Tillman's county of Edgefield, for example, reported two thousand more votes for the Democrats than the total population. As more of these reports emerged, Grant felt comfortable telling journalists that he was confident Hayes had really won the election.[23]

The Democrats, of course, sent their own distinguished figures to the disputed states to mirror the actions of Garfield, Sherman, and other Republicans. The "visitors" from both sides tried to influence the counts. When the Republicans pointed to missing African American votes and repeated white votes, the Democrats produced evidence that African Americans allegedly did not want to vote, and they demanded that every ballot cast get counted.

The two sides appealed to state and federal courts, triggering a crowd of confusing, and often contradictory, lawsuits. Mountains of sworn affidavits about alleged fraud were submitted to the courts, often from witnesses who were obviously lying. Legitimate witnesses, especially African Americans, reported death threats if they testified. And rumors quickly circulated of partisan efforts to bribe canvassing officials and judges.

Senator Sherman, for example, apparently tried to buy off members of the board counting votes in Louisiana with promises of patronage and perhaps cash. On November 20, he wrote to two of them: "Neither

Mr. Hayes, myself, the gentlemen who accompany me, or the country at large can ever forget the obligation under which you will have placed us should you stand firm in the position you have taken." Even more damning, Sherman continued: "I am justified in assuming responsibility for promises made and for guarantees that you shall be provided for as soon after the 4th of March [Inauguration Day] as may be practicable."

The recipients of Sherman's letter responded that they wanted more from the Republicans because the Democrats had also offered them a lucrative bribe. They were in a position to play one desperate party against the other. The election had become a competitive bidding war for the fealty of local officials.[24]

The Republicans had the advantage in the bidding war because they held the most powerful federal and state offices. Florida, Louisiana, and South Carolina were the only three Southern states that still had Republican governors, elected when African Americans were able to vote in large numbers. (All three states replaced their Republican governors with Democrats in 1877.) Grant's position as president also mattered enormously. Together, he and the governors could coordinate the deployment of resources, including soldiers. They could also speak with authoritative voices in the press, even if half the country distrusted what they said. Most important, they had political and financial leverage over the counting boards, many of which were composed of officials they had appointed or helped get elected.

On December 6, when the electors in every state met, the governors of Florida, Louisiana, and South Carolina affirmed that Hayes had received the most votes in their jurisdictions. The secretaries of state appointed each state's electors for the Republican Party, and the electors then chose Hayes. The Oregon governor tried to give one of his state's electors to the Democrats, but that act was reversed by his secretary of state, who appointed all three of the electors for the Republicans. These were now the official, legal votes to make Hayes the next president with 185 total electoral votes, one more than Tilden's 184 electoral votes.

The Democrats refused to give up. Each of the three disputed states, and Oregon, sent an alternative set of electors to Congress. In South

Carolina, the Democrats convened a separate meeting of their state legislators to appoint their own electors. In Florida and Louisiana, Democratic candidates for governor—who claimed victory in the 1876 elections but still had not taken office—designated alternative electors. In Oregon, the sitting governor did the same, trying to overrule his secretary of state.

The Democrats challenged the obvious partisanship in choosing electors where the vote counts remained unclear. Of course, the Democrats were equally partisan. Their arguments were self-serving, especially after they had restricted African American voter access and cast multiple ballots in many places. Nonetheless, the actual ballots did not obviously favor Hayes. In Louisiana, for example, the counting of rejected ballots would have given Tilden the lead. The Democrats had similar data for Florida and South Carolina.

They were not looking to "find" new ballots but demanding that all votes get counted, even if they appeared to be coerced or repeated. The standards for counting or rejecting a ballot varied from state to state, and they changed based on who judged the ballots. With the votes so close and the decisions so dependent on local authorities, the outcome seemed arbitrary. There was no objective count.

The Democrats argued forcefully that it was unfair to give all the contested electors to one side. They only needed one of the twenty electors in dispute for Tilden to become president. They would not give up their fight in Congress or in the streets. Talk of armed insurrection grew among Southern Democrats, encouraged by the many former Confederates in their ranks.

Abram Hewitt, a congressman from New York and chairman of the Democratic Party, warned that "the terrors of civil war were again to be renewed." He and Tilden feared that the most extreme elements were activated by the depth of the perceived injustice. They felt they had lost control of their own party, despite a very disciplined campaign.[25]

Senator Sherman agreed. In a letter to Hayes, he invoked the trauma of Lincoln's election when describing the current moment: "The same influence now rules the House and *its galleries* that did in 1860–61, and I feel that we are to encounter the same enemies that we did then." Sherman gave extra emphasis to the sentiment in the "galleries," alerting Hayes to the spread of militaristic attitudes among angry ex-Confederates, still the heart of the Democratic Party. The 1876 election proved that voting does not heal deep political divisions; it hardens them and often adds to the violence.[26]

As the old battle lines hardened, members of Congress struggled to find a way out. Every elected official remembered the dark days of early 1861, and few wanted to replay that history sixteen years later. Senator Sherman, Representative Garfield, and other leading Republicans began to search for Democrats willing to consider some sort of compromise that would make Hayes president, with conditions. A number of Southern Democrats, many of whom had former connections to the Whig Party, showed tentative interest. Informal discussions began in December, often mediated through respected journalists.

Former Confederates were never personally committed to Tilden. He had spent his entire career in New York, with few connections to their region. Although he echoed white supremacist arguments about the "higher type of mankind" and its right to special privileges, he was neither a former slaveholder nor a part of the landed gentry. He was an urban professional who made his money through finance—precisely the kind of politician who inspired resentments from figures like Benjamin Tillman. When the men in white sheets and red shirts terrorized the South Carolina and Georgia countryside, they did not think they were following the governor of New York. In 1876, Tilden's leadership of the party of the Confederacy was circumstantial, at best.

The contested election changed the circumstances. Southern Democratic leaders stared at the possibility of another Republican president or another military conflict, or both. Without conceding defeat in the election, former Confederates looked to secure their priorities. They clarified their demands in return for accepting Hayes as a possible president. What they wanted was to ensure that a Hayes presidency would be much more like Andrew Johnson's than Grant's or Lincoln's.[27]

The most obvious and important Southern demand was the removal of the U.S. Army. Democrats wanted all remaining federal soldiers in

Florida, Louisiana, South Carolina, and other former Confederate states withdrawn, and they wanted pledges of no future interference in local politics. This meant a renunciation of the Ku Klux Klan Act and other enforcement laws by the new president. Like Johnson, Hayes would be expected to stymie congressional legislation.

Southern Democrats also wanted to strip the executive branch of "carpetbaggers" and African Americans appointed to work on issues affecting their states. This demand required a rapid reversal of former attorney general Amos Akerman's heroic efforts to build a U.S. Department of Justice presence in the South to protect citizens' rights. Federally appointed sheriffs and marshals who showed sympathy for mistreated African American citizens would be purged.

Southern Democrats wanted to accompany these removals with the presence of at least one of their members in the president's cabinet. That would guarantee patronage appointments to their supporters throughout the region. For the first time since secession, former Confederates might gain control of the federal appointments they cared most about.

And they wanted money. All political deals involve the transfer of cash, in some form. The Civil War had impoverished many former wealthy Southern communities, and it deepened the suffering of the already poor. Although Democrats criticized U.S. government intervention in their region, they still wanted resources from the U.S. Treasury. They demanded extensive federal subsidies to help white communities improve their conditions. Claims about "states' rights" were really calls for more public resources, not less, but without federal conditions attached. Then and now, the loudest critics of "big government" were often the recipients of the most benefits.

Democrats wanted the new president to sponsor economic development in their region, following the model of federal investments in the West. This plan included rebuilding the expensive levies along the Mississippi River to prevent flooding and facilitate transportation. Well-connected Southern businessmen demanded their own railroad subsidies, particularly for the proposed Texas and Pacific Railway, which would transport cotton from East Texas to the shores of Southern California. The wealthy supporters of the Democratic Party who invested in the railroads would, of course, benefit most from the federal subsidies. These government financing plans marked the beginning of a century of lucrative government investments in the South without any civil rights conditions attached.

In late December, Hayes was briefed in detail on the negotiations. He did not reject the Southern proposals. He was careful not to accept them either. He deftly encouraged continued discussions while he waited to see how Congress reacted to the competing electoral votes. Hayes conveyed clear sympathy for Southern Democrats and a willingness to work closely with them, but he gave himself the classic politician's escape—vagueness: "I do not wish to be committed to details. It is so desirable to restore peace and prosperity to the South that I have given a good deal of thought to it. The two things I would be exceptionally liberal about are education and internal improvements of a national character."

Civil rights were the main source of division. Hayes pledged to focus on prosperity—helping white citizens in the South. He hoped that they would share that prosperity with African Americans, but he was clear he would do little to ensure it. He conveyed this position to the negotiators as well: "Too much politics, too little attention to business, is the bane of that part of our country." Southerners recognized Hayes's words as coded language for ignoring race.[28]

President Grant was not intimately involved with the negotiations between Southern Democrats and Hayes's team, but he played an important role in efforts to break the congressional stalemate. Each party objected to the other side's electors from the disputed states. With Republicans in control of the Senate and Democrats in control of the House, Congress could not proceed to count the votes of the electors and announce a new president. Grant encouraged his ally Senator Roscoe Conkling from New York to propose a joint committee that would advise both houses. The president did not expect easy agreement, but he hoped that a new political body would give cover for compromise.

On January 26, 1877—more than two months after Election Day—Congress created an Electoral Commission to help select the next president. Nothing like this had existed in American history before, and its creation raised many hesitations from both Hayes and Tilden. They were desperate, however, to try something.

The composition of the Electoral Commission was entirely partisan. The Senate appointed three Republicans and two Democrats from its ranks. The House appointed three Democrats and two Republicans. Five Supreme Court justices joined the commission as well. Two were known to be loyal Republicans, and two loyal Democrats. The final Supreme Court justice, and the deciding fifteenth vote on the commission, was Joseph Bradley. He had been appointed to the court by President Grant, but Bradley was considered neutral in his politics, or at least as close as someone could be in a very partisan environment.

The fifteen members of the Electoral Commission did not have sole power to choose the next president. Their role was advisory to the Senate and the House of Representatives, who still had to vote separately to accept one set of electors or another for each of the contested states. The Electoral Commission was charged to help determine which electors were most legitimate. To break the stalemate in Congress, the legislation creating the Electoral Commission stipulated that the electors designated as legitimate could only be denied if *both* the Senate and the House of Representatives objected. No longer could one house alone veto certification. The commission would identify the presumed electors, and it would be very hard for either party to reject them. Many Democrats would come to regret this change of procedure.

Throughout the month of February, the Electoral Commission examined the disputed returns, with testimony from both Republicans and Democrats. In separate votes, the commission affirmed the Republican electors in each state. The alternative Democratic electors were rejected. The vote on the Electoral Commission was 8–7 each time, with Judge Bradley joining all the Republicans against all the Democrats. Predictably, the Democratic House of Representatives rejected the commission's findings, but the Senate approved.

That should have made Hayes president, but it didn't. Democrats in the House could not overturn Senate approval of the Republican electors, but they could stall on their final vote. The two branches of

Congress could not meet in joint session to announce the new president until the House completed its work. The Senate, and the country, simply had to wait. Garfield and other Republicans condemned this obstructionist filibuster.

If the House did not vote by March 4, the official Inauguration Day, Grant's term as president would end without a replacement. No one knew what to do if that happened.

The negotiations between Southern Democrats and Republicans, begun in December, saved the republic. Hayes's advisers accepted the demands of their counterparts. On the night of February 26, Sherman, Garfield, and three other confidants of Hayes (all from Ohio) met in Washington's Wormley Hotel with the head of Louisiana's Democratic Party and two Democratic congressmen. Garfield's diary recorded a "political bargain" that he was hesitant to endorse, especially because of the backlash it would inspire from Republican proponents of civil rights.[29]

Garfield's second thoughts were just that. The presidency was a big enough carrot to convince key party figures, especially Hayes, to accept Southern demands. Ohio representative Charles Foster put the agreement in writing: "We can assure you in the strongest possible manner of our great desire to have him [Hayes] adopt such a policy as will give to the people of the States of South Carolina and Louisiana the right to control their own affairs in their own way." Foster confirmed that he and his colleagues were "authorized, from our acquaintance with and knowledge of Governor Hayes" to "pledge ourselves to you for him and that such will be his policy."[30]

Hayes had indeed given his Ohio mafia the power to speak for him, with assurance that he would follow through. Less than two weeks before the Wormley Hotel meeting, he wrote Sherman: "You may say, if you deem it advisable, that you *know* that I will stand by the friendly and encouraging words" for Southern interests "and by all that they imply." Hayes closed his letter by encouraging Sherman to share this message: "You can not express that too strongly."[31]

Many of the details remained vague, at least in writing, but the correspondence made a clear commitment to the core Southern demand:

freedom from federal enforcement of civil rights under President Hayes—what many Southerners called "home rule." Hayes never renounced this agreement, nor did Garfield and others who later expressed regrets. To hold the country together after an unresolved election, the Republicans gave the Democrats much of what they demanded.[32]

In response, a handful of Southern Democrats agreed to force a final vote on the electors in the House of Representatives. During the early hours of March 2, at about 4:00 a.m., Congress finally certified that the governor of Ohio had won 185 electoral votes—one more than Tilden and enough to become the next president of the United States. Almost four months after citizens had voted, the election was over.

Hayes learned that he had triumphed as he traveled by train to the nation's capital from his home in Columbus, Ohio: "At Marysville, near Harrisburg, we were wakened to hear the news that the two houses had counted the last State and that I was declared elected!" President-elect Hayes reached Washington later that morning, around 9:50 a.m., where he was greeted by Senator Sherman and General Sherman (the two most powerful brothers in Washington) and a heavy police guard. He met with President Grant and his cabinet and then traveled to the Capitol, where he made a point of talking with a group of influential Southern Democrats.[33]

The next evening, Hayes took the oath of office in the Executive Mansion, under tight security. Morrison Waite, the chief justice of the Supreme Court, administered the oath a few hours before March 4 because the inauguration date fell on Sunday that year. Grant and Hayes agreed on an early oath to ensure that there was no gap between the expiration of the current president's term at noon and the start of the new president's term immediately after.

Hayes's public inauguration echoed those of Lincoln and Grant, with the same aspiration to unity in a time of conflict. On Monday, March 5, Hayes took the oath again on the East Portico of the Capitol. The *New York Times* described the massive crowd that lined the streets and "thronged" the Capitol, including "colored people" who "insisted on their rights." The newspaper reported that they expressed "approval, hope, and support" for the new president. They needed him.

President Rutherford B. Hayes reads his inaugural address to the assembled crowd at the U.S. Capitol after a divisive, contested election. *Source: Bain News Service*

Despite the optimism, partisan divisions were unmistakable. The *New York Times* recounted that many figures, including two Democratic Supreme Court justices (Nathan Clifford and Stephen Field) who served on the Electoral Commission, "refused to be present." They held to the "partisan feeling that has characterized their actions" and evidently remained quite raw. Hayes's contested rise to the presidency left deep scars in an already divided country.[34]

The election of 1876 was a failure. Turnout was high, but the restrictions on voting and the disputes in counting the ballots made it impossible to know who had more support. The convoluted, decentralized American election process—with separate rules in each state and electors who choose the president after the people had voted—encouraged conflict. There were almost three hundred thousand more ballots counted for Tilden across the country, but not necessarily in the states that mattered for a majority of electors. Under the rules in the Constitution, we still do not know who really won the election. We just know how it ended.

Hayes became president because of a backroom deal that tore away many of the assumptions about representative government—assumptions already undermined in earlier contested elections. The negotiations to make Hayes president occurred between party leaders, with the intention of leaving political differences unresolved and the country permanently divided, largely at the cost of the weakest groups—especially African Americans.

In return for control of the presidency, Republicans kept their end of the bargain. Congress voted to fund the levies on the Mississippi River, new railways, and other infrastructure projects in the South. Federal support included more money for landholders and federal patronage jobs. On taking office, Hayes removed the last U.S. Army forces from the South, and he abandoned federal enforcement of most Reconstruction laws, especially those protecting voting, property, and basic human dignity for African Americans. The hard-fought civil rights accomplishments of Republicans since Appomattox were reversed by their own party leader, collaborating with the veterans of the Confederacy.

Republicans retained national leadership to pursue economic expansion in the North and West, and Democrats regained unchallenged political power in the South. They now controlled all Dixie's governorships, state legislatures, and congressional delegations—in addition to police departments, courts, and school boards. The country was deeply divided by region and party, as it had been before the Civil War. Neither the election nor its outcome served the majority of citizens, or what Abraham Lincoln had articulated as democracy's promise: "government of the people, by the people, for the people."

Instead, the election seeded another "corrupt bargain" among elites, revealing a fatal weakness in the U.S. constitutional system. American democracy concentrated power in the hands of a few, and it excluded more than half the population through restrictions on voting and a Senate and electoral college that represented territories, not people. Southern white men, like Benjamin Tillman, were overrepresented; minorities, women, and the poor were excluded.

The political parties assembled themselves around regional cleavages, creating permanent political antagonisms. There were two Americas: Democratic and Republican. The third America, often unheard and unseen, was the one that included the vast majority of the population who neither voted nor benefited from the government programs that served the few wealthy and well connected.

Hayes inherited these divisions and the negotiated limits on his presidency. He aspired to unite the country but had few options. After a long and hard-fought election, the presidency became his poisoned chalice. He soon felt that way, as did his successors.

CHAPTER 9

Caretaker

The dispute over the 1876 election did not end after Rutherford Hayes became president. Samuel Tilden faded from public view, but other Democrats continued to challenge the legitimacy of the Republican president—"His Fraudulency," as opponents called him. The Democratic House of Representatives passed a resolution denying that Hayes had been elected to the position he now held. Few people contested that Hayes *was* president after the bargain in Congress; many, however, questioned his right to hold the office.

Hayes had his doubts as well. Although he believed that the majority of eligible voters would have supported him if they could vote, the president criticized the election process—including the partisan roles played by local and state officials, as well as the prevalence of bribery and violence. Just a few days after citizens voted, Hayes complained in his diary about the chaos accompanying American elections. He called for "amendments of the Constitution" or "proper legislation, against a recurrence of the danger."[1]

Hayes was remarkably open in his concerns. His inaugural address described the "closeness" and "uncertainty" of the election. To the surprise of many Republicans, Hayes admitted "good men differ as to the facts and the law no less as to the proper course to be pursued." When discussing the Electoral Commission, which sided with him, Hayes empathized with his adversaries: "Human judgment is never unerring, and is rarely regarded as otherwise than wrong by the unsuccessful party in the contest." Instead of affirming the righteousness of his side against the other, Hayes candidly appealed for peaceful compromise.

He also called for "a change of great importance": "an amendment to the Constitution prescribing a term of six years for the Presidential office and forbidding a reelection." The purpose of this proposal was to liberate the elected president from the continuing ties of party. In principle, a single-term president was beholden to no one for his future. He could unify the country and focus on the general welfare, as the founders intended.[2]

Andrew Jackson had advocated major changes to American elections in his first message to Congress almost fifty years earlier. He had called for direct popular election of the president in a single national vote: "As few impediments as possible should exist to the free operation of the public will." Jackson excluded African Americans, American Indians, and many others from participation. A simpler process would allow fewer opportunities for local tampering with the results. It would also give clear legitimacy to the candidate with the most total votes across the country.[3]

Hayes did not echo Jackson's proposal in precise detail, especially because it was the votes of electors and not the popular vote that had made him president. He searched for a nonpartisan alternative— "integrity and intelligence"—to the hyper-partisan battles all around him. If Jackson appealed to the popular base of the Democratic Party for legitimacy, Hayes wanted to build his presidency around some kind of broader consensus, even though the country was deeply divided. In his diary, Hayes criticized "extreme party action," especially from Republicans. "Moderation," he wrote, was the "only chance."[4]

Hayes was both pragmatic and idealistic, and many would say that he was also naive. After a bitterly contested election, he desperately wanted to escape or to wish away the hardened divisions that surrounded his rise to power.

The former governor of Ohio was well known for his midwestern sobriety, quite literally. He and his wife (the original "Lemonade Lucy") did not drink, they lived simply, and they spoke plainly. For many

Republicans, Hayes offered a welcome example of modesty and integrity after the corruption swirling around Grant's administration.

Hayes's inaugural address did not skirt the divisive issue of race. He spoke idealistically of how "a moral obligation rests upon the National Government to employ its constitutional power and influence to establish the rights of the people it has emancipated, and to protect them in the enjoyment of those rights when they are infringed or assailed." Hayes defended the principle of universal male suffrage and public education, but he admitted that federal action would not follow his strong words. He rejected President Grant's use of the U.S. Army to enforce civil rights. Hayes pledged that the "superstructure of beneficent local government can be built up, and not otherwise," and he emphasized that "local self-government" was the "true resource" of democracy, the wellspring for the "contentment and prosperity of their citizens."

The president recognized the obvious and uncomfortable contradiction: that in the South, the local governments he championed had supported the resistance he condemned. Hayes hoped the contradiction would resolve itself because his administration would not actively address it, and his speech departed into what for a plainspoken Ohio man was clearly magical thinking: "It is my earnest desire to regard and promote their truest interest—the interests of the white and of the colored people both and equally—and to put forth my best efforts in behalf of a civil policy which will forever wipe out in our political affairs the color line and the distinction between North and South."

In his inaugural address, his diary, and subsequent speeches, Hayes called his vision of change "pacification"; *self-delusion* might have been a more accurate description. Despite all the evidence to the contrary, Hayes believed that he could somehow persuade civil rights activists, Ku Klux Klansmen, and everyone in between.[5]

Hayes badly underestimated the depth of the country's partisan divisions. He simply could not persuade the white supremacists who dominated the Democratic Party to accept their former slaves as equal, or even near-equal, citizens. This was not a point of negotiation for former Confederates, like Benjamin Tillman, who now had more control over their state governments than in any period since Appomattox. In South Carolina, for example, the Red Shirts widened their vigilante activities against African Americans. They collaborated with state militias, murdered opponents, and consistently escaped prosecution under the watch of friendly judges.

Just one year after Hayes took office, the *Edgefield Advertiser*, published in Tillman's hometown, extolled the heroism of violent men who led "the struggle for supremacy between the races." It openly encouraged its readers to join the war for white rule. This aggressive language spread throughout the South, cowering more inclusive voices. The region became increasingly hostile to the basic rights of African Americans.[6]

Hayes had withdrawn U.S. Army forces from South Carolina and Louisiana, as promised in the deal to make him president. Instead of winning goodwill, this retreat had liberated racial violence. Tillman and other Democrats treated the departure of the army as a long-overdue vindication for their resistance to Northern intervention. Their resistance had prevailed, and now they had finally sent Lincoln's and Grant's soldiers home. Local violence and intolerance appeared to work; compromise seemed unnecessary and contrary to their goals.

Hayes initially denied this reality. As he "ordered away" the troops, he expressed "hope for peace and what is equally important, security and prosperity for the colored people." He recounted in his diary that he planned "to get from those states by their governors, legislatures, press, and people pledges that the Thirteenth, Fourteenth, and Fifteenth Amendments shall be faithfully observed; that the colored people shall have equal rights to labor, education, and the privileges of citizenship."[7]

Although the president was "confident this is good work," he had little leverage over the influential figures who promoted the Red Shirts and other violent groups. He told himself that he would "maintain the authority of the United States and keep the peace between the contending parties," but he never explained how. He repeatedly invoked the phrase *peaceful methods*, without details about what those methods were or if they existed at all. He had no plan and quickly found that he had backed himself into a corner.[8]

Hayes raised expectations that compromise with Southern Democrats would be possible once U.S. Army forces retreated. He blamed the soldiers who protected peace and civil rights for the violence of their adversaries and intentionally neglected the reason they had been deployed in the first place. The misrepresentation of federal law enforcement efforts was dishonest and self-serving.

The argument that the army provoked Southern resistance was designed to justify withdrawal, despite continued lawbreaking. It allowed a way out for Republicans who cared about civil rights but not enough to continue paying the costs of enforcement. They could focus on other priorities, including Northern business expansion, and pretend they were not ignoring racial violence. It was a convenient fiction.

Hayes promoted this lie. He had to—it was the only way out of the contested election, the only path to his presidency. It is hard to assess how much he convinced himself of the distortion and how much he knowingly created a false impression. Regardless, it is clear that he recognized withdrawing federal forces would increase violence against African Americans, and he let that happen.

Hayes's diary is filled with passages in which he demands both a withdrawal of the U.S. Army in the South and more law enforcement in the region. He repeatedly advocates giving white men the right to rule themselves and guaranteeing the protection of African American citizens. In one sentence, he proclaims that "local self-government means the determination by each State for itself of all questions as to its own local affairs," only for his next sentence to add: "The real thing to be achieved is safety and prosperity for the colored people."[9]

The two thoughts were as incompatible as slavery and free labor were in Lincoln's time, but unlike his predecessor, Hayes refused to admit the contradiction. He pretended otherwise, and many other Republicans joined the charade. His policy extolled progress through compromise, but it really allowed regression. It was a principled retreat—in the sense that Northern principles retreated.

The Southern Democrats did not demobilize, they did not pursue peace with African American citizens in their communities, and they did not seek to rebuild a trusting relationship with the federal government. Just the opposite. They exploited the power vacuum created by the federal retreat to advance their power and to diminish all African American and Republican challengers. The struggle for racial inclusion in the South—the central issue of the Civil War—suffered its largest setback since Appomattox when Hayes removed his troops from the key sites of battle.

The president's commitment to "local self-government" was hardly absolute. As he removed soldiers from the South, he deployed more federal forces in Northern cities than any president since Lincoln confronted draft riots in 1863. The summer of 1877 was much worse.

In July, Northern railroad workers began to strike on various lines, protesting poor working conditions, reduced pay, and callous indifference from the wealthy owners of what were the largest American corporations. The troubles began in Martinsburg, West Virginia, on July 16, 1877, when workers stopped the trains at this high-traffic junction for the Baltimore and Ohio Railroad. Local police could not handle the strikers, so the governor mobilized a state militia and requested U.S. Army support.

The head of the railroad, John Garrett, made similar demands to the U.S. president. He called the strike an "insurrection," even though the workers made no demands to overthrow anyone from power. They only sought better pay and treatment in the workplace.[10]

Hayes was responsive to Garrett and the needs of Northern business leaders in ways unimaginable for African Americans facing graver dangers in the South. Hayes ignored the demands of the strikers and approved military intervention to force them back to work. Three hundred federal troops arrived in Martinsburg on July 19 to restore order and assist strikebreaking substitutes brought in to drive the trains.

The arrival of federal forces sparked wide resistance, especially from poor, white laborers across the country. Within days, more than one hundred thousand railroad workers in cities as far away as Chicago and Omaha went on strike. Miners, dockworkers, bakers, and other wage laborers left their jobs out of sympathy and in opposition to what they viewed as government-supported tyranny by big business. The cities of

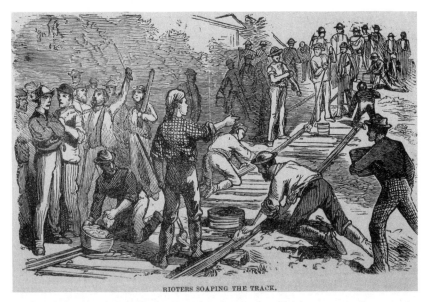

RIOTERS SOAPING THE TRACK.

Striking workers (called "rioters" in this drawing) rubbed soap on railway tracks to make it difficult for trains to move, particularly up steep grades. *Source: Annals of the Great Strikes in the United States (Chicago: L. T. Palmer, 1877)*

St. Louis and Pittsburgh were essentially shut down, taken over by workers. Some observers saw echoes of the Paris Commune of 1871 in what was widely called the "Great Strike." The sympathetic *Pittsburgh Leader* proclaimed a new "civil war in this country, between labor and capital."[11]

Hayes and his closest advisers saw it that way too. In cabinet meetings, they spoke of the "riots" and "mobs" that threatened commerce, including the delivery of the mail by the railroads. The latter was the legal justification the administration used to force the trains back into service. Hayes's handwritten notes show that he was ready to send the army wherever order was threatened in the North. On July 26, for instance, he commented favorably on sending troops to Indiana, Pennsylvania, Illinois, and Wisconsin. The army eventually entered cities in fourteen states. Many of the soldiers sent to repress the strikers had recently left garrisons in the South.[12]

By August 1, most railway lines were restored and most strikers had returned to work. Many did so with guns pointed at them by the U.S. Army, accompanied by local police and vigilante groups. The workers did not get the increased wages or the better conditions that they had demanded. More than one hundred people had died from violence during the strikes; many more were injured.

The resentment of workers did not dissipate as they returned to their jobs. The next three decades would witness a series of large-scale strikes by the growing population of men and women who toiled in factories, mines, and railways to fuel the growth of the American economy. This was a generation of what Lincoln had called "penniless beginners," and they pursued the Republican promise of wealth through hard work, but they frequently felt that they did not see the fruits of their labor. They remained poor as the men who owned the corporations—men like Cornelius Vanderbilt, Andrew Carnegie, and George Pullman—became unimaginably rich. Only a very select few owned the gold in the Gilded Age. By 1894, with another national strike beginning near Pullman's headquarters in Illinois, violence between workers and their employers had become pervasive in the Northern cities first shut down during the Great Strike.

The U.S. Army consistently stepped in to force workers back to their jobs. It became the most powerful instrument for protecting the property of business owners and ensuring the functioning of the American economy. Hayes set the precedent in 1877. He renounced military enforcement of civil rights in the South, but he promoted the use of soldiers to keep workers on the job in the North. The federal government had two separate military policies, entrenching two cultures of violence—one vigilante-based for keeping African Americans down, another centralized for keeping industrial labor controlled. Both policies favored the white elites who owned the land and the factories.

Hayes's commitment to military withdrawal and local self-government was not as consistent or benign as he made it sound. He rationalized inaction against Black repression and then reversed himself when intervention was necessary to quell labor unrest. For all his conciliatory rhetoric, Hayes used force not to unite but to divide.

The president continued to talk of bringing the country together. In September 1877, he embarked on a nineteen-day tour of the Southern states—the first Northern-born president to spend so much time in the region since the start of the Civil War. He covered almost three thousand miles by train and horse-drawn carriage, visiting Virginia, Georgia, Tennessee, and Kentucky, before going north to his home in Ohio. His wife, Lucy, three cabinet members, and two governors joined the traveling party. The trip was grueling, and Hayes made a point of speaking to large audiences filled with former Confederates. He wanted them to embrace him as their president.

Hayes's goal was reconciliation. He wanted credit from Southerners for withdrawing federal troops, and he asked for their adherence to basic protections for African Americans. If former Confederates showed their adherence to the Constitution, Hayes believed that Northerners would renounce future interventions. "Our aspiration," he wrote, "is for the reign of peace and goodwill over the whole of our recently agitated (disturbed) and afflicted land."[13]

The president told African American audiences that they were better off without protection from the U.S. Army: "I believe that your rights and interests would be safer if this great mass of intelligent white men were left alone by the general government." Then he falsely claimed that Southern Democrats have "no desire to invade the rights of colored people." Listeners must have wondered how he could deny the obvious.[14]

That was the president's hope—to talk away the pervasive racial brutality. He appealed to what he called the "better classes" of Southern white gentlemen, whom he believed were potential Republican voters. By showing goodwill and placing his faith in them, he hoped they would lead public opinion against the "ruffian class, the implacables, and the press"—the violent supporters of the Ku Klux Klan and the Red Shirts. The "better classes" would welcome the removal of federal "bayonets," push out the vigilantes, and restore lawful governance. Hayes expected them to perceive the constitutional protections for African Americans as a lever for boosting themselves over the lower groups of white citizens. The president proposed a partnership of well-reasoned elites against the violent extremes.[15]

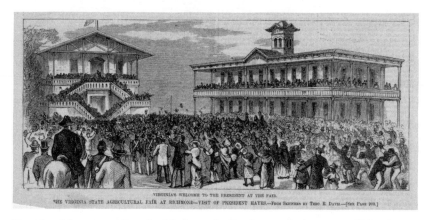

VIRGINIA'S WELCOME TO THE PRESIDENT AT THE FAIR.
"THE VIRGINIA STATE AGRICULTURAL FAIR AT RICHMOND—VISIT OF PRESIDENT HAYES.—From Sketches by Theo. R. Davis.—[See Page 909.]

President Hayes was pleased with the enthusiastic crowds that greeted him during his Southern tour. The politeness of the crowds disguised the violent opposition to his calls for civil rights and reconciliation. *Source: Richmond Nineteenth-Century Print Collection, Virginia Commonwealth University Libraries*

If the North could restrain its instinct to intervene, couldn't the South restrain its impulse to exclude?

Large cheering crowds greeted the president in most places. Many listeners heard only one part of the message—the renunciation of federal intervention *or* the support for civil rights. Hayes saw what he wanted to see—evidence of popular sentiment for reconciliation, even partnership. Caught up in the moment, he wrote the most exuberant diary entry of his presidency: "Received everywhere heartily. The country is again one and united! I am very happy to be able to feel that the course taken has turned out so well."[16]

The president's friends reinforced these triumphant words. William Henry Smith, a journalist and longtime adviser to Hayes, sent him a letter calling the trip his "greatest success." Smith praised the president's speeches for their directness and personal touch. He believed the "implacables are at last dumbfounded. They never believed that you would talk plainly to the Southern people of the Constitutional amendments and education as you did. Let them pass. They are now powerless for evil."[17]

Hayes was not the last president to believe that his words moved opponents when they didn't. He had only persuaded those in his circle who did not need persuading. He had not broken new ground in convincing white Southern listeners—including "the better classes"—that they had to change their ways. If anything, the praise from the president gave former Confederates cover to continue on their current path. Congressman James Garfield was more accurate than Smith when he observed that his fellow Ohioan had lent Democrats respectability and alienated Republicans who cared about civil rights. Hayes was "losing friends every hour," without new partners to be found in the still hostile, if superficially polite, South.[18]

The elections for Congress and state offices in 1878 echoed Garfield's premonitions. Southern Democrats followed the old Confederate script, and it worked. State officials depicted Hayes's defense of constitutional rights as yet another round of Yankee interference in their communities. Congressmen described his calls for unity as disguised repression. They praised themselves, not Hayes, for forcing the removal of U.S. Army soldiers.

Just as Republicans continued to campaign in the North on their heroic commitment to the Union, Democrats ran hard in the South on their unbending defense of white supremacy. Resistance to a Republican president, especially one selected in contested circumstances, was an intoxicating platform for former Confederates. Hayes was, in fact, a very useful villain for motivating voters who connected him with the hated policies of Lincoln and Grant.

Without the army and Justice Department on the ground, Republicans could not organize their voters. African American participation continued to plummet as white turnout remained very high—near 80 percent. Southern Democrats remained loyal to their party, backing violent advocates of Black repression throughout the region. They enthusiastically attended rallies, joined marches to intimidate opponents, and came out to vote. Hayes's appeals to moderation and compromise had a negligible effect. The South only became more solidly Democratic after 1876.[19]

Hayes's opponents used the circumstances of his election as a reminder of the perceived Republican injustice against their region. In May 1878—just six months before the next Election Day—the

Democratic majority in the House empowered a special committee, headed by New York congressman and next-door neighbor of Samuel Tilden, Clarkson Potter. Known as the Potter Committee, the eleven-member group was charged "to inquire into the alleged fraudulent canvass and return of votes at the last presidential election in the states of Louisiana and Florida." Democrats later expanded the charge to include additional states.[20]

New evidence of bribery and other malfeasance had emerged, but no one expected the committee to resolve the disputed votes. The real purpose of the investigation was to diminish Hayes's authority and motivate angry voters to come out for Democratic candidates. Republican claims that they were the party of the Constitution became less persuasive when evidence circulated showing their own unconstitutional behavior—including bribery of state officials and efforts to reject Democratic ballots. The inquiry also detracted from Hayes's efforts to push reconciliation. How could Democrats reconcile with someone they believed stole power from them?

Hayes's diary took a dark turn during the ten months of Potter Committee hearings. He realized, at last, that the leaders of the Democratic Party were determined to resist his overtures and exploit his weaknesses. Anger and resentment motivated Democratic voters, and candidates believed that more of both would improve their prospects. The president wanted to move on from the contested election, but his opponents had every reason to dig up all the dirt they could find. Hayes lamented that his hopes for reconciliation would be extinguished by a "partisan proceeding for merely partisan ends."[21]

He grew more alarmed as Democratic newspapers speculated about his possible removal from office: "There is a purpose with the real authors to reverse the result of the last election. If they are sustained in the elections there is danger. It is another rebellion!" Hayes called the Potter Committee an act of "civil war": "I should defend my office and the independence of the Executive against any intruder."[22]

The president finally understood that the Civil War was not over. The Potter Committee was a new battlefield, dominated by Democratic members of Congress. They began every day looking to land body blows against the president and his Republican supporters. They had no interest in reconciliation or compromise. They were after blood for the sake of protecting their white voters against any federal limits. If Lee fought to defend Southern secession, the Potter Committee was part of an organized campaign for white democracy and resistance to any forms of multiracial inclusion.

In more than two hundred interviews, the Potter Committee interrogated politicians close to Hayes, including Senator John Sherman and Representative James Garfield. It also acquired hundreds of telegrams, many written in cipher by campaign officials. All this material was released to the press, and it turned the 1878 congressional elections into a replay of 1876. Voters were asked to cast their ballots based on who they believed was telling the truth, when no one really was. As a result, the electorate largely defaulted to partisan loyalties.

The country split again. The Democrats lost nine seats in the House of Representatives, but they still maintained a slim majority. In the Senate, the Democrats were able to win a majority for the first time since before the Civil War. They benefited from the retirement of six incumbent Republican senators in states with Democratic legislatures. Although very few votes shifted, the Democrats gained control of both houses of Congress, isolating the president and his party. Hayes's popularity among Republicans plummeted from his failure to generate more votes. He was now a president very much on his own.

Hayes had begun his presidency seeking to escape the divisions surrounding his election, but he quickly became a victim of them. His moderation was exploited by Democrats and rejected by Republicans. Violence and voter suppression increased in the South under his watch. Republicans did not benefit from promised civil rights advances or improved economic conditions. Hayes's rejection of traditional patronage in pursuit of a nonpartisan civil service meant that many party leaders, especially Maine senator James Blaine and New York senator Roscoe Conkling, felt they did not get the personal benefits they deserved from a Republican president.

Hayes's nonpartisan ambitions undermined his power in a highly partisan moment. Reconciliation sounded nice, but it was not possible.

Arguably, it was an irresponsible dream. Hayes learned from the 1878 midterm elections that he had to use his powers in more determined ways to push back against Southern lawbreaking, even as he tried to avoid a return to military occupation. By the time he realized this, it was too late to shift course. The Democrats controlled Congress, all the state legislatures in the South, and several in the North. The U.S. Army and the Justice Department were largely absent from the region, and Hayes could not send them back.

Hayes had signed the Posse Comitatus Act in June 1878, which severely constrained his powers as commander in chief. Under the act, the president could no longer deploy the army "for the purpose of executing the laws." Any enforcement of the law by the military against disobedient states and citizens required express authorization from the text of the Constitution or a special act of Congress. Hayes had reached out to the South by withdrawing federal forces, and now Democrats had cut off his arm. After 1878, many Republicans regretted the president's approval of this act, which has remained a source of controversy ever since—including during recent moments of national protest and organized insurrection.[23]

Sensing weakness in Hayes, Democrats pushed for still more restrictions on federal power. Looking toward the next presidential election, the party of the Confederacy wanted to ensure that a Republican could not win. In addition to the removal of U.S. Army forces, they sought to eliminate all federal supervision of elections for national offices. States alone would set the rules for who voted and how ballots were counted. There would be no federal marshals or observers. In cases of violence, federal judges would not have any jurisdiction, and federal soldiers would not be available for emergency needs. For those seeking to run for office, Democrats demanded the end of the mandatory "test oath," instituted by Congress in 1862, requiring all federal officeholders to declare their loyalty to the U.S. government and renounce any acts of disloyalty.

For obvious reasons, Hayes opposed these measures, designed to replace illegal voter repression in the South with legal and permanent exclusion of African Americans and other Republican voters. Exasperated, Hayes commented in his diary: "Constitutional provisions which guarantee equal citizenship have been practically nullified."[24]

The president and members of his party rallied to prevent further erosion of basic voting rights in the South. There was no more talk of reconciliation or moderation after 1878. Hayes was now entering a war to defend the basic law enforcement powers of the federal government, which had been the foundation for all Lincoln's and Grant's actions. The future of a united democracy was at stake if one party was determined to give states the ability to defy the Constitution and prevent free elections.

In his strongest language yet, Hayes announced: "No means within my power will be spared to obtain a full and fair investigation of the alleged crimes" against lawful voters. He spoke of peace but no longer through compromise. The president now sought to force white supremacists to accept a more open democracy.[25]

Democrats in Congress doubted Hayes's resolve. They used their control over government spending to coerce the president into approving a prohibition on any federal enforcement of election laws. In 1878, House Democrats had attached the Posse Comitatus Act as a rider to the annual appropriations bill for the army. If the Republican Senate and the president wanted money for the army, they had to accept restrictions on its use. Hayes agreed because he did not intend to deploy the army for law enforcement, as Grant had before him. He saw this as a onetime agreement, but Democrats treated it as a starting point for the wider restrictions they wanted on federal authority.

In the early weeks of the new year, Democrats refused to pass legislation to keep the army and other government employees paid unless Republicans accepted new riders that eliminated the use of civilian agencies for election law enforcement. The states would have full freedom to conduct elections as they wished; the federal government would have no recourse. Since Republicans controlled the U.S. Senate until March 4, 1879, when the newly elected Democratic majority would be inaugurated, they rejected this proposal, and it died temporarily in the upper chamber.

Most years, members of Congress did not meet after March 4 until December, but President Hayes called a rare special session on March 18 to address the needed government expenditures. Without any action, the money available for federal spending would run out on June 30. The Democrats now controlled both houses of Congress so they could manage all legislation, but Hayes made it clear that he would oppose any concessions on federal election laws.

Hayes condemned Democratic hardball tactics as a "revolutionary" attack on the constitutional powers of the president. Ironically, he echoed Andrew Johnson, who had resisted congressional efforts to force reform on the president when the Republicans were in control a decade earlier. Now Hayes was resisting Democratic domination. "No precedent shall be established," he vowed, "to coercion of the Executive." In perhaps the most defiant words of his presidency, he wrote: "I must resist it to the last extremity."[26]

Like Johnson, Hayes relied on his veto powers. Unlike his predecessor, he had the advantage of a large enough minority in both houses to prevent a veto override. Five times, Hayes rejected congressional legislation that tied government expenditures to the nullification of federal election laws. No president vetoed essentially the same piece of legislation so many times. Hayes faced potential impeachment, but he knew that he was secure from conviction because Democrats could not cross the needed two-thirds threshold. This latest struggle between the congressional majority and the president produced a deadlock familiar from the previous decade. The conflict had not changed very much; the parties had only traded institutional beachheads on different sides of Pennsylvania Avenue.

"If the proposed legislation should become the law," Hayes explained in one of his veto messages, "the National Government will be powerless to enforce its own statutes." This would mean the end of the Union as Lincoln understood it. The conditions the Democrats placed on appropriations would lead to what Hayes called "a consolidation of unchecked and despotic power in the House of Representatives. A bare majority of the House will become the Government. The Executive will no longer be what the framers of the Constitution intended—an equal and independent branch of the Government."[27]

That was the goal of former Confederates since Booth's assassination of Lincoln: to diminish the power of the president and increase the freedom for states to ignore federal laws. Through the spring of 1879, Democrats repeatedly threatened to shut down the entire U.S. government, holding up appropriations for the military, the judicial branch, and all executive agencies until the president agreed to nullify the federal election laws. Hayes continued to resist, with the backing of Republicans in Congress. He began to feel that his vetoes had restored his popularity within his own party at least. Standing up to the Democrats drew praise from those who had criticized him only months before. The *New York Herald*, a frequent detractor, commended his "cool hand" and "shrewd" maneuvers. It was Hayes's best press since he entered office.[28]

After months of gridlock, the Democrats backed down because, in the end, they needed the federal government too. White Southerners were dependent on Washington's money for railroads and river levees, as well as food, cotton, and other purchases by federal agencies, especially the army and navy. The national government was a big customer for Southern agriculture and industry. Federal judges also played essential roles in business and criminal disputes that crossed state lines.

Denying federal appropriations was perhaps most harmful to the region still trying to rebuild from the economic devastation of the past two decades. Those who hated the national government needed it most, and they could not cope without it.

In the days before June 30, 1879, when the money ran out, the Democrats in Congress finally passed legislation to fund the military and most of the federal government. Hayes welcomed but also condemned them for their retreat. "The Democrats instead of squarely backing out of their awkward position, or manfully sticking to it, seem disposed to creep out of it in a way to enable them to say that they have gained something by their contest." Although they recognized the limits of their power, the Democrats continued to trumpet demands for freedom from all federal requirements. They retreated but did not admit defeat, continuing their two-decade-long struggle to protect an exclusive democracy for the few in the South.

To symbolize their continued resistance, Southern Democrats insisted on denying pay to federal marshals when they enforced election laws. They funded every other service except this one. Hayes continued to appoint marshals across the country, and they still collected salaries, but they would now have to "volunteer" when working around election facilities. The strange arrangement allowed the Democrats to claim that they had cut federal funding for election enforcement, even though they had not cut personnel or changed the law.

Hayes felt vindicated, but it was a hollow win—the victory of a man willing to celebrate that he has avoided a greater defeat. He confessed to his diary: "I am now experiencing one of the 'ups' of political life. Congress adjourned on [July] 1st after a session of almost 75 days mainly taken up with a contest against me. Five vetoes, a number of special messages and oral consultations with friends and opponents have been my part of it. At no time—not even after the [Republican Party] nomination at Cincinnati, has the stream of commendation run so full."[29]

Hayes was a controversial president, weakened by his narrow election and then by his strategic ineptitude. He was diminished by the implacable opposition of the Democrats in the South and by his naive failure to recognize that they would not be persuaded to any kind of compromise. Hayes just barely prevented a complete renunciation of civil rights, and he ultimately pushed back somewhat against Democratic efforts to weaken the presidency. He was, however, perpetually on the defensive, and he failed to reverse the damaging trends for African Americans and Republicans.

Hayes's presidency is overlooked because he accomplished so little: His signature move was the withdrawal of Union forces from the South—a colossal mistake. He was a well-intentioned caretaker for a divided democracy, but he was in no way up to the task of managing the divisions he inherited, let alone healing them. He was the wrong commander in chief for the times, who misunderstood the entrenched nature of the conflict. And he lost. His successor would fare even worse.

CHAPTER 10
Death Again

In the late spring of 1879, Rutherford Hayes told his beloved wife, Lucy: "I am heartily tired of this life of bondage, responsibility, and toil. I wish it was at an end! I rejoice that it is to last only a little more than a year-and-a-half longer.'" Hayes would not seek a second term.[1]

He was a badly damaged president. His contested election and his battle with Congress had sucked the energy from him. Fighting to survive left little time for anything else. Hatred of Hayes had only grown among Democrats, especially former Confederates. Republicans appreciated his personal integrity, but his abandonment of the South was frustrating. African Americans did not trust that Hayes would protect them.

The party had an alternative: Ulysses Grant. Since he left the presidency in 1877, the old general's fame had only risen. He spent two and a half years touring the world, meeting with all the major figures in Europe and Asia. American newspapers published frequent accounts of Grant's intimate conversations with the British monarch, the Russian czar, the Ottoman sultan, and the Japanese emperor, among many others. Grant was the first American president treated as an equal by the world's aristocrats. His travels brought pride to Americans, North and South, who believed their country had finally arrived at the pinnacle of civilization. Grant encouraged this perception when he commented: "The attentions I am receiving are intended more for our country than for me."[2]

In the years after his presidency, Ulysses Grant traveled around the world, meeting with foreign leaders, including Chinese general and diplomat Li Hongzhang. Note the aristocratic appearance of this photo. Grant's world tour was covered widely in American newspapers. *Credit: Liang Shitai, Japan, 1879*

That was only partially true. Grant used his travels to escape the miseries of his last years in the presidency. But as he sailed from one foreign port to another, he kept his eyes on the United States and the possibility of a return to the nation's highest office. After the Democrats captured both houses of Congress in November 1878 and began their efforts to nullify federal election laws, Grant wrote from Paris to Elihu Washburne, a leading Republican politician in Illinois: "It seems to me to put the Republican party right for [18]80. Providence seems to direct that something should be done just in time to save the party of progress and national unity and equality."[3]

Washburne and other Republicans agreed. They were already working to resurrect the Civil War hero, once more, to boost their party. They believed that only Grant could motivate Northern voters and push back against Democratic offenses, especially in Congress. In the fall of 1878, Republican Party meetings in Illinois and other states witnessed large crowds of attendees waving "Grant for President in 1880" banners. The former president encouraged these crowds.[4]

Grant timed his return to the United States for the early fall of 1879, one year before the next presidential election. His ship docked in San Francisco on September 20 and was greeted with a boisterous welcome, including foghorns, factory whistles, and cheering crowds onshore. A parade of smaller sailing ships escorted his steamship into the city as cannons fired off in celebration. It felt like the arrival of a king.

"From the pier," Grant's wife, Julia, recounted, "we drove through vast throngs of people who greeted the General with enthusiastic cheers again and again, and which were renewed as my carriage passed until I was compelled to half-rise many times in acknowledgment of their hearty and glorious welcome." The Grants rested in "luxurious apartments" provided for free by the city. "Every moment of General Grant's time was taken up in receiving delegations, committees, and the different officials of most royal San Francisco."[5]

Grant remained the "popular favorite" as he traveled throughout the country for the next nine months, meeting with enthusiastic crowds and enjoying lavish banquets in his honor. In Chicago, for example, he rode at the head of a parade that included three thousand soldiers. He gave several speeches and attended a dinner for the six hundred most powerful people in the growing city at the Palmer House Hotel. The event lasted until early the next morning, and it included countless toasts to Grant as a warrior, a leader, and a man of the people. Mark Twain attended the extravaganza and commented: "I doubt if America has ever seen anything quite equal to it. I am well satisfied I shall not live to see its equal again."[6]

Grant traveled east from Chicago in a custom-built railway car. He eventually made his way south to Jacksonville, Savannah, New Orleans, Galveston, San Antonio, and other cities in the heart of the old Confederacy. Each of these communities had thousands of families who lost husbands and sons at the hands of Grant's Union army. They had received President Hayes politely two years earlier, but now the enthusiasm for Grant was much greater. Julia recounted that in Texas her husband was "greeted with hearty cheers and a great tossing up of wide-brimmed hats."[7]

Southern resistance to civil rights had not receded, and resentment toward the North was as sharp as ever. Remembering Lincoln's assassination less than a decade and a half earlier, Julia feared for her husband's safety. Grant was, however, a celebrity—a figure of fascination even among his enemies. He drew more attention than any other politician. He was the presumptive Republican nominee for president, again, in 1880.

The Republican Convention opened in Chicago in June. Grant's support was strong and consistent, led by New York senator Roscoe Conkling, who controlled access to the wealthiest and best-connected members of the party—most of whom served in Grant's prior administrations and looked forward to lucrative government appointments again. These were the same men associated with the corruption of the early 1870s.

The Grant "stalwarts," as they called themselves, faced determined opposition from another faction of the party, following Maine senator James Blaine. This second group opposed the old patronage system protected by Grant. They sought to open the party to new figures, based on merit. They favored civil service reform, originally championed by President Hayes, to turn government employees into experts rather than appoint friends of powerful figures.

A third, smaller faction allied with Treasury Secretary John Sherman and backed civil service reform but not with the same zeal as Blaine's supporters. Sherman's group reassembled Hayes's "Ohio mafia" and reminded party members that the Buckeye State was essential for Republican presidential prospects. These midwesterners showed deference to Grant, but they voiced concerns about the stench of corruption around his supporters. They also noted the public expectation that a president would serve no more than two terms. This was a tradition created by George Washington, and it remained compelling for many voters who suspected anyone in power too long. The Republican Party's small-town roots still held tight to this wisdom.

Grant had the most votes at the convention but never enough to win the party nomination; Blaine's and Sherman's supporters denied him a majority in thirty-five consecutive ballots. The convention was deadlocked. Out of desperation, Grant's opponents came together behind an alternative: James Garfield.

He was a decorated Civil War veteran who had represented northeastern Ohio in the House of Representatives for almost seventeen years. He was close to Hayes and Sherman, and highly regarded by most Republicans for his hard work and integrity. Garfield was a strong proponent of civil rights, going back to his early opposition to slavery, but he was also a pragmatist who worked well with the moderate wings of the party and industrial leaders in Chicago, Cleveland, Buffalo, and other growing Great Lakes cities. Garfield had fewer enemies than the more prominent party leaders, and that made him attractive to the rank and file.

On June 8, 1880—the seventh day of the convention—Garfield received a majority of the party's votes to become the next Republican nominee for president. Grant's supporters, especially Conkling, did not join the bandwagon. They continued to argue that the former president was the best candidate.

To mollify their opposition, the party nominated a close Conkling confidant, Chester Arthur, as vice president. He was the former tax collector for the port of New York, pushed out of office by President Hayes for alleged corruption. Arthur's selection was small consolation for Grant and Conkling, but it allowed them to maintain some control over party leadership.

Garfield was the rare presidential candidate who was honest when he wrote that he "neither sought nor desired the nomination." He was, however, ambitious and believed that he could promote prosperity, civil rights, and freedom—the core Republican principles. Seeking Grant's support, Garfield told the former president: "I am anxious to do my whole duty to the country."[8]

He managed his campaign from his farm in Mentor, Ohio, northeast of Cleveland. Garfield followed the model of previous candidates, staying close to home and relying mostly on surrogates to sell his life story to the public. The Republican Party sent speakers to nearly every town, published countless newspaper articles, and circulated numerous biographies. Horatio Alger, the famous writer of "rags-to-riches" fables for boys, penned a powerful yarn about the candidate. It was based in fact, but the portrait was idealized for an audience eager to find hope in their difficult lives.

Garfield was born in a log cabin, the fifth child of a poor, devout settler family on the Ohio frontier. His hardworking father, Abram, died when Garfield was only two—a casualty of pneumonia and poor medical care in a town of six hundred struggling inhabitants. Garfield made it out through hard work, piety, and a little luck—the formula for individual success espoused by the Republican Party. He educated himself, gained professional status as a teacher and lawyer, attained a leadership position in the Union army, and then entered politics with the support of his neighbors, who knew and revered him. Garfield fit the model of the self-made American. He was Lincoln's "penniless beginner" who benefited from the opportunities of an open, inclusive society. (Abraham Lincoln's image replaced the memory of the other Abram in Garfield's early life.)

Garfield's story was compelling, but it was not enough. He recognized that he could only win by uniting his party and its voters in the North and West. He had to motivate them after four uninspiring years. In contrast to Hayes, who had emphasized conciliation with the South, he returned to strong arguments about the rightful power of the federal government and the enforcement of constitutional law. Garfield rejected "the pernicious doctrine of State supremacy, which so long crippled the functions of the national government" and "brought the union very near to destruction."

He was more explicit than Hayes had ever been about the federal government's obligation to act against local violence. "The wounds of the war cannot be completely healed," Garfield explained, "until every citizen, rich or poor, white or black, is secure in the free and equal enjoyment of every civil and equal right guaranteed by the constitution and the laws." Garfield hoped for change but recognized it would require more federal action, not less.

The Republican presidential candidate took direct aim at his Democratic opponents, blaming them for supporting lawlessness and disunity: "The most serious evils which now afflict the South arise from the fact that there is not such freedom and toleration of political opinion and action that the minority party can exercise an effective and wholesome restraint upon the party in power. Without such restraint, party rule becomes tyrannical and corrupt."[9]

Northern audiences remained reluctant to support costly federal interventions in the former Confederacy, but Garfield sensed a growing frustration with Democratic obstructionism, especially in Congress. He recognized that Republican voters no longer accepted the fiction of a self-reforming South once the army departed. To the contrary, former Confederates had shown that they would take advantage of every opportunity to increase their power and repress Republican voters. Garfield never spoke of returning to military enforcement, but he made it clear that he favored a firmer federal hand.

Garfield used his campaign speeches to argue that he would stand up to those who challenged the chief executive. His personal biography showed his toughness against great odds, and that fit with his statements about protecting the Constitution. He was not a flagrant militarist who would expand the long-standing sectional conflict, but he was not a naive pacifier either. Garfield made a strong case for affirmative Republican leadership, lacking since Grant's first election more than a decade earlier.

Election Day on November 2, 1880, drew heavy turnout across the country. More than 75 percent of eligible voters cast ballots, but hundreds of thousands of African Americans in the South were denied their say. In some nearly all-Black counties of Mississippi, Georgia, and South Carolina, the majority of votes cast were from white residents. African Americans were again frequently threatened by white gangs if they tried to vote, and if they voted, their ballots often disappeared.

The results in 1880 were even closer than before. Garfield and his Democratic opponent, Winfield Scott Hancock, split nearly nine million votes in thirty-eight states. The difference in total votes was less than two thousand—a narrower popular vote margin than in any other presidential election in U.S. history.

Each candidate won nineteen states: the Democratic ticket won every Southern state, plus the border states and New Jersey, Delaware, California, and Nevada. The Republican ticket held the rest of the North, including New York and Oregon. The clear regional divide translated into the U.S. Senate, which was evenly divided between the parties. Republicans gained a majority in the House of Representatives, but the margin there was tight.

The popular vote was a virtual tie. "It is very close," Garfield observed in his diary. He became president because the nineteen states that he won had more electoral votes, based on their population, than the nineteen states won by Hancock. The Republican candidate gained 214 electoral votes to the Democrat's 155. Suppression of African American voters in the South surely reduced Garfield's totals there, but the allocation of electors distorted the outcome to his advantage. Garfield's victory, like Hayes's four years earlier, reflected the undemocratic character of American elections.[10]

Garfield lacked a popular mandate or anything close to a national consensus for his leadership. He commented in his diary that President Hayes was "very happy" with the outcome, seeing continuity from one Ohio Republican to another. Garfield's transition was expected to be much smoother than the near disaster in 1876.[11]

But a smooth transition did not translate into easy leadership. The divisions in the electorate had only hardened. As in prior elections, very few citizens changed their votes from one party to the other; their preferences were predictable. What mattered most was who turned out, who didn't, and who couldn't.

Although Democrats generally accepted that Garfield had received the most electoral votes in 1880, they continued to resist presidential and federal power. The virtual tie in the popular vote strengthened their claims against the "winner." Southern Democrats, in particular, wanted to be governed by the white leaders they had voted for overwhelmingly in their states.

President James Garfield. *Credit: Mathew Brady*

Garfield began his presidency with half the country opposed to him, often violently so. Despite that, he spoke of African American rights as essential to the full flowering of free labor. No president since Lincoln was so explicit. Even the poorest-born men, like young Garfield, should work, receive pay for their sweat, and participate fully in American democracy, the new president argued. He offered one of the most powerful statements of this promise in his inaugural address:

> The elevation of the negro race from slavery to the full rights of citizenship is the most important political change we have known since the adoption of the Constitution of 1787. No thoughtful man can fail to appreciate its beneficent effect upon our institutions and people. It has freed us from the perpetual danger of war and dissolution. It has added immensely to the moral and industrial forces of our people. It has liberated the master as well as the slave from a relation which

wronged and enfeebled both. It has surrendered to their own guardianship the manhood of more than 5,000,000 people, and has opened
to each one of them a career of freedom and usefulness. It has given
new inspiration to the power of self-help in both races by making labor
more honorable to the one and more necessary to the other.

He pledged: "So far as my authority can lawfully extend," African
Americans "shall enjoy the full and equal protection of the Constitution and the laws." Garfield called Southern efforts to deny voting
rights a "crime": "If in other lands it be high treason to compass the
death of the king, it shall be counted no less a crime here to strangle
our sovereign power and stifle its voice."[12]

What was Garfield going to do about the frequent Southern crimes
against African Americans and other groups? He matched his tough
language with a striking silence on enforcement. He followed his calls
for protecting constitutional rights with a reminder that he would carefully avoid "invading" what Democrats called the "rights of the states."

Garfield never once mentioned the army or the Justice Department
in his inaugural speech. It was as if he was convinced that his words
alone would somehow create compliance. No one listening could have
believed that, especially after the previous years of consistent resistance.
Although Garfield's language was much stronger than Hayes's, his plan
of action looked eerily similar.

Garfield tried to offer one alternative: universal education. This was
a core Republican proposal, dating back to Lincoln's presidency. Garfield spoke from his own experience of how access to schooling could
open opportunities for prosperity and improve one's commitment to
constitutional principles. He believed that by educating more white
and Black citizens, especially in the South, his administration would
help remove "ignorance and vice," which, he argued, encouraged "corruption and fraud in the suffrage."[13]

Hayes had hoped that he could appeal to "better classes" in the
former Confederacy for reconciliation; Garfield wanted to use federal
resources to create those classes within both races. This was a worthy
and sincere vision, with strong support in many Republican circles, and

it had been the aim of the Freedmen's Bureau in the years after Appomattox. The problem was, again, that Garfield offered no mechanism for overcoming Southern resistance.

Poor white and Black children faced high hurdles to decent education due to the frequent denial of land and basic security. African American communities struggled to keep their schools open in the face of violent opposition. Famous Black schools, especially Booker T. Washington's Tuskegee Institute (founded the year of Garfield's inauguration), were the exception. More than half the African Americans living in the South remained illiterate in the last decades of the nineteenth century. And as long as they were illiterate, they were denied the right to participate in elections. Garfield offered no solution. For the African American citizens of the former Confederacy, the daily limitations were much more real than the distant promises of presidential rhetoric.[14]

During Garfield's presidency, African Americans left the South in rising numbers, seeking opportunities in Kansas, Indiana, and other parts of the country. In 1880, fifteen thousand African Americans left Mississippi, Louisiana, and Texas alone. The numbers remained high in 1881 and 1882. The *New York World*, a Democratic newspaper, called the fleeing of African Americans a "very serious matter" that reflected their poor treatment in the former Confederacy. When white Southern landowners used violence, including targeted killings, to stop this migration, Garfield's government did not act.[15]

The president also ignored African American pleas for help emigrating from the South to Liberia, a settlement for freed slaves in Africa, first founded by the American Colonization Society before the Civil War. Henry Adams, the former slave who had led African American efforts to acquire land in Louisiana, was one of many advocates demanding that the federal government offer transportation to the suffering Black laborers in the South who wanted to escape. He published a letter from another former slave who had already reached Liberia and called on others to join "who believe that they are not the white man's inferior."[16]

More than four thousand former slaves followed this call to return to Africa. Many more left the former Confederacy but stayed within the United States. They had little to attract them to a poor new nation across the ocean or hostile American communities outside the South. The desperate departure of thousands of African Americans was evidence that they were brutalized and hopeless in their former homes.

When a journalist in St. Louis asked a migrating mother, holding her child, if she would consider returning, she responded: "Oh no; I'd sooner starve here!" An African American minister from Louisiana explained that he and others were fleeing "because they were terrorized, robbed, and murdered by the bulldozing desperadoes" unleashed by Democrats in the South.[17]

For all the strong words in his inaugural address defending civil rights, Garfield showed no inclination to act against the increasing violence of the "bulldozing desperadoes," like Benjamin Tillman. The Democrats tightened their grip on the former Confederacy as African Americans tried to leave and the president struggled with limited options. Without military forces stationed in the South or a well-resourced Justice Department, he could not do much. Garfield had inherited a weak hand.

The new president did not have time to change his cards. He spent his first weeks in office struggling to respond to the wave of Republican Party members seeking appointed positions, often with lucrative salaries and other benefits. The office seekers surrounded him each day, they badgered him with written requests, and they had their allies in Congress hound him whenever possible. Garfield expressed exasperation in his diary. "Again and again," he wrote, "we were compelled to shut the doors, with the files of people extending to the avenue." He found the "office hunters" contemptuous: they "drew papers on me as highway men draw pistols."[18]

Garfield confessed that he felt overwhelmed, even depressed. "I must resist a very strong tendency to be dejected and unhappy," he told himself. The new president wanted to focus on the policy issues he articulated in his inaugural address, but he was continually diverted.[19]

This was not a new phenomenon, but it was more trying for Garfield than for his predecessors. The deep divisions in the Republican Party between Roscoe Conkling's "stalwarts," James Blaine's reformers, and the Ohio mafia in between made every major appointment an extended battle. Conkling still believed he should be the kingmaker while Blaine and the Ohio group resisted. Garfield clearly favored Blaine, appointing him secretary of state and giving him influence over other major positions. Conkling demanded control of key offices, particularly the powerful collector of the port of New York—a position Vice President Chester Arthur had held as Conkling's protégé.

Garfield recognized that he could not pursue his agenda, including breaking the patronage system, if he bent to Conkling's will. He rejected the senator's demands and sought to free himself from his influence. "The civil service must be regulated by law," Garfield pleaded to his diary, "or the president can never devote his time to administration." He pushed to create a nonpartisan merit basis for hiring, where possible. Conkling's supporters responded by blocking many of the president's appointments in the Senate, often breaking ranks to work with the Democrats.[20]

Garfield was stalemated by his own partisans as he struggled to fill important positions. The president's frustration peaked during the spring of 1881. "My day is frittered away by the personal seeking of people," he complained to his diary. "Four years of this kind of intellectual dissipation may cripple me for the remainder of my life."[21]

The president was also distracted by the illness of his wife, Lucretia. Washington, DC, remained a small, swampy town in the late nineteenth century, and the First Lady contracted malaria from the mosquitoes that infested the area. Lucretia spent the first months of her husband's presidency convalescing in bed with a dangerously high fever. The many doctors who attended to her could only counsel for rest and hope for the best.

Lucretia's sickness hit her husband hard, and he wrote tenderly about it. "I awoke this morning, and found my precious one a little better, but very weak," Garfield recounted in May. "I went through the duties of the office, very anxiously getting away every few moments to see her." The concerned husband had "no heart" for congressional politics while his wife struggled before his eyes.[22]

Garfield was deeply in love with Lucretia. He was emotionally drained by her suffering and regretted bringing her to Washington. His worries pervade his diary, where he describes how her sickness distracted him from his duties.[23]

After a long, influential career in Congress, Garfield felt shackled by his executive and personal burdens. He was unable to make progress on "the great problems which concern the whole country." He admitted that he frequently "felt like crying" because of the "agony of my soul." He contrasted his hopes for a more vibrant and prosperous democracy with "the greed for office" and "its consumption of my time." Garfield was personally offended by the vulgarity of it all: "My services ought to be worth more to the government than to be thus spent." Few presidents have been so unhappy with their new role so soon.[24]

Charles Guiteau was one of the many vulgar office seekers who hounded Garfield. Born in Illinois in 1841, he had latched on to Republican politics in Boston and New York in 1880. Deeply indebted and unemployed, Guiteau believed he could show his true genius by helping the party elect its presidential candidate. He felt God called on him to do this work, and he believed, without any evidence, that he could move audiences. Guiteau was in fact a loner who alienated everyone around him.

He wrote a speech, "Garfield Against Hancock," which was distributed among New York Republicans before the election. Guiteau read the speech on one occasion at a small campaign event, with little reaction. He met Chester Arthur at several gatherings, where Guiteau often lurked around the edges of major figures. He became familiar enough that Republican Party leaders recognized Guiteau, warily.

He believed that he had made a major contribution to Garfield's election. Guiteau convinced himself that his obscure speech had, somehow, motivated thousands of people to vote for Republicans. After the election, he wrote to the president-elect, congratulating him and asking for compensation: "I, Charles Guiteau, hereby make application for the Austrian Mission." He had no foreign policy experience, and he did not speak German (his ancestors were French Huguenots), but Guiteau described his successful legal practices in Chicago and New York, his extensive work for the party, and his impending marriage to a "wealthy and accomplished heiress." None of these claims were true. Guiteau was in debt, he had a criminal record, and he was largely alienated from other people, including any potential spouses. He was a pathetic ne'er-do-well who imagined he was a powerful party figure.[25]

Determined to make his case in person, Guiteau traveled by train to Washington, DC, on the day after Garfield's inauguration. He joined the daily lines of office seekers that the president so deeply detested. Garfield's private secretary remembered him for his repeated efforts to get an audience: "I saw Mr. Guiteau probably fifteen times altogether at various places, about on the street and about in the Executive Mansion and on the grounds." Guiteau also stalked other powerful figures, including Secretary of State Blaine and various members of Congress.[26]

His relentlessness paid off, in part. Guiteau maneuvered his way into a short meeting with Garfield. He introduced himself as a strong supporter and handed the president a copy of the speech he had written with the words *Paris Consulship* scribbled on the first page—apparently, Guiteau had changed his requested position. Garfield accepted the document but did nothing.

When Guiteau encountered Blaine, the secretary of state was more explicit. He told Guiteau that he had "no prospect whatever" of getting an appointment. Annoyed by the office seeker's pestering, Blaine exclaimed: "Never speak to me about the Paris consulship again!"[27]

Guiteau had faced failure and rejection his entire life, but he did not take it well. He blamed Garfield for ignoring the role of his speech in the election. He believed the president stood in the way of the position he would receive if the New York Republicans—Conkling's faction— were in charge.

This line of thinking led a clearly troubled man to a reckless act of pointless violence. Guiteau decided that he would assassinate the ungrateful Republican leader and make Vice President Chester Arthur the president. As Conkling's close ally, Arthur would surely recognize Guiteau's contributions and reward him. Guiteau had become obsessed with the disputes inside the Republican Party, and he decided to prove himself to Conkling's group once and for all.

A troubled office seeker with delusions of grandeur, Charles Guiteau believed Republican Party bosses would reward him for assassinating President James Garfield.

Garfield had been eager to escape the nation's capital and the political battles all around him. On June 18, he had taken Lucretia to a beach resort in Long Branch, New Jersey, for her continued convalescence. He enjoyed it at least as much as she did: "The worry and work of Washington seems very far away and I rest in the large silence of the sea air." Garfield was pleased to leave the lines of office seekers behind.[28]

He traveled back to Washington on June 27 for meetings with his cabinet. Garfield planned to return to his wife and the sea air in just five days. Guiteau would make that impossible.

On July 2, Guiteau stalked the president again, but this time with a loaded gun. When Garfield entered the Baltimore and Potomac Railroad station that morning to catch his train back to New Jersey, Guiteau slithered behind him and fired two shots. Like Lincoln sixteen years earlier, the president was not protected, except for the secretary of state and his two teenage children who accompanied him. The first shot passed through Garfield's right arm and then loudly pierced a toolbox that a worker was carrying through the station. The second shot was fatal. It lodged in Garfield's back, initially to the right of his spinal column, and then traveled behind his pancreas. The president immediately sank to the ground. Vomiting, he began bleeding from his back. He remained conscious but just barely.

After the initial shock, the people in the station ran to help Garfield and apprehend his assassin. A ticket agent grabbed Guiteau by the neck, holding him until a police officer arrived. Guiteau carried a letter explaining his deed: "The President's tragic death was a sad necessity, but it will unite the Republican party and save the Republic." A second letter, addressed from Guiteau to General William Sherman, called upon the military leader to rescue him from jail. Guiteau expected that Chester Arthur and Roscoe Conkling would reward him.[29]

Guiteau was utterly deluded. He was taken to prison, tried for murder, and executed by hanging a year later. Although his trial attracted wide attention and assessments of his insanity drew curiosity after his death, Guiteau did not become a hero for Garfield's opponents, on the model of John Wilkes Booth. Guiteau shot a president who was far less threatening to the privileges of white men in the South.

Unlike Lincoln, Garfield could have been saved. The gunshot wounds did not kill him outright. Poor medical treatment caused a second presidential death in less than two decades. Garfield received care from the best-connected physicians, not the most skilled or knowledgeable.

Scientific research on bacteriology, infections, and antiseptic surgery had become a standard part of medicine in Europe and among young American doctors, but it was still resisted by the leaders of the medical profession in the United States. Distinguished American physicians continued to place their patients on filthy floors, probe their wounds with dirty hands, and insert unsanitized instruments into their bodies.

Garfield was subjected to a doom loop of malpractices. From the moment that the first doctor tended to him in the train station, his wounds were probed in ways that brought infection, not relief, to his body. More than a dozen physicians stuck their germ-filled hands and instruments deep into his back. When he quickly developed the symptoms of an infection—high fever and pus-filled discharges—his main physician, Dr. D. Willard Bliss, confidently predicted recovery. In the end, scientific ignorance among powerful people caused the president's death.[30]

Garfield suffered terribly in the process. For eighty agonizing days, he endured high fevers, acute body pains, weight loss, and brain fog. Since he could not keep food down, Dr. Bliss resorted to rectal feeding—injecting a beef bouillon cocktail into the president's anus every four hours. The personal embarrassment and psychological trauma of slow decline, broken by moments of false hope, wore the president and his family down.

Garfield's body was decaying, but his doctors refused to see it or do anything about it. They continued to expect that he would, somehow, revive. He did not. He slipped away on the night of September 19, first losing consciousness before his heart ceased beating. Garfield was two months shy of fifty, a self-made man of enormous accomplishment and a figure undone by the presidency. He was another victim of the nation's divisions.

Garfield's death was not as sudden as Lincoln's, but it had many echoes. Lincoln's eldest son, Robert, was present at both assassinations. He was with his father at Petersen House, after his ailing body was moved from Ford's Theatre. As secretary of war, he was in the railway station when Garfield was shot. (When President William McKinley was shot in Buffalo in 1901, he was also there. Robert Lincoln witnessed every presidential assassination before John F. Kennedy's.)

Lincoln's and Garfield's deaths exposed unresolved problems of succession in the executive branch. Vice presidents Andrew Johnson and Chester Arthur were ill prepared to take over. They were not close to the dead presidents, they did not share in their goals, and they did not have the political capital to influence members of Congress. Yet since Lincoln and Garfield died early in their terms, their unelected successors had more than three years in office. Although Lincoln's and Garfield's deaths encouraged periods of public mourning throughout the country, soon after, the divisions hardened. Their successors inherited presidencies that were weaker as a consequence.

Chester Arthur was the second vice president in sixteen years to succeed a slain president within a year of his election. *Credit: Charles Milton Bell*

Vice President Chester Arthur was at his home in New York when he learned of President Garfield's death. At 2:15 a.m. on September 20, 1881, New York Supreme Court judge John R. Brady administered the oath of office, making Arthur president. He returned to Washington and quickly found himself embroiled in the same fights as his predecessor with Democrats and within the Republican Party. Arthur possessed even less leverage because he had few followers. He was not well liked. He also suffered from degenerative kidney disease for much of his presidency, although that was kept secret from the public.

Arthur did, however, represent an enduring shift in the Republican Party. Garfield was a president in Lincoln's mold—born to small-town frontier circumstances, self-made, and committed to free labor as a source of opportunity for the penniless beginner. Arthur came from the growing urban and industrial wing of the party, committed more to big business than to the cause of free labor. Future Republican presidents, especially William McKinley and Theodore Roosevelt, would exhibit far less attachment to free labor. They would emphasize economic growth and foreign expansion above all.

The Republican Party remained committed to civil rights but with ever-less vigor. Garfield had done little, but at least he made strong statements. Those statements became less common, especially after the first Democratic president since before the Civil War, Grover Cleveland, took office in 1884. Focused on economic growth and wary of further alienating white voters in a series of tight presidential races, the Republican Party lifted almost all pressure on Southern states.

Garfield's death marked the end of Republican efforts to build an inclusive, multiracial democracy. Many party members still held this aspiration, but the resistance from Democrats and some Republicans had finally worn them down. African Americans were more ignored by Republicans and repressed by Democrats than at any time since Appomattox.

The Democrats exploited this moment to turn back the clock. The Confederate exiles who had refused to surrender in 1865 and joined forces with Maximilian in Mexico returned to leading positions in the South. Their traitorous behavior was treated as heroism, and their attacks on civil rights were made lawful.

Alexander Terrell, the judge and Confederate officer who volunteered to spy for the Mexican emperor, reemerged as one of the most prominent legislators in Texas during Garfield's presidency and later years. He served in the Texas Senate, where he proudly represented the "white man's vote" in Austin and nearby communities. He disdained what he called the "mass of ignorant negro voters," and he made a name for himself as one of the leading advocates to "purify the ballot box." That meant preventing African Americans from voting through poll taxes, which discouraged poor men from casting what became an expensive ballot. Other measures included onerous requirements for voter registration and scarce voting locations in Black neighborhoods.[31]

Terrell also supported a closed Democratic Party primary, which allowed only white male voters to select the nominees who would run for office on Election Day. The closed primary made it impossible for African American candidates to get on the ballot. All these measures were eventually codified as the Terrell Election Law in Texas—one of the most discriminatory voting systems in the United States, with clear legacies in the twenty-first century.

Terrell wrote many other pieces of important legislation, including the bill creating the University of Texas, but he continued to prioritize the exclusion of African Americans. Despite constitutional guarantees, he consistently sought mechanisms to keep the Black population down. He never abandoned that basic Confederate position. In 1883, he referred to African Americans as the "most terrible enemy"—"not controlled by intelligence and patriotism."[32]

The last comment was rich with irony, considering that he was referring to former slaves who had fought courageously in the Union army while he was a mediocre Confederate officer and a traitor who lent his services to a foreign government. By the 1880s, white Southerners did not probe these contradictions. Men like Terrell were popular for defying the federal government time and again to protect the privileges of traditional landholders. Texas and other states instituted laws that restored as much of the Confederacy as possible.

Another Republican president was dead, and this time, it started to look like the Democrats had won, at least in the South. Garfield was the last president for more than fifty years to condemn the denial of freedom to nonwhite citizens. He called it an "evil" and a "crime." His successors would not use such words. They negotiated a truce that kept the Confederacy alive.

Two presidents and more than half a million people had died over the question of who should be included in America's democracy. After Garfield's death, it was a question that remained unresolved. The conflict over who should have say, and how, continued. It still does.

Legacies

In the years after Lincoln's death, American democracy tried to become something new. Slavery ended rapidly, turning four million people into citizens, but only because the United States government fielded the largest army in the world and occupied hostile cities and towns across the southern and western parts of the country. Rich plantation families were impoverished by the war, and few had any prospect of recovering the extravagant wealth and high position that they had inherited but now lost. The Republican Party, founded only a few years earlier and led by white men of modest means from the middle of the country, controlled all the institutions of the federal government and attracted a new following among former slaves. The United States was leaving the founders' republic of slaveholders and white family farmers behind.

In its place was a surly new democracy still dominated by white men. They still owned the land. They still had most of the guns. They still controlled local offices. And they still had the power to determine who voted and who didn't. The Fifteenth Amendment to the U.S. Constitution only prohibited voter disqualifications based explicitly on race. Opponents found other ways to justify keeping Black men from the polls.

Two different futures contested for the soul of America in the 1870s. Some Republican leaders like Ulysses Grant wanted to build a nation that included Black men more fully. They had already proven themselves as courageous soldiers in the Union army. After the war, African Americans could be independent farmers, teachers, and business owners. To achieve the Republican ideal of "free labor," Black men had to have some say in government through their votes, and they had to feel represented.

This multiracial vision did not require integrated living among the races, nor did it call for full equality. Grant and his contemporaries in the Republican Party never went so far. They did, however, believe that former slaves were now citizens, entitled to the basic protections and privileges for participation in American democracy. From the most powerful federal institutions, Grant's Republicans defended the civil rights of African Americans as never before in the nation's history.

Many disagreed. Civil rights progress was a nightmare for those who felt they had the most to lose: the traditional white gentry in the South. More participation for Black men meant less power for them. Landholders no longer possessed their slaves; now they feared they would have to cede their control of local government too. They fought against multiracialism with the same determination they had shown on the battlefields, except now the fights were inside their communities.

White supremacy emerged as a popular ideology devoted to defending self-rule for white men against rising African Americans in their midst. Their claims of racial superiority were not new, but numerous citizens—from John Wilkes Booth to Benjamin Tillman—organized around this vision with increased fanaticism. They became vigilantes, using lynching, nighttime raids, and other forms of mass terror to gang up on reformers.

Resistance spread as a reaction to civil rights reforms, and it thrived not only because it was popular among former Confederates. It had many advantages in the American democratic system. First, white supremacy had longevity and tradition on its side—slavery was part of the nation's founding. Racial and gender hierarchies were central to American political rhetoric from its earliest origins when Native Americans were pushed off their land and denied basic rights. For early white American settlers, the historian Edmund Morgan famously observed, their freedom justified subjugation of those who did not deserve to be free.[1]

Second, Southern resistance to reforms raised the costs of enforcement for Republicans. Northern communities had to levy troops for occupying the South, and they had to pay the taxes for equipment, supplies, and salaries. They also had to devote time and attention to this intractable issue rather than toward the prospects for economic growth in the West. As Grant learned during his frustrating second term, the Northern advocates of civil rights had other priorities, and their willingness to sacrifice for former slaves diminished with each passing year.

This was a severe shortcoming of Republican civil rights advocacy. The party was built primarily to help Lincoln's "penniless beginners" in the North, not suffering African Americans in the South. That lineage gave an advantage to Southern Democrats, who dug in for a long struggle, waiting for Northern zeal to dissolve into empty rhetoric and then passive neglect.

Third, and most important, the structure of the American government lent former Confederates numerous advantages, which they keenly exploited. Through their states, they controlled the rules for voting, deciding who cast a ballot and how. They also determined how congressional and state legislative districts were drawn, dividing up the population to diminish the influence of minority groups. Under the legal separation of powers in the United States, reducing Black votes and representation was acceptable.

Even with war powers, the federal government had very few tools to enforce fairness at the ballot box or in the drawing of legislative districts. State, county, and municipal officials provided the most direct oversight. State courts offered primary adjudication for disputes. Southern landholders worked diligently through these institutions to suppress African American voters and gerrymander them out of representation. These discriminatory actions gained extra force from the presence of paramilitary groups, ready to silence anyone who tried to challenge the system or bring in the federal government.

The democratic structures favoring white supremacy were exacerbated by the U.S. Senate and the electoral college. Both institutions gave disproportionate representation to the states controlled by Democrats and less leverage to the denser Republican states in the North. Senators were chosen by white legislators; electors were certified by white secretaries of state and counting boards. In the 1876 and 1880 presidential elections, these racially biased institutions, not the popular vote, determined the outcome. That would remain a recurring problem into the twenty-first century.[2]

The essentials of American democracy were contested intensely for a decade and a half after the Confederate surrender at Appomattox. The war moved from the muddy battlefields to the marble halls of Congress, various statehouses, a theater, and a train station. The latter two locations witnessed the first presidential assassinations in American history. They would not be the last.

After 1881, the debates between multiracial and white supremacist visions of democracy continued, often with increased local violence and stubborn national denial. In the early twentieth century, President Theodore Roosevelt tried to address these seething tensions, promoting progressive reforms through a stronger federal government. He detested citizens who relied on landed wealth, rather than intelligence and hard work, for their fortunes. He disguised his multiracial vision behind rhetoric of national power, foreign expansion, and manly prowess. He was a bully of a different kind.

President Woodrow Wilson, the first Southerner elected president since more than a decade before the Civil War, pushed back in the other direction. He was a respected academic but also a child of the former Confederacy. He opposed civil rights legislation, defended Jim Crow laws, and advocated for white supremacy. Wilson hid his racism behind eloquent calls for worldwide democracy and peace between nations after a terrible world war. From the White House, he defended Southerners who felt threatened by rising Black men and other minorities. Wilson advocated what he called the "New Freedom"—an idealistic cover for giving local segregationists more say and rejecting federal action to stop lynching or voter suppression.

The years between Abraham Lincoln's and James Garfield's assassinations were the moment when these warring perspectives on democracy were planted firmly in the soil of the modern American nation. The country became more multiracial and more white supremacist at the same time.

This division would remain unresolved. In later periods, the conflicting beliefs were submerged beneath preoccupations with foreign expansion, economic depression, world war, and anti-communism. Skilled politicians, like Franklin Roosevelt, diverted attention from America's democratic deficiencies into other conflicts.

But the deficiencies were never hidden for long. They burst into the open and "surprised" Americans time and again, as evidenced by the conflicts around civil rights in the 1950s and 1960s, and then again in recent years. With economic uncertainty and deepening diversity, the public eagerness for inclusive reforms has become overwhelming again. Black Lives Matter is a twenty-first century echo of the Union Leagues, the Freedman's Bureau, and African American Republican organizations across the old Confederacy. Donald Trump and QAnon are twenty-first-century replays of Andrew Johnson and the Ku Klux Klan—red hats this time born of older white hoods.

History allows us to map the intricate roots buried in the soil, to understand how they were planted, and to appreciate how they have sprouted today. It also reminds us that what we see in front of us is not all that matters. American democracy is not just defined by the people and controversies of our time. It is driven by recurring problems— problems of inclusion and exclusion—that remain deep below our eyes, growing unattended to eventually disrupt our current and future eras.

If we want to escape the recurring patterns of civil war, we must dig up the roots to remove the rot. In particular, there are key parts of American political life that have long been rotting from neglect and misuse:

Voting. Freed slaves never benefited from a right to vote. The Fifteenth Amendment, ratified in 1870, prohibited discrimination in voting based on race. Other forms of voter discrimination—based on sex, wealth, education, criminal record, debt, and many additional prejudices—were still permitted by the Constitution. The Nineteenth Amendment, ratified in 1920, only eliminated sex as an acceptable form of voting discrimination. The states retained enormous power to deny ballots to millions of citizens.

They have taken advantage of that power, building on the precedents created in 1870s. The number of white male voters in the United

States grew to a historic high at the end of the nineteenth century, as the Democratic and Republican Parties worked closely with local businesses and bosses to motivate, and frequently coerce, men to cast their ballots. Urban workers were told their jobs depended on voting for the preferred candidates, early and often. Rural farmers warily eyed county militias that policed polling places, keeping a close account of who voted and for which party. Citizens deposited ballots, color coded by party in many cases, making voting hardly an anonymous or voluntary task.

For African Americans and many other minorities, the workings of the American democratic system kept them away from the polls. The lesson white leaders took from the 1870s was that the vote could be kept white, even as the population diversified and the laws appeared to be more inclusive. Burdensome requirements—including tests, taxes, and identification checks enforced only for Black voters—lowered their turnout. Hard-to-reach polls, with limited voting hours on a workday (Tuesday), kept numbers for certain groups low. And physical intimidation made voting for many African Americans unsafe.

There was no secret about this, as this book has shown. Northern Republicans took some action to protect Black voters but not enough. After 1872—the fairest election for the next century—voter suppression was accepted as a normal part of American politics. As late as 2020, states with nonwhite majorities, like Texas, still saw more white citizens at the polls. Voter turnout is skewed to this day, and some states continue to adjust voting laws to make certain that continues.[3]

Although the rotten roots of voter suppression go back to slavery and property requirements at the nation's founding, they spread more deeply in American soil during the nineteenth century because emancipated men still did not have a right to vote. The Constitution protected the former slave's right to speak and worship, but the right to cast a ballot was absent, and never guaranteed. That gap in American democracy was used to exclude millions of people from a say in their government. It was partially closed by the Voting Rights Act of 1965, but it has widened again through new voter restrictions, making American elections more about privileged access than full participation. *This history makes clear that our democracy needs a constitutional amendment guaranteeing all citizens the right to vote.*[4]

Powerful state and local groups have used violence to discourage nonwhite citizens from voting in the United States since 1865. This pattern of exclusion continues today, especially the violent efforts to prevent the counting and certifying of votes from the 2020 elections. *Source: Harper's Weekly, October 1876*

Elections. Voting is not the only problem with American elections. Too often, the electoral process allows the candidate with fewer votes to win. This is particularly true in presidential elections. The electoral college is perhaps the strangest institution in the country. It does not actually exist as an organization or even a network. Few people understand how it works. No one can justify its existence in terms of democratic values.

Every four years, a mysterious group of party leaders in each state selects an even more obscure collection of party members to serve as designated *electors.* They are allocated to each state in proportion to its number of congressional representatives, which allows lower-population states a surplus number of electors because the Senate gives every state two members, regardless of size. The state electors then cast their votes for the candidate whom they believe received the most votes in their states, or they sometimes don't, depending on the certification and electoral laws, which differ from state to state.[5]

This chaotic system disrupts the democratic presumption that the voters should elect their president. They don't. The electors elect the president. The process is so convoluted and messy that it widens disputes in close, contested elections. The 1876 election was the most obvious case, when the country almost did not elect a president because of the electoral college. The 1880 election had many similar problems because the popular vote for the two candidates was within a few thousand total ballots.

The same would be true for the next three elections after that, including 1888, when the electoral college winner, Benjamin Harrison, had fewer popular votes than the loser, incumbent president Grover Cleveland. With close elections in the early twenty-first century, the old problem plagued American democracy again, contributing to a widening belief that the arbitrariness of the system permitted a "win at all costs" attitude from candidates.

President George W. Bush in 2000 and Donald Trump in 2020 did not care who received the most votes—neither of them did. Instead, they focused on arguing that they had somehow "won" with fewer votes. Echoing the candidates in 1876, Bush and Trump worked to legally steal the election. That is what the American system encourages when the vote is close and the electoral college is contested.

American elections have additional problems, dating back to the nineteenth century. Large groups of citizens in non-state territories do not have a right to vote in presidential and congressional elections. The disenfranchised parts of the country included the western territories in Grant's time; they include Washington, DC, Puerto Rico, the Virgin Islands, Guam, American Samoa, and the Northern Mariana Islands today. The excluded population totals more than three and a half million current citizens. The fact that they are often nonwhite is predictable and atrocious.

The counting of the votes in elections adds yet another layer of arbitrariness. Every state has its own rules and its own certification procedures. No two are exactly alike. Within the states, different counties adopt their own practices. This system makes the counting difficult to follow, and it offers numerous opportunities for cheating (as was often the case in the nineteenth century) or false allegations of cheating (promoted by losers in the twenty-first century).

American elections remain undemocratic. The beneficiaries of the existing system have every incentive to continue fighting for it as they have for 150 years. In this sense, American elections perversely encourage attacks on democracy. *This history makes clear that our democracy needs to eliminate the electoral college and create a system of national rules for all elections, ensuring that only the candidates with the most votes win.*[6]

Representation. Electing popular leaders is an incomplete step toward democracy. The leaders must actually represent the people. That means there must be some connection between an elected representative and the voters who elected her. That connection need not be direct; the representative can come from a different background. The connection should, however, include some bond of identity; the elected leader and the voters must feel they are part of the same community. And citizens must be able to hold the elected leader accountable if she does not really represent them.

Confederate authorities believed that they were representing their communities, but the political changes of the 1870s allowed them to neglect and harm the other citizens residing in their cities, counties, and states. Southern Democrats not only corrupted voting and elections, they also distorted the lines of representation. They used their control of state legislatures to draw congressional and state legislative districts that diluted potential non-Democratic voters. Republicans did the reverse in the North and often in the West. Although the process of gerrymandering was not new, it was weaponized for explicitly racial purposes.

The constitutional non-representation of minorities before the Civil War was replaced by gerrymandered non-representation thereafter. That remains true today. The state of Texas, for example, experienced rapid population growth in the early twenty-first century, and it gained additional seats in Congress with each decennial census. The population growth in the state occurred largely in nonwhite communities, yet the state legislature has drawn new districts to guarantee that each has a majority of white voters. Through the creative grouping of citizens for voting purposes, state leaders have used an increased minority population to empower more white representatives.[7]

Computer technology has made this process especially nefarious, giving state legislatures the tools to shape district lines precisely for white majorities, selecting particular families for one district or another. State leaders dilute nonwhite populations by spreading them across multiple oddly drawn districts. Congressional maps look less like colorful collages of neighborhoods and more like islands of isolated families thinly connected by long, irregular lines. The ugliness of the maps captures their unreasonableness.

Since the 1870s, and with redoubled determination in the twenty-first century, the effort to deny representation to voting citizens has defined the working of American democracy. That's how the lines are drawn. Elected leaders, mostly white, choose their voters, and they prevent other voters from choosing their leaders. Millions of Americans have no chance to gain real representation in Congress or their state legislature or their city council. *Partisan gerrymandering is a democratic cancer, and it has to stop.*[8]

Presidential succession. The Civil War expanded the powers of the American president. He deployed a massive army across the South and the West, killing hundreds of thousands of Confederates, freeing millions of slaves, and occupying countless communities. Although members of Congress controlled the president's purse strings, he often made monumental decisions—from emancipating slaves to pardoning secessionists—without consulting them. For more than half of these pivotal years, Congress was not even in session. The president had near-dictatorial powers during those months.

The growth of executive power and the spread of political turmoil exposed a serious weakness in the rules governing presidential succession.

When John Wilkes Booth murdered Abraham Lincoln, Lincoln's successor, Andrew Johnson, gained all the powers of the presidency, and he held them for almost four years. He allowed former Confederates to reestablish political control in the South, even though the Republican Party had been elected to do just the opposite. Congress could not stop him, and removing him from office failed, as it has for every impeached president. Executive power slipped into unelected and ill-prepared hands, and it remained there to the great harm of the country.

Less than two decades after Andrew Johnson's disastrous presidency, the same thing happened again. Executive power slipped into Chester Arthur's hands after James Garfield's assassination. No one had intended for Arthur to become president, including Arthur himself. He was a machine politician, placed in the vice presidential slot as a form of graft for party bosses in New York. Yet he held the presidency for more than three years and prevented any effort at civil rights reform.

In the twentieth century, Theodore Roosevelt, Calvin Coolidge, Harry Truman, and Lyndon Johnson each initially became president by the death of the elected executive. Gerald Ford entered the White House after Richard Nixon and his vice president, Spiro Agnew, resigned. Roosevelt, Truman, and Ford served more than half a presidential term before they faced voters. Ford, like Andrew Johnson and Chester Arthur, was never elected president, yet he served more than two years.

For purposes of stability, it makes sense that the vice president succeeds a slain, sick, or inaccessible president temporarily. Routine succession ensures some basic continuity. But allowing a person without electoral legitimacy to wield so much power is dangerous for policy and destructive for democracy. It places the possession of office ahead of how one arrived there. In a well-functioning democracy, the most consequential decisions should have the most electoral legitimacy. A president who did not get elected to office appears arbitrary and non-representative, especially when his policies contradict the president who was actually elected to office. That was the case with Andrew Johnson, and his prolonged succession fed continuing divisions.

Citizens need to believe that the nation's chief executive was elected to that office by the people when he takes controversial actions.

Short-term substitutes for the elected president should be just that: provisional successors who offer temporary stability and do not make transformative decisions without standing for election. *Our democracy needs a process for new presidential elections when the elected president is unable to serve for more than half the elected term.*

Hearts and minds. Politics is about much more than presidents. The Civil War strengthened the grip of white supremacy on the hearts and minds of millions of citizens. Southerners took up arms to protect their dominance and their right to keep other people down. They supported secession, exile, and even the enlistment of foreign governments, especially Mexico, against their own. At countless locations, most notoriously Fort Pillow, they murdered defenseless enemy soldiers, displaying a descent into fanaticism and what later observers would call war crimes.

The Confederate army's surrender at Appomattox did not diminish the fanaticism. Just the opposite. From the moment when John Wilkes Booth murdered Lincoln, large numbers of Southerners expressed a willingness, even a desire, to continue fighting against federal authority. They organized behind former Confederate figures in the Democratic Party, and they created new terrorist groups, like the Ku Klux Klan. Repeatedly, the Democrats and the Klan encouraged violent attacks on African American communities, especially those who dared to vote and elect their own leaders.

Southern politics encouraged more division, hate, and violence. Men like Benjamin Tillman made their careers promoting conflict, and their influence was not confined to the former Confederacy. As this book has shown, many Northern politicians shared these attitudes. They were reluctant to challenge racial violence when they saw personal and party benefits from acquiescence.

In the century and a half since then, this history has been covered up. Academics have written about it for sure, but most Americans have learned little about the violent white supremacy of the years after Appomattox and the subsequent decades of Jim Crow. The United States might have fought to "save democracy" in two world wars, but it was not a democracy at home when millions of citizens still could not vote and hundreds were lynched for the color of their skin—even those who had valiantly fought America's enemies. Ignorance of the past has perpetuated hateful attitudes and hidden continued injustices.

Historical ignorance confers power on those who benefit from continuing to keep certain groups down. The mighty and insecure cling to ignorance for this reason. That was true in the decades after Appomattox, as it is also true in the early twenty-first century. How else can we explain the popular desire to glorify the past and censor discussion of injustices? How else can we explain the push to tell a whiter history at a time when the country is more diverse than ever before? The history of hate and violence is dangerous for those who are fighting to hoard power against the claims of rising, multiracial citizens.

Americans must come to terms with their past as an aspiring but imperfect democracy. This reckoning requires a willingness to learn more openly about our history, identify our inherited flaws, and work to repair them. We cannot erase the past, but we can adjust our present to the lessons history teaches. Instead of denying or condemning old offenses, we should seek to understand them. We must not allow injustices to recur out of ignorance or wishful thinking.

Learning history is really about hearts and minds—teaching ourselves to look beyond appearances and probe deeply into who we are as a society. That begins with asking where we came from. There are many answers to that question, but for Americans, they all include some relationship to the years in this book, the years when the divisions within our society hardened and planted roots for our troubles today. We have all inherited that history in some way. It is everywhere around us—in our institutions, our rhetoric, our statues, and our symbols. The continued presence of the Confederate flag is the most obvious, and problematic, testimonial.

Visualizing the persistence of violent white supremacy is necessary to eradicate it, at last. The alternative possibilities—the courage of former slaves, the idealism of reformers, and the leadership of Lincoln and Grant—offer us the historical hope we need for our own difficult days. Democracies do not come together when they glorify their past but when they strive to repair it. We have lots of good work to do.

Acknowledgments

Every book is a journey; this one was an unpredictable exploration into the American heart of darkness. I began by examining the sources of resilience for democracy, but I uncovered much more evidence for the old scars that have not yet healed. We live in a time when these scars are bleeding anew.

Despite the darkness of the subject, I find hope in the hunger of so many people to learn and change. My work has benefited from the inspiration and assistance they offered to me. At the top of the list are my students—undergraduates, graduate students, executive students, and others. I am blessed by their energy and optimism every day. Their questions keep me sharp; their ambitions remind me of why we should care so deeply about our democracy.

The incredible staff of Liberal Arts Instructional Technology Services (LAITS) at the University of Texas at Austin deserve special praise for how much they have helped me to learn about teaching and studying history. Above all, they support the weekly podcast that I co-host with my seventeen-year-old son, Zachary: *This Is Democracy*. Each week, we explore a different topic in the past, present, and future of our society. Each week, the LAITS staff help us to produce a worthwhile episode and reach a young and growing audience. Thank you especially to Marla Gilliland, Heather Van Ligten, Jacob Weiss, William Kurzner, William Shute, Anne Burke, and the other amazing people who work with them. This book emerged, in part, from our collaborations over the years.

A number of my PhD students have contributed to my understanding of the history in this book. These extraordinary scholars are writing their own groundbreaking monographs. They include Benjamin Allison, Diana Bolsinger, Jon Buchleiter, Augusta Dell'Omo, Paul Edgar, Bryan Frizzelle, John Gleb, Ashlyn Hand, Jeremy Kasper, Ryan Kendall, Daniel Samet, Cali Slair, and Emily Whalen. My numerous other former PhD students are distinguished professors, writers, and policy makers, striving to make our democracy more vibrant.

I am fortunate to work in an intense and collegial academic community at the University of Texas at Austin, where so many of my colleagues are world-leading thinkers. Their insights and questions greatly improved this book. Their commitment to merging rigorous research with serious public engagement helps to guide me. Thank you to Barry Bales, Bill Brands, Robert Chesney, James Galbraith, Robert Hutchings, William Inboden, Peniel Joseph, Mark Lawrence, Aaron O'Connell, Craig Pedersen, Richard Reddick, Mark Updegrove, and Selena Walsh.

The wider intellectual community in Austin is more eclectic than the university and often more committed to pursuing ideas for changing the world. I have learned a lot about innovation and its limits from Robert Campbell, Paul Huggins, Brett Hurt, Bryan Jones, David Judson, and Barry Kahn. Steven Schragis, the indefatigable founder of One Day University and many other ventures, coached me on how to communicate with a rapidly changing audience, especially during the unending COVID pandemic. My dear friends in Madison, Wisconsin—Dan Checki, David Fields, John Hall, B. Venkat Mani, Andrew Seaborg, and Andrew Thompson—helped me to see the bigger picture and think critically about my own biases. One of my oldest friends, Dylan Tyson, exposed me to different viewpoints and tested my arguments as no one else can.

The writing (and rewriting) of this book benefited enormously from the tireless efforts of my editor, Clive Priddle. He had a powerful vision for this book from the start, and he helped me conceptualize and then refine the narrative. His international perspective on American history opened my eyes to many parts of the story that I had seen too narrowly or neglected entirely. Anupama Roy-Chaudhury helped to discipline my writing (and my exuberant metaphors!). She also kept me on track.

My literary agent, Andrew Wylie, continues to educate me on what it means to be a writer for both scholars and the wider public. His wisdom on the subject and format for this book shaped my thinking from an early stage.

All my work in this book reflects the encouragement and patience of my family. I wrote nearly every page from home during the pandemic. On most days, all of us were in the same house, often on four separate Zoom meetings. If the book kept me focused, my wife and kids kept me sane. We grew closer and more acutely aware of how important it is to bring kindness and empathy into our harsh world. Alison does that every day as a leader of the Austin City Government. Natalie does the same in college and in her community work. Zachary, my podcast partner, puts kindness and empathy into poetry each week, and then he applies it in high school, German language school, synagogue, and elsewhere. I talk and write a lot, but my wife and kids know more about what needs to be said. I am fortunate to learn from them. They are in every word of this book, although they are obviously not to blame for my shortcomings in choosing the words. I love them more than any words can express.

Notes

Introduction

1. Winston Churchill, "The Lord Mayor's Luncheon, Mansion House," Churchill Society, http://www.churchill-society-london.org.uk/EndoBegn.html.
2. Capitol Police officer James Blassingame, quoted in the *New York Times*, September 18, 2021, A13.
3. See "Description of the Delaware Confederate Monument," Delaware Grays, https://www.descv.org.
4. Brice Stump, "A Monumental Honor: Giving Confederate Soldiers Their Due," *Delmarva Now*, March 31, 2014, https://www.delmarvanow.com/story/news/war-on-the-shore/2014/03/29/a-monumental-honor-giving-confederate-soldiers-their-due-/7068879/.
5. United States Attorney's Office, District of Columbia, Capitol Breach Case, Kevin Seefried, Case Number 1:21-cr-287-2, Statement of Facts, https://www.justice.gov/usao-dc/defendants/seefried-kevin.
6. Delaware Grays, updated August 24, 2021, https://www.descv.org.

Chapter 1: Dying for Country

1. Terry Alford, *Fortune's Fool: The Life of John Wilkes Booth* (New York: Oxford University Press, 2015), 313.
2. "John Wilkes Booth's Diary," Abraham Lincoln's Assassination, https://rogerjnorton.com/Lincoln52.html; William Shakespeare, *Julius Caesar*, act 1, scene 2, 95–96.
3. "Last Public Address," Abraham Lincoln Online, April 11, 1865, http://www.abrahamlincolnonline.org/lincoln/speeches/last.htm.
4. Alford, *Fortune's Fool*, 257–261.
5. Ibid., 257, 260.
6. Booth originally left this handwritten letter in a sealed envelope with his brother-in-law, John S. Clarke, in late 1864. The envelope was opened and shared with the U.S. marshal for the Eastern District of Pennsylvania after

Lincoln's assassination and Booth's death. The letter was originally printed in the *Philadelphia Inquirer*, then reprinted in countless other newspapers. "The Murderer of Mr. Lincoln," *New York Times*, April 21, 1865, 3, https://www .nytimes.com/1865/04/21/archives/the-murderer-of-mr-lincoln-extraordinary -letter-of-john-wilkes.html.

7. Jeremi Suri, *The Impossible Presidency: The Rise and Fall of America's Highest Office* (New York: Basic Books, 2017), 73–101.

8. The full text of *Our American Cousin*, originally performed in 1858, at "Gutenberg eBook of Our American Cousin, by Tom Taylor," Project Gutenberg, http://www.gutenberg.org/files/3158/3158-h/3158-h.htm.

9. "Statement of an Actor Who Was on the Stage in Ford's Theatre—Additional Facts," *New York Times*, April 26, 1865, 2, https://timesmachine.nytimes.com /timesmachine/1865/04/26/88155031.html?pageNumber=2.

10. Alford, *Fortune's Fool*, 265–269.

11. Ibid., 309. On the many other Confederate exiles to Mexico, see Chapter 3.

12. Ibid., 315.

Chapter 2: Martyrs

1. Walt Whitman, "O Captain! My Captain!," Poetry Foundation, https://www .poetryfoundation.org/poems/45474/o-captain-my-captain.

2. *Texas Republican*, May 5, 1865. For more on the history and influence of the *Texas Republican*, see Max S. Lale, "Marshall Texas Republican," Texas State Historical Association, https://tshaonline.org/handbook/online/articles/eemhq.

3. *Texas Republican*, May 5, 1865.

4. *Columbia Daily Phoenix*, May 18, 1865.

5. Elizabeth Keckley, *Behind the Scenes: Thirty Years a Slave, and Four Years in the White House* (New York: New York Printing Company, 1868), 190–191, https:// docsouth.unc.edu/neh/keckley/keckley.html#keckley174.

6. "Second Inaugural Address of Abraham Lincoln," Avalon Project, https://avalon .law.yale.edu/19th_century/lincoln2.asp.

7. Quoted in Martha Hodes, *Mourning Lincoln* (New Haven: Yale University Press, 2015), 162, 326n33.

8. *Weekly Union Record* (Oroville, CA), April 22, 1865; *Weekly Trinity Journal* (Weaverville, CA), May 13, 1865.

9. *Texas Republican*, May 5, 1865.

10. *Houston Telegraph* article reprinted in *Dallas Herald*, May 4, 1865.

11. *Texas Republican*, May 5, 1865.

12. *Dallas Herald*, May 4, 1865.

13. *Texas Republican*, May 5, 1865.

14. *Columbia Daily Phoenix*, May 18, 1865.

15. *Chattanooga Daily Rebel* (printed in Selma, AL), April 25, 1865.

16. Scholars still debate whether Stanton used the word *ages* or *angels*. The latter is obviously more religious, but both imply martyrdom. See Adam Gopnik's excellent essay, "Angels and Ages," *New Yorker*, May 21, 2007.

17. Quoted in Terry Alford, *Fortune's Fool: The Life of John Wilkes Booth* (New York: Oxford, 2015), 325.

18. Quoted in ibid., 329.

19. *Baltimore American and Commercial Advertiser*, June 9, 1870.

Chapter 3: Exiles

1. Shelby's speech is reprinted in full in the *Texas Republican*, May 5, 1865.

2. Ibid.

3. *Dallas Herald*, May 4, 1865.

4. Shelby's announcement that "he was not going to surrender, but was going to Mexico" is recounted in the unpublished memoirs of Thomas W. Westlake, one of his soldiers. Quoted in Deryl P. Sellmeyer, *Jo Shelby's Iron Brigade* (Gretna, LA: Pelican Publishing, 2007), 281.

5. Information about weapons from Daniel O. Flaherty, *General Jo Shelby: Undefeated Rebel* (Chapel Hill: University of North Carolina Press, 2000), 235.

6. Abraham Lincoln to Matías Romero, secretary of the Mexican Legation in Washington, DC, January 21, 1861, reprinted in Roy P. Basler, ed., *The Collected Works of Abraham Lincoln*, Vol. IV (New Brunswick, NJ: Rutgers University Press, 1953), 177–178.

7. Lincoln, annual message to Congress, December 6, 1864, in Basler, *Collected Works of Abraham Lincoln*, Vol. VIII, 137.

8. Quoted in Flaherty, *General Jo Shelby*, 247.

9. Maury's letter to Reverend F. W. Tremlett, August 8, 1865, reprinted in the biography of Maury prepared by his daughter, Diana Fontaine Maury Corbin, *A Life of Matthew Fontaine Maury* (London: Sampson Low, Marston, Searle, and Rivington, 1888), 230–231.

10. Quoted in Todd W. Wahlstrom, *The Southern Exodus to Mexico: Migration Across the Borderlands After the American Civil War* (Lincoln: University of Nebraska Press, 2015), 16.

11. Maury's letter to Tremlett.

12. Quoted in Wahlstrom, *The Southern Exodus to Mexico*, 16.

13. Maury's letter to Tremlett.

14. Ibid.

15. Flaherty, *General Jo Shelby*, 296.

16. Quoted in ibid., 298.

17. *Texas Republican*, May 19, 1865.

18. Quotations and poem in Lewis Gould, *Alexander Watkins Terrell: Civil War Soldier, Texas Lawmaker, American Diplomat* (Austin: University of Texas Press, 2004), 49–50.
19. On Terrell's "double game," see ibid., 50.
20. Philip H. Sheridan, *Personal Memoirs*, Vol. 2 (New York: Charles L. Webster, 1888), Chapter 9, https://www.gutenberg.org/files/4362/4362-h/4362-h.htm#linkch9b.
21. Ibid.
22. "Proclamation 179—Granting Full Pardon and Amnesty for the Offense of Treason Against the United States During the Late Civil War," American Presidency Project, https://www.presidency.ucsb.edu/documents/proclamation-179 -granting-full-pardon-and-amnesty-for-the-offense-treason-against-the.
23. Quotation from *Confederate Veteran*, published in Nashville, TN, Vol. 11, January 1903. See additional accounts of the exiles in Vol. 14, January 1906; Vol. 22, January 1914; and Vol. 23, January 1915.
24. Thomas M. Settles, *John Bankhead Magruder: A Military Reappraisal* (Baton Rouge: Louisiana State University Press, 2009), 303, 305.

Chapter 4: Citizens

1. Frederick Douglass, "Our Martyred President," speech delivered in Rochester, NY, April 15, 1865, quoted in David W. Blight, *Frederick Douglass: Prophet of Freedom* (New York: Simon and Schuster, 2018), 462.
2. W. E. B. Du Bois, *The Souls of Black Folk* (New York: Library of America, 1986), 359, 372.
3. Quoted in Blight, *Frederick Douglass*, 395, 460.
4. Abraham Lincoln, annual message to Congress, December 8, 1863, in Roy P. Basler, ed., *The Collected Works of Abraham Lincoln*, Vol. 7 (New Brunswick: Rutgers University Press, 1953), 50; Blight, *Frederick Douglass*, 395.
5. Ira Berlin, Barbara J. Fields, Steven F. Miller, Joseph P. Reidy, and Leslie S. Rowland, *Slaves No More: Three Essays on Emancipation and the Civil War* (New York: Cambridge University Press, 1992), 206.
6. Ibid., 203.
7. Ibid., 222.
8. Union first lieutenant Mack Leaming's account of the Battle of Fort Pillow, TN, written April 15, 1893: "Unpublished Manuscript Relating Events of the Battle of Fort Pillow, Tennessee," Gilder Lehrman Institute of American History, https://www.gilderlehrman.org/sites/default/files/inline-pdfs/t-05080.01.pdf.
9. Joseph T. Glatthaar, *Forged in Battle: The Civil War Alliance of Black Soldiers and White Officers* (Baton Rouge: Louisiana State University Press, 1990), 157–158.
10. Quotations from ibid., 168.
11. "The Ovation to the Black Regiment," *New York Times*, March 7, 1864, 4. This article is also quoted, in more abbreviated form, in Glatthaar, *Forged in Battle*, 141–142.

12. Ibid.

13. "Last Public Address," Abraham Lincoln Online, April 11, 1865, http://www
    .abrahamlincolnonline.org/lincoln/speeches/last.htm.

14. Report on the Memphis Riots and Massacres, U.S. House of Representatives,
    Thirty-Ninth Congress, session 1, report 101, July 25, 1866, 6.

15. Ibid., 8, 11–12; "The Freedmen's Bureau Report on the Memphis Race Riots of
    1866," Teaching American History, https://teachingamericanhistory.org/library
    /document/the-freedmens-bureau-report-on-the-memphis-race-riots-of-1866/.

16. "The Freedmen's Bureau Report," Teaching American History.

17. Report on the Memphis Riots and Massacres, U.S. House of Representatives,
    35–36.

18. Ibid., 3.

19. Ibid., 33.

20. Ibid.

21. Quotation from Nell Irvin Painter, *Exodusters: Black Migration to Kansas After
    Reconstruction* (New York: W. W. Norton, 1976), 73–74.

22. Quotations from ibid., 74.

23. Frederick Douglass, *Narrative of the Life of Frederick Douglass, an American
    Slave. Written by Himself* (Boston: Anti-Slavery Office, 1845), 35.

24. Quotation from Steven Hahn, *A Nation Under Our Feet: Black Political Struggles
    in the Rural South from Slavery to the Great Migration* (Cambridge, MA: Harvard University Press, 2003), 319.

25. Quoted in Painter, *Exodusters*, 77.

26. On voting demographics see Hahn, *A Nation Under Our Feet*, 198; Eric Foner,
    Reconstruction: America's Unfinished Revolution, 1863–1877 (New York: HarperCollins, 1988), 291, 294.

27. Quoted from Cincinnati *Commercial*, February 1868, in Foner, *Reconstruction*,
    291.

28. Quoted in Hahn, *A Nation Under Our Feet*, 205.

29. Quoted in Foner, *Reconstruction*, 330.

30. Quoted in Hahn, *A Nation Under Our Feet*, 215.

31. Report on the Memphis Riots and Massacres, U.S. House of Representatives,
    13–14.

32. Quoted in Foner, *Reconstruction*, 288.

33. This section draws on Hahn, *A Nation Under Our Feet*, 242–244.

34. For more on the Ku Klux Klan Act and related federal enforcement measures,
    see Chapter 7.

35. Quoted in "RAINEY, Joseph Hayne," U.S. House of Representatives, https://
    history.house.gov/People/Detail/20095.

36. Quoted in Ron Chernow, *Grant* (New York: Penguin Press, 2017), 707.

37. Quoted in ibid., 709.

38. J. B. Smith to Senator Charles Sumner, March 31, 1870, cited in David Donald, *Charles Sumner and the Rights of Man* (New York: Alfred Knopf, 1970), 427; Declaration of Independence, July 4, 1776; James McPherson, *Abraham Lincoln and the Second American Revolution* (New York: Oxford University Press, 1991).

Chapter 5: Republicans

1. *Springfield Republican*, November 1, 1856, quoted in William E. Gienapp, *The Origins of the Republican Party, 1852–1856* (New York: Oxford University Press, 1987), 356.

2. See Gienapp, *The Origins of the Republican Party*, esp. 347–373; Eric Foner, *Free Soil, Free Labor, Free Men* (New York: Oxford University Press, 1970).

3. Abraham Lincoln to Jesse W. Fell, enclosing autobiography, December 20, 1859, in Roy Basler, ed., *The Collected Works of Abraham Lincoln*, Vol. 3 (New Brunswick: Rutgers University Press, 1953), 511; fragment on Free Labor, September 17, 1859, in ibid., 462.

4. Abraham Lincoln's address before the Wisconsin State Agricultural Society, Milwaukee, WI, September 30, 1859, in Basler, ed., *The Collected Works of Abraham Lincoln*, Vol. 3, 478–479.

5. Ibid., 478.

6. Fragment on Free Labor, September 17, 1859, in ibid., 462–463.

7. Abraham Lincoln, speech at Dayton, OH, reprinted from Dayton *Journal*, September 19, 1859, in ibid., 436–437.

8. Abraham Lincoln to Mark W. Delahay, May 14, 1859, in ibid., 378–379.

9. Abraham Lincoln, speech at Cincinnati, OH, in ibid., 460; address at Cooper Institute, New York City, February 27, 1860, in ibid., 537.

10. See Hans L. Trefousse, *Thaddeus Stevens: Nineteenth-Century Egalitarian* (Chapel Hill: University of North Carolina Press, 1997), 168–170; repeated proposals to provide former slaves with pensions for their years of unpaid labor were also defeated by Republicans in Congress, see Miranda Booker Perry, "No Pensions for Ex-Slaves," *Prologue Magazine* 42 (Summer 2010), https://www.archives.gov/publications/prologue/2010/summer/slave-pension.html.

11. Quoted in Eric Foner, *Reconstruction: America's Unfinished Revolution, 1863–1877* (New York: HarperCollins, 1988), 344.

12. Speech by Senator Andrew Johnson in the U.S. Senate, December 18–19, 1860, Hathi Trust Digital Library, https://babel.hathitrust.org/cgi/pt?id=mdp.39015035903064&view=1up&seq=1.

13. Quotation from Annette Gordon-Reed, *Andrew Johnson* (New York: Times Books, 2011), 112; "The Vice President's Speech at the Inauguration," *New York Times*, March 20, 1865, 5.

14. The first quote in this paragraph is the assessment of biographer Annette Gordon-Reed in *Andrew Johnson*, 124. The next two quotes are from Johnson's

correspondence, which are quoted in another excellent biography: Hans L. Trefousse, *Andrew Johnson* (New York: W. W. Norton, 1989), 236.

15. *New York Times*, April 16, 1865, 1.

16. David Donald, *Charles Sumner and the Rights of Man* (New York: Alfred Knopf, 1970), 219.

17. Quoted in Foner, *Reconstruction*, 189.

18. Andrew Johnson, "Cleveland Speech, September 3, 1866," American History: From Revolution to Reconstruction and Beyond, http://www.let.rug.nl/usa/presidents/andrew-johnson/cleveland-speech-september-3-1866.php.

19. Benjamin F. Flanders, quoted in Foner, *Reconstruction*, 199.

20. "Black Codes of Mississippi," Teaching American History, https://teachingamericanhistory.org/library/document/black-codes-of-mississippi.

21. "South Carolina's 'Black Code,'" LDHI, http://ldhi.library.cofc.edu/exhibits/show/after_slavery_educator/unit_three_documents/document_eight.

22. See James B. Browning, "The North Carolina Black Code," *Journal of Negro History* 15 (October 1930): 461–473.

23. Basler, ed., *The Collected Works of Abraham Lincoln*, Vol. 3, 478.

24. Abraham Lincoln, speech at Dayton, OH, reprinted from Dayton *Journal*, September 19, 1859, in ibid., 436–437.

25. "An Act to Protect All Persons in the United States in Their Civil Rights, and Furnish the Means of Their Vindication," Thirty-Ninth Congress, session 1, 1866, https://www.loc.gov/law/help/statutes-at-large/39th-congress/session-1/c39s1ch31.pdf.

26. Andrew Johnson, "Veto Message," February 19, 1866, American Presidency Project, https://www.presidency.ucsb.edu/documents/veto-message-437.

27. Andrew Johnson, "Veto Message," March 27, 1866, American Presidency Project, https://www.presidency.ucsb.edu/documents/veto-message-438.

28. Quoted in Eric Foner, *The Second Founding: How the Civil War and Reconstruction Remade the Constitution* (New York: W. W. Norton, 2019), 70.

29. Fourteenth Amendment to the U.S. Constitution, https://constitutioncenter.org/interactive-constitution/amendment/amendment-xiv.

30. See "Reconstruction Acts," Teaching American History, https://teachingamericanhistory.org/library/document/reconstruction-acts/.

31. Ibid.

32. *Army and Navy Journal*, June 22, 1867, quoted in Gregory P. Downs, *After Appomattox: Military Occupation and the Ends of War* (Cambridge, MA: Harvard University Press, 2015), 181.

33. Quoted in Dan T. Carter, *When the War Was Over: The Failure of Self-Reconstruction in the South, 1865–1867* (Baton Rouge: Louisiana State University Press, 1985), 251.

34. "Philip H. Sheridan to Ulysses S. Grant, New Orleans, August 1, 1866," House Divided, http://hd.housedivided.dickinson.edu/node/46024.

35. "Philip H. Sheridan to Ulysses S. Grant, New Orleans, August 2, 1866," House Divided, http://hd.housedivided.dickinson.edu/node/46025.

36. Quoted in Ron Chernow, *Grant* (New York: Penguin, 2017), 584.

37. Grant quoted in Downs, *After Appomattox*, 184.

38. The above four paragraphs draw on the important research of Downs, *After Appomattox*, 184–197.

Chapter 6: Impeachment

1. Alexander Hamilton, *Federalist* 70, March 18, 1788.

2. Alexander Hamilton, *Federalist* 77, April 4, 1788.

3. David Donald, *Charles Sumner and the Rights of Man* (New York: Alfred Knopf, 1970), 280–281.

4. *Atlantic Monthly*, January 1868, 112, and *New York Tribune*, February 25, 1868, 1. Both publications are cited in Jennifer L. Lowe, "The Interaction Between Andrew Johnson and the Press," master's thesis in communications, December 2004, University of Tennessee, Knoxville, 36, 41.

5. See Stanley I. Kutler, "Reconstruction and the Supreme Court: The Numbers Game Reconsidered," *Journal of Southern History* 32 (February 1966): 42–58.

6. Charles L. Black Jr. and Philip Bobbitt, *Impeachment: A Handbook*, new ed. (New Haven, CT: Yale University Press, 2018), 4.

7. "An Act Regulating the Tenure of Certain Civil Offices," March 2, 1867, Thirty-Ninth Congress, session 2, chapter 154, 1867, https://www.senate.gov/artandhistory/history/resources/pdf/Johnson_TenureofOfficeAct.pdf.

8. Quoted in Hans L. Trefousse, *Andrew Johnson: A Biography* (New York: W. W. Norton, 1989), 295.

9. Ibid., 308–309.

10. Ibid., 309.

11. Gideon Welles, *Diary of Gideon Welles*, Vol. 3 (Boston: Houghton Mifflin, 1911), 285.

12. Donald, *Charles Sumner*, 332.

13. Hans Trefousse, *Thaddeus Stevens: Nineteenth-Century Egalitarian* (Chapel Hill: University of North Carolina Press, 1997), 224.

14. The full text of the eleven articles of impeachment, March 3, 1868, at "History of the Impeachment of Andrew Johnson," Avalon Project, https://avalon.law.yale.edu/19th_century/john_chap_07.asp#articles.

15. Ibid.

16. U.S. Constitution, Article I, Section 3; Article II, Section 4.

17. Quoted in Hans Trefousse, "Ben Wade and the Failure of the Impeachment of Johnson," *Historical and Philosophical Society of Ohio Bulletin* 18 (October 1960): 245.

18. *New York Times*, March 4, 1868, 1.

19. Dickens quoted in Robert J. Cook, *Civil War Senator: William Pitt Fessenden and the Fight to Save the American Republic* (Baton Rouge: Louisiana State University Press, 2011), 228.

20. *New York Times*, March 7, 1868, 1.

21. President Johnson's answer to the articles of impeachment, March 23, 1868, at "History of the Impeachment of Andrew Johnson," Avalon Project, https://avalon.law.yale.edu/19th_century/john_chap_07.asp#johnsons_answer.

22. *New York Times*, March 13, 1868, 4.

23. Quotation from Cook, *Civil War Senator*, 228.

24. Quoted in Stephen W. Stathis, "Impeachment and Trial of President Andrew Johnson: A View from the Iowa Congressional Delegation," *Presidential Studies Quarterly* 24 (Winter 1994): 40–41.

25. Welles, *Diary of Gideon Welles*, Vol. 3, 338.

26. Ibid., 339.

27. Stathis, "Impeachment and Trial of President Andrew Johnson," 41; Donald, *Charles Sumner*, 335, 337.

28. On Fuller's bribery of the Kansas state legislature in 1867, see David O. Stewart, *Impeached: The Trial of President Andrew Johnson and the Fight for Lincoln's Legacy* (New York: Simon and Schuster, 2009), 264.

29. David O. Stewart, "Edmund G. Ross Was a Profile in Impeachment Corruption, Not Courage," History News Network, December 15, 2019, https://historynewsnetwork.org/article/173849; David Greenberg, "Andrew Johnson: Saved by a Scoundrel," *Slate*, January 21, 1999, https://slate.com/news-and-politics/1999/01/andrew-johnson-saved-by-a-scoundrel.html; Jeremi Suri, "Pence's Outrageous Op-Ed Holds Deeper Meaning," CNN, January 18, 2020, https://www.cnn.com/2020/01/18/opinions/mike-pence-wsj-oped-is-wrong-suri/index.html.

30. Quoted in Trefousse, *Thaddeus Stevens*, 234.

31. Quoted in Stewart, *Impeached*, 298.

Chapter 7: Will to Power

1. Ulysses S. Grant, *Memoirs and Selected Letters* (New York: Library of America, 1990), 744.

2. Ibid., 761.

3. Ibid., 753.

4. *Texas Republican*, January 22, 1869, 2.

5. "First Inaugural Address of Ulysses S. Grant," Avalon Project, https://avalon.law.yale.edu/19th_century/grant1.asp.

6. Grant, *Memoirs and Selected Letters*, 753.

7. Quoted in Eric Foner, *The Second Founding: How the Civil War and Reconstruction Remade the Constitution* (New York: Norton, 2019), 97.

8. Quotations from ibid., 111; David W. Blight, *Frederick Douglass: Prophet of Freedom* (New York: Simon and Schuster, 2018), 525.

9. "March 30, 1870: Announcement of Fifteenth Amendment Ratification," UVA Miller Center, https://millercenter.org/the-presidency/presidential-speeches/march-30-1870-announcement-fifteenth-amendment-ratification.

10. Quoted in Blight, *Frederick Douglass*, 526–527.

11. Testimony of Abram Colby, in Shawn Leigh Alexander, ed., *Reconstruction Violence and the Ku Klux Klan Hearings* (Boston: Bedford St. Martin's, 2015), 48–51; "White Mob Kidnaps and Whips Black Georgia Legislator," Equal Justice Initiative, https://calendar.eji.org/racial-injustice/oct/29.

12. See, for example, "Negro Rising in Georgia," *Texas Republican*, January 22, 1868, 2.

13. Steven Hahn, *A Nation Under Our Feet: Black Political Struggles in the Rural South from Slavery to the Great Migration* (Cambridge, MA: Belknap Press of Harvard University Press, 2003), 275.

14. Carole Watterson Troxler, " 'To Look More Closely at the Man': Wyatt Outlaw, a Nexus of National, Local, and Personal History," *North Carolina Historical Review* 77 (October 2000): 417.

15. Quotes from Lou Falkner Williams, *The Great South Carolina Ku Klux Klan Trials, 1871–1872* (Athens: University of Georgia Press, 1996), 20.

16. Ibid., 38.

17. Testimony of Harriet Simril in Alexander, *Reconstruction Violence*, 45–48.

18. Williams, *The Great South Carolina Ku Klux Klan Trials*, 30.

19. John Y. Simon, ed., *The Papers of Ulysses S. Grant*, Vol. 21: November 1, 1870–May 31, 1871 (Carbondale: Southern Illinois University Press, 1998), 264.

20. Ibid., 258.

21. For the data on African Americans elected to state and federal office, see J. Morgan Kousser, *Colorblind Injustice: Minority Voting Rights and the Undoing of the Second Reconstruction* (Chapel Hill: University of North Carolina Press, 1999), 19.

22. *Weekly Clarion* (Jackson, MS), September 28, 1871.

23. Representative James Garfield, quoted in Ron Chernow, *Grant* (New York: Penguin Press, 2017), 705.

24. Grant to Akerman, December 12, 1871, in Simon, *The Papers of Ulysses S. Grant*, Vol. 22: June 1, 1871–January 31, 1872, 288–289.

25. Quoted in William S. McFeeley, *Grant: A Biography* (New York: W. W. Norton, 1981), 373.

26. "Second Inaugural Address of Ulysses S. Grant," Avalon Project, https://avalon.law.yale.edu/19th_century/grant2.asp.

27. Mark Twain and Charles Dudley Warner, *The Gilded Age: A Tale of To-Day* (San Francisco: American Publishing Company, 1873).

28. Richard White, *Railroaded: The Transcontinentals and the Making of Modern America* (New York: W. W. Norton, 2011), 50.

29. The federal government did not pay standard pensions for Union veterans until 1890. The two previous paragraphs draw on Richard White, *The Republic for*

Which It Stands: The United States During Reconstruction and the Gilded Age, 1865–1896 (New York: Oxford University Press, 2017), 260–273.

30. Quoted in Nicholas Lemann, *Redemption: The Last Battle of the Civil War* (New York: Farrar, Straus and Giroux, 2006), 20.

31. Ibid., 21.

32. Quotation from Eric Foner, *Reconstruction: America's Unfinished Revolution, 1863–1877* (New York: HarperCollins, 1988), 530.

33. Lemann, *Redemption*, 26.

34. Quotation and photo of the plaque in Danny Lewis, "The 1873 Colfax Massacre Crippled the Reconstruction Era," *Smithsonian Magazine*, April 13, 2016, https://www.smithsonianmag.com/smart-news/1873-colfax-massacre-crippled -reconstruction-180958746/.

35. Chernow, *Grant*, 763.

36. President Grant to the U.S. Senate, January 13, 1875, in Simon, *The Papers of Ulysses S. Grant*, Vol. 26: 1875, 3–16.

Chapter 8: Contested Election

1. Ulysses Grant to General Harry White, May 29, 1875, in Simon, *The Papers of Ulysses S. Grant*, Vol. 26: 1875, 132–134. See also Grant's draft letter to Edwin Cowles, May 29, 1875, in ibid., 128–129. The Twenty-Second Amendment to the Constitution, ratified on February 27, 1951, limited presidents to two terms in office.

2. Letter from Frederick Douglass, May 31, 1875, quoted in ibid., 135.

3. Roscoe Conkling, quoted in Joel H. Silbey, *The American Political Nation, 1838–1893* (Stanford, CA: Stanford University Press, 1991), 220.

4. Silbey's description from ibid., 221.

5. Quotation from Michael F. Holt, *By One Vote: The Disputed Presidential Election of 1876* (Lawrence: University Press of Kansas, 2008), 74.

6. Tilden quoted in Alexander Clarence Flick, *Samuel Jones Tilden: A Study in Political Sagacity* (New York: Dodd, Mead, and Company, 1939), 170.

7. Ibid., 169.

8. Ibid.

9. Samuel Tilden, "The Outrage Upon the Sovereignty of Louisiana," January 12, 1875, in *The Writings and Speeches of Samuel J. Tilden*, Vol. 2, ed. John Bigelow (New York: Harper and Brothers, 1885), 80–84.

10. Quoted in Holt, *By One Vote*, 111.

11. Quoted in Stephen Kantrowitz, *Ben Tillman and the Reconstruction of White Supremacy* (Chapel Hill: University of North Carolina Press, 2000), 68.

12. Ibid., 76.

13. Hayes diary entry, November 7, 1876, in *Diary and Letters of Rutherford Birchard Hayes*, Vol. 3 (Columbus: Ohio State Archeological and Historical Society, 1924), 373.

14. Hayes diary entry, November 11, 1876, in ibid., 376.

15. On the rules for selection of electors in each state, see the U.S. Constitution, Article II, Section 1. For the quote from Tilden's associate, see Flick, *Samuel Jones Tilden*, 331.

16. Hayes diary entry, November 11, 1876, in *Diary and Letters of Rutherford Birchard Hayes*, Vol. 3, 377.

17. President Grant to General Sherman, November 10, 1876, in John Y. Simon, ed., *The Papers of Ulysses S. Grant*, Vol. 28: November 1, 1876–September 30, 1878 (Carbondale: Southern Illinois University Press, 2005), 17. See the accounts of Democratic efforts at fraud, sent to Grant, ibid., 19.

18. Grant to Sherman, November 10, 1876, in ibid., 19–20.

19. Grant to Sheridan, November 10, 1876, in ibid., 36.

20. Reprinted in ibid., 34.

21. See Sherman's correspondence, in ibid., 37.

22. James Garfield, handwritten diary, November 11, 1876, series 1, diaries, 1848–1881, Vols. 13–19, James A. Garfield Papers, Library of Congress, Washington, DC [Hereafter Garfield diary].

23. On repeated Democratic voters in Edgefield County, many from nearby Augusta, Georgia, see Holt, *By One Vote*, 181. On Grant's November 11 comments to reporters, see Brooks D. Simpson, "Ulysses S. Grant and the Electoral Crisis of 1876–77," *Hayes Historical Journal* 11 (Winter 1992), https://www.rbhayes .org/research/hayes-historical-journal-ulysses-s.-grant/.

24. For quotations and more background on the bribery allegations in Louisiana, see Holt, *By One Vote*, 196–197.

25. Quotation in C. Vann Woodward, *Origins of the New South, 1877–1913* (Baton Rouge: Louisiana State University Press, 1951), 25.

26. John Sherman to Rutherford B. Hayes, January 18, 1877, in *Diary and Letters of Rutherford Birchard Hayes*, Vol. 3, 405.

27. See Garfield's revealing diary entry from his December 18, 1876, meeting with Andrew Kellar, a Democratic newspaper editor from Tennessee, who served as an intermediary between some Southern Democrats and Hayes's team. Garfield diary, December 18, 1876.

28. Rutherford B. Hayes to William Henry Smith, December 24, 1876, in *Diary and Letters of Rutherford Birchard Hayes*, Vol. 3, 393.

29. Garfield diary, February 26, 1877.

30. Quoted in Holt, *By One Vote*, 241.

31. Rutherford B. Hayes to John Sherman, February 15, 1877, in *Diary and Letters of Rutherford Birchard Hayes*, Vol. 3, 415.

32. Although much has been written about the election of 1876, the most important book on the election and its aftermath remains C. Vann Woodward, *Reunion and Reaction: The Compromise of 1877 and the End of Reconstruction* (Boston: Little, Brown, 1951). I am deeply indebted to this book for my analysis in this chapter.

33. Hayes diary entry, March 14, 1877, in *Diary and Letters of Rutherford Birchard Hayes*, Vol. 3, 425. For a detailed account of Hayes's first days in Washington, DC, see "The First Days of the Hayes Administration: Inauguration to Easter Sunday," compiled by Webb C. Hayes and Watt P. Marchman, *Hayes Historical Journal* 1 (Fall 1977), https://www.rbhayes.org/research/hayes-historical-journal-the-first -days-of-the-hayes-administration-inauguration-to-easter-sunday-1877/.

34. *New York Times*, March 6, 1877, 1.

Chapter 9: Caretaker

1. Hayes diary, November 11, 1876, in *Diary and Letters of Rutherford Birchard Hayes*, Vol. 3 (Columbus: Ohio State Archeological and Historical Society, 1924), 377. See also letter from Hayes to Carl Schurz, December 6, 1876, in ibid., 386. [Hereafter Hayes diary.]

2. "Rutherford Hayes Inaugural Address," Rutherford B. Hayes Presidential Library & Museums, https://www.rbhayes.org/hayes/rutherford-b.-hayes-s-inaugural -address/.

3. Andrew Jackson, "First Annual Message," https://www.presidency.ucsb.edu /documents/first-annual-message-3.

4. Hayes diary, March 12, 1878.

5. "Rutherford Hayes Inaugural Address," Hayes Presidential Library.

6. Quoted in Stephen Kantrowitz, *Ben Tillman and the Reconstruction of White Supremacy* (Chapel Hill: University of North Carolina Press, 2000), 92.

7. Hayes diary, April 22, 1877.

8. Ibid., March 23, 1877.

9. Ibid.

10. Quoted in Robert V. Bruce, *1877: Year of Violence* (New York: Bobbs-Merrill, 1959), location 1031.

11. Quoted in ibid., location 1722.

12. "President Hayes's Notes of Four Cabinet Meetings," ed. George Frederick Howe, *American Historical Review* 37 (January 1932): 286–289.

13. Hayes diary, August 26, 1877.

14. Quoted in Brooks D. Simpson, *The Reconstruction Presidents* (Lawrence: University of Kansas Press, 1998), 213.

15. Ibid.; Hayes diary, March 21, 1878. Hayes referred later to his hope that the "better class of Southern people" would "suppress the violence of the ruffian class" and "protect colored people in their rights." See Hayes diary, May 25, 1879.

16. Hayes diary, September 6, 1877.

17. Letter to Hayes from William Henry Smith, September 27, 1877, excerpted in *Diary and Letters of Rutherford Birchard Hayes*, Vol. 3: 443.

18. Quoted in Simpson, *Reconstruction Presidents*, 216.

19. On voter turnout and the consistency of party preferences in this period, see Joel H. Silbey, *The American Political Nation, 1838–1893* (Stanford, CA: Stanford University Press, 1991), 141–175.

20. Quoted in Karen Guenther, "Potter Committee Investigation of the Disputed Election of 1876," *Florida Historical Quarterly* 61 (January 1983): 283.

21. Hayes diary, May 14, 1878.

22. Ibid., May 19, 1878; Hayes's comments to friends quoted in Harry Barnard, *Rutherford B. Hayes and His America* (New York: Bobbs-Merrill, 1954), 468–469.

23. Original text of the Posse Comitatus Act, 1878, in Matt Mathews, *The Posse Comitatus Act and the United States Army: A Historical Perspective* (Fort Leavenworth, KS: Combat Studies Institute Press, [2006]), 32–33, https://www.armyupress.army .mil/Portals/7/combat-studies-institute/csi-books/matthews.pdf. On recent controversies, see Jeremi Suri, "'We the People' Trumps 'Commander-in-Chief,'" CNN, June 2, 2020, https://www.cnn.com/2020/06/02/opinions/trump-military-force -insurrection-act-resistance-suri/index.html; Ryan Goodman and Justin Hendrix, "Crisis of Command: The Pentagon, the President, and January 6," *Just Security*, December 21, 2021, https://www.justsecurity.org/79623/crisis-of-command-the -pentagon-the-president-and-january-6.

24. Hayes diary, November 12, 1878.

25. Rutherford Hayes, second annual message to Congress, December 2, 1878, reprinted in Arthur Bishop, ed., *Rutherford B. Hayes, 1822–1893: Chronology–Documents–Bibliographical Aids* (Dobbs Ferry, NY: Oceana Publications, 1969), 50.

26. Hayes diary, March 9 and 18, 1879.

27. Hayes, Veto message for an army appropriation bill, April 29, 1879, in Bishop, ed., *Rutherford B. Hayes*, 57–59.

28. Quoted in Barnard, *Rutherford B. Hayes and His America*, 484.

29. Hayes diary, July 3, 1879.

Chapter 10: Death Again

1. Hayes diary, June 6, 1879, in *Diary and Letters of Rutherford Birchard Hayes*, Vol. 3 (Columbus: Ohio State Archeological and Historical Society, 1924), 557. [Hereafter Hayes diary.]

2. Quotation from Meredith Hindley, "The Odyssey of Ulysses S. Grant," *Humanities* 35 (May-June 2014), https://www.neh.gov/humanities/2014/mayjune /feature/the-odyssey-ulysses-s-grant.

3. John Y. Simon, ed., *The Papers of Ulysses S. Grant*, Vol. 29: October 1, 1878–September 30, 1880 (Carbondale: Southern Illinois University Press, 2008), 38.

4. William Hesseltine, *Ulysses S. Grant: Politician* (New York: Dodd, Mead, 1935), 432.

5. Julia Dent Grant, *The Personal Memoirs of Julia Dent Grant*, ed. John Y. Simon (Carbondale: Southern Illinois University Press, 1975), 307–308.

6. Hayes diary, December 18, 1879; Twain quoted in Ron Chernow, *Grant* (New York: Penguin, 2017), 887.

7. Grant, *Personal Memoirs of Julia Dent Grant*, 317–318.

8. Garfield letter to Grant, July 26, 1880, excerpted in *The Diary of James Garfield*, Vol. 4: 1878–1881, eds. Harry James Brown and Frederick D. Williams, (East Lansing: Michigan State University Press, 1967), 439. [Hereafter Garfield diary.]

9. "James Garfield's Letter Accepting the 1880 Republican Presidential Nomination," National Park Service, https://www.nps.gov/articles/000/james-a-garfield-s-letter-accepting-the-1880-republican-presidential-nomination.htm.

10. Garfield diary, November 3, 1880.

11. Ibid., November 4, 1880.

12. James Garfield, "Inaugural Address, March 4, 1881," UVA Miller Center, https://millercenter.org/the-presidency/presidential-speeches/march-4-1881-inaugural-address.

13. Ibid.

14. For the statistics on illiteracy and educational deprivation in the South, see Robert A. Margo, *Race and Schooling in the South, 1880–1950: An Economic History* (Chicago: University of Chicago Press, 1990), 6–28.

15. Quoted in Heather Cox Richardson, *The Death of Reconstruction: Race, Labor, and Politics in the Post–Civil War North, 1865–1901* (Cambridge, MA: Harvard University Press, 2001), 168.

16. Quoted in Nell Irvin Painter, *Exodusters: Black Migration to Kansas After Reconstruction* (New York: W. W. Norton, 1976), 103.

17. Quotations from ibid., 191–192.

18. Garfield diary, March 8, 1881.

19. Ibid., March 14, 1881.

20. Ibid., March 26, 1881.

21. Ibid., June 13, 1881.

22. Ibid., May 12, 1881.

23. Ibid., May 8, 1881.

24. Ibid., June 13, 1881, and June 8, 1881.

25. Quotations from Candice Millard, *Destiny of the Republic: A Tale of Madness, Medicine, and the Murder of a President* (New York: Random House, 2011), 110.

26. Quoted in ibid., 113.

27. Quoted in ibid., 125.

28. Garfield diary, June 19, 1881.

29. Quotations from Millard, *Destiny of the Republic*, 149.

30. Ira Rutkow, *James A. Garfield* (New York: Henry Holt, 2006), 110–111.

31. Quotations from Lewis L. Gould, *Alexander Watkins Terrell: Civil War Soldier, Texas Lawmaker, American Diplomat* (Austin: University of Texas Press, 2004), 74.

32. Ibid., 85.

Chapter 11: Legacies

1. Edmund S. Morgan, *American Slavery, American Freedom: The Ordeal of Colonial Virginia* (New York: W. W. Norton, 1975).

2. See Alexander Keyssar, *Why Do We Still Have the Electoral College?* (Cambridge, MA: Harvard University Press, 2020).

3. See Carol Anderson, *One Person, No Vote: How Voter Suppression Is Destroying Our Democracy* (New York: Bloomsbury, 2018).

4. See Alexander Keyssar, *The Right to Vote: The Contested History of Democracy in the United States,* revised ed. (New York: Basic Books, 2000), esp. 291–293; Ari Berman, *Give Us the Ballot: The Modern Struggle for Voting Rights in America* (New York: Picador, 2015), esp. 207–314. The Brennan Center for Justice follows state voting laws closely. In October 2021, they reported: "In an unprecedented year so far for voting legislation, 19 states have enacted 33 laws that will make it harder for Americans to vote." See "Voting Laws Roundup: October 2021," Brennan Center, https://www.brennancenter.org/our-work/research-reports/voting-laws-roundup-october-2021.

5. See Robinson Woodward-Burns, *Hidden Laws: How State Constitutions Stabilize American Politics* (New Haven, CT: Yale University Press, 2021). In 2016, ten electors pledged to Donald Trump or Hillary Clinton tried to choose other candidates. This had happened 157 times before 2016. See "The One Election Where Faithless Electors Made a Difference," National Constitution Center, https://constitutioncenter.org/blog/the-one-election-where-faithless-electors-made-a-difference.

6. See Jesse Wegman, *Let the People Pick the President: The Case for Abolishing the Electoral College* (New York: St. Martin's, 2020).

7. See Steve Bickerstaff, *Gerrymandering Texas,* ed. C. Robert Heath (Lubbock: Texas Tech University, 2020), esp. Chapters 6–8.

8. See Stephen K. Medvic, *Gerrymandering: The Politics of Redistricting in the United States* (Medford, MA: Polity Press, 2021).

Index

Jeremi Suri holds the Mack Brown Distinguished Chair for Leadership in Global Affairs at the University of Texas at Austin. He is a professor in the university's Department of History and the LBJ School of Public Affairs. Dr. Suri is the author and editor of eleven books on contemporary politics and foreign policy, most recently *The Impossible Presidency: The Rise and Fall of America's Highest Office.* His other books include *Henry Kissinger and the American Century, Liberty's Surest Guardian: American Nation-Building from the Founders to Obama,* and *Power and Protest: Global Revolution and the Rise of Détente.* He writes widely for many publications and is also the host of the podcast *This Is Democracy.*

PublicAffairs is a publishing house founded in 1997. It is a tribute to the standards, values, and flair of three persons who have served as mentors to countless reporters, writers, editors, and book people of all kinds, including me.

I. F. STONE, proprietor of *I. F. Stone's Weekly*, combined a commitment to the First Amendment with entrepreneurial zeal and reporting skill and became one of the great independent journalists in American history. At the age of eighty, Izzy published *The Trial of Socrates*, which was a national bestseller. He wrote the book after he taught himself ancient Greek.

BENJAMIN C. BRADLEE was for nearly thirty years the charismatic editorial leader of *The Washington Post*. It was Ben who gave the *Post* the range and courage to pursue such historic issues as Watergate. He supported his reporters with a tenacity that made them fearless and it is no accident that so many became authors of influential, best-selling books.

ROBERT L. BERNSTEIN, the chief executive of Random House for more than a quarter century, guided one of the nation's premier publishing houses. Bob was personally responsible for many books of political dissent and argument that challenged tyranny around the globe. He is also the founder and longtime chair of Human Rights Watch, one of the most respected human rights organizations in the world.

• • •

For fifty years, the banner of Public Affairs Press was carried by its owner Morris B. Schnapper, who published Gandhi, Nasser, Toynbee, Truman, and about 1,500 other authors. In 1983, Schnapper was described by *The Washington Post* as "a redoubtable gadfly." His legacy will endure in the books to come.

Peter Osnos, *Founder*